T0355190

Aesthetics of the Familiar

Yuriko Saito explores the nature and significance of the aesthetic dimensions of people's everyday life. Everyday aesthetics has the recognized value of enriching one's life experiences and sharpening one's attentiveness and sensibility. Saito draws out its broader importance for how we make our worlds, environmentally, morally, as citizens and consumers. Saito urges that we have a social responsibility to encourage cultivation of aesthetic literacy and vigilance against aesthetic manipulation. Yuriko Saito argues that ultimately, everyday aesthetics can be an effective instrument for directing the humanity's collective and cumulative world-making project for the betterment of all its inhabitants.

Everyday aesthetics has been seen as a challenge to contemporary Anglo-American aesthetics discourse, which is dominated by the discussion of art and beauty. Saito responds to controversies about the nature, boundary, and status of everyday aesthetics and argues for its legitimacy. She highlights the multi-faceted aesthetic dimensions of everyday life that are not fully accounted for by the commonly-held account of defamiliarizing the familiar.

Yuriko Saito, born and raised in Japan, is Emerita Professor of Philosophy at the Rhode Island School of Design in the United States. She has written and lectured widely on everyday aesthetics, environmental aesthetics, and Japanese aesthetics. Her *Everyday Aesthetics* was published by Oxford University Press in 2008. In addition to serving as an editorial consultant for a number of journals on aesthetics and environmental ethics, she works as Editor of the first free-access, peer-reviewed, online journal on aesthetics, *Contemporary Aesthetics*.

Aesthetics of the Familiar

Everyday Life and World-Making

Yuriko Saito

Great Clarendon Street, Oxford, OX2 6DP,
United Kingdom

Oxford University Press is a department of the University of Oxford.
It furthers the University's objective of excellence in research, scholarship,
and education by publishing worldwide. Oxford is a registered trade mark of
Oxford University Press in the UK and in certain other countries

First Edition published in 2017
First published in paperback 2019

Published in the United States of America by Oxford University Press
198 Madison Avenue, New York, NY 10016, United States of America

British Library Cataloguing in Publication Data
Data available

Library of Congress Cataloging in Publication Data
Data available

ISBN 978–0–19–967210–3 (Hbk.)
ISBN 978–0–19–885291–9 (Pbk.)

Contents

Acknowledgments

My first book, *Everyday Aesthetics* (Oxford University Press, 2007), was published almost ten years ago. Its aim was to begin a discussion about opening the scope of aesthetics to include those aspects of our lives previously neglected in the aesthetics discourse. I have been gratified by the increasingly lively debate over everyday aesthetics in recent years. In this regard, I feel that it's "mission accomplished." At the same time, I am motivated more than ever to continue exploring this area of our aesthetic lives, not only to contribute to the ongoing conversation among aestheticians but also, perhaps more importantly, to pursue what I take to be the social responsibility of aesthetics.

Teaching R(hode) I(sland) S(chool) of D(esign) students continues to provide a constant intellectual nourishment for me. Their work, whether comments in class, papers, presentations, or studio projects, has been a perpetual source of inspiration, stimulation, and challenges to my own thinking. My RISD colleagues, too numerous to name, have also been my cheerleaders with their steady encouragement, support, and food for thought. In particular, they helped me widen my horizons and open my eyes through their different disciplinary approaches, global perspectives, and, most importantly, their commitment to teaching and practicing socially and ethically responsible work.

While at times missing having a philosophy department and students majoring in philosophy, I have come to truly appreciate and cherish the privilege and advantage of teaching at an art and design school. Being at RISD forces me to think about aesthetics as a practice, not only as a scholarly endeavor, and to write in a way that is accessible and relevant to readers across disciplinary and cultural boundaries.

The feedback I have received on my first book has been extremely rewarding, particularly because it came from readers from diverse disciplines and different corners of the world. They included professional artists and other practitioners such as architects, designers, writers, stage set designers, and medical professionals, as well as academicians in fields ranging from sociology, education, film criticism, art, and architecture to, of course, philosophy. Although I cannot list all of them by name, I thank them for reaching out to me and informing me how my writing was useful in their own work.

Over the years, my professional colleagues and friends have helped me develop and test my ideas. I want to give special thanks to Yrjö Sepänmaa, Ossi Naukkarinen, Pauline von Bonsdorff, and Arto Haapala, who together provided many opportunities to present my ideas in what I now call my third home (after Japan and US), Finland.

I am most indebted to the two reviewers of the first draft of this book, Arnold Berleant and Tom Leddy: a dream team! Their suggestions, comments, and challenges were invaluable and I hope I did justice to the care they took in reading the manuscript. As it should become clear throughout the book, my own thinking on everyday aesthetics, or aesthetics in general, owes much to their works. Tom has been a supporter of everyday aesthetics not only by encouraging my work but also by his own work that culminated in *The Extraordinary in the Ordinary: The Aesthetics of Everyday Life* (Broadview Press, 2012). The process of reinforcing each other's work and building the field of everyday aesthetics together has been exciting and rewarding.

In addition to his numerous comments and suggestions on the first draft of this book, I specifically owe Arnold the three-part organization of this book with respective titles: Concepts, Cases, and Consequences. His suggested framework helped create an improved sequence, as well as a balance between and among each part. My indebtedness to Arnold goes much deeper than his help with this book, however. Arnold was pioneering everyday aesthetics without using that particular term many years before I started formulating my own thoughts. Without his trailblazing work, I would not have had any guidance or direction. The impact of Arnold's work on my thinking in aesthetics is both profound and pervasive. The overall influence and inspiration I gained from his extensive *oeuvre* is beyond measure and cannot be adequately reflected in my occasional specific references to his work.

My thinking on aesthetics has also benefitted from collaborating with Arnold on *Contemporary Aesthetics*, a free access, online, and peer-reviewed journal that he started as its Editor in 2003. This journal (from which I have cited many articles in this book) has encouraged and provided home for good and innovative works in aesthetics that helped enlarge this discipline's domain, approach, and cultural boundary. It has been a labor of love for Arnold, and I, working as Associate Editor, have been the beneficiary of sharing in this exciting and rewarding journey.

Finally, I want to thank my editor at Oxford University Press, Peter Momtchiloff, for his support and patience throughout the process of preparing the manuscript. As with my first book, I am grateful to the freedom he gave me regarding the content of this book and an ever-extending deadline!

As was the case when I was writing the first book, my family, Gerry, Sarah, and Adam, provided much support in many ways, support that I particularly needed during the last stage of completing this manuscript. For the last several months of writing, my father was suffering from terminal illness, and most of the revision work with the reviewers' feedback was done in Japan while caring for him. Unfortunately he never had a chance to see the publication of this book. I am dedicating this book to him who taught me a work ethic, professionalism, social grace, and, above all, how to live and die.

July, 2019

List of Figures

Note: All figures are author's photographs

Introduction

Everyday aesthetics is becoming established as a subdiscipline of aesthetics. In one sense, it is ironic that such a subdiscipline be created anew, because neither the original Greek meaning of the term *aesthesis* nor Baumgarten's formulation of aesthetics as a discourse regarding senses excluded any dimensions of our lives from deliberation. Furthermore, until about a century ago, the subject matters of aesthetics in the Western philosophical tradition ranged from natural objects and phenomena, built structures, utilitarian objects, and human actions, to what is today regarded as fine arts.

In addition, although not formulated as aesthetic theories, many cultural practices outside the Western tradition are concerned with the aesthetics of daily lives. In some, such as Inuit and Navajo, aesthetic considerations are thoroughly integrated in their daily activities, including making things such as tools. Even in other traditions, such as Chinese and Japanese, with distinctive art-making practices of painting, literature, theater, and the like, aesthetic practices permeate people's daily lives. In these cultural traditions, there may not be a need for an aesthetics discourse specifically devoted to everyday life.

Thus, the perception that everyday aesthetics is a newly emerging field needs to be understood as a specific response to twentieth-century Anglo-American aesthetics, which is almost exclusively focused on issues related to fine arts. As observed by Liu Yuedi, "in the West the aesthetics of everyday life is 'reflexive' or in other words is a reaction against a certain tendency in Western aesthetics itself, while in Oriental aesthetics it is a reaction against 'the Other,' namely the invading heterogeneous elements of Western aesthetics."[1] Instead of opening a new frontier, the everyday aesthetics discourse emerging in Western aesthetics today should be considered as *restoring* aesthetics to its original task: investigating the nature of experiences gained through sensory perception and sensibility. It is a reaction against the predominant tendency to equate aesthetics with the philosophy of art in contemporary Western aesthetic discourse. It can also be considered an attempt to distinguish "aesthetic" and "artistic."[2]

A number of recent thinkers have expressed their dissatisfaction with the limited scope of aesthetics that led them to promote everyday aesthetics. For example, Ben Highmore, a cultural studies scholar specializing in everyday studies, makes the following observation.

Once upon a time the word 'aesthetics' was less freighted with the task of policing the corridors of art or evaluating the experiences associated with it.... Emerging as a named area of inquiry only in the mid-eighteenth century, the history of aesthetics can be seen to follow a wayward path of increased intellectual specialization, increasingly limiting itself to only certain kinds of experience and feeling, and becoming more and more dedicated to finely wrought objects.[3]

Another advocate of everyday aesthetics, Hans Ulrich Gumbrecht, also observes that "the number and the forms of those situations that Western culture has marked as appropriate for the production of aesthetic experience have been astonishingly small and rigid" and the "traditional frames of aesthetic experience are not only strangely inflexible but have reached a high degree of exhaustion."[4] Finally, in her most rigorous and sustained critique of mainstream aesthetics, Katya Mandoki offers a series of "the fetishes" and "the myths" of aesthetics, which include "the fetish of the artwork" and "the myth of the synonymity of art and aesthetics."[5] These voices collectively express dissatisfaction with mainstream Anglo-American aesthetics for its unduly limited scope, which takes art as its focus and marginalizes everything else.

However, there has been considerable disagreement over whether or not, and how to, expand the scope of aesthetic inquiry, and what such an expanded scope means to existing aesthetics discourse. This book joins this ongoing debate over the nature, value, and implications of everyday aesthetics.

Part I addresses conceptual issues regarding the nature of 'everyday' and 'aesthetics' in everyday aesthetics. Controversies regarding the nature of 'everyday' in everyday aesthetics range from what is included in or excluded from its purview to how everyday life is generally characterized, a dreary drudgery or comforting stability. I argue that, in light of the diversity of people's life experiences, 'everyday' should be defined not in terms of a specific list of items and activities but rather by reference to the typical, usually practical, attitude that people take toward what they are experiencing. Furthermore, most people experience everyday life sometimes as a dreary and monotonous routine and some other times as a familiar safe haven. Both offer aesthetic textures, negative or positive, if we understand 'aesthetic' in the classificatory, rather than the usual honorific, sense.

The narrative currently dominating the discourse on everyday aesthetics requires defamiliarization of the familiar to render the ordinary in our life extraordinary. While I agree with the existence and importance of this mode of experiencing the ordinary, I offer another possibility. I argue that we can capture the aesthetic texture of ordinariness experienced as such, as long as we pay attention to what we are experiencing rather than acting on autopilot. Being attentive is a prerequisite for any kind of aesthetic experience and it does not necessarily compromise the ordinariness of ordinary life.

Such experience of the ordinary is also captured by attending to the aesthetic experience of doing things, such as cooking and laundering. This activity-based aspect of our life experience is generally neglected in traditional aesthetics discourse because it is oriented toward objects and the spectators' judgments regarding them. It also highlights the aesthetic relevance of proximal senses and bodily engagement, another area that has traditionally been excluded from the reach of aesthetic investigation.

If the conceptual analysis of Part I can be characterized as 'talking about' everyday aesthetics, Part II can be regarded as 'doing' everyday aesthetics. The three chapters comprising Part II explore specific examples to illustrate how familiar and seemingly ordinary objects and activities from our everyday life can provide rich materials for aesthetics. The first example comes from the recent art projects that facilitate our aesthetic experience of the sky. Although I promote the aesthetic appreciation of the ordinary as ordinary in Part I, it is proposed as an additional dimension of everyday aesthetics, not as a rejection of experiencing the ordinary as extraordinary. Various examples of what I call 'sky art' demonstrate how art helps render the otherwise ordinary part of our everyday life, namely the sky and various celestial and meteorological phenomena within, extraordinary.

The second case study regards controversies over the presumed eyesore effect of wind turbines that are becoming increasingly common in many parts of the world. This example of environmental aesthetics offers a good case to explore the relationship between the sensuous and the conceptual, as many opponents of wind turbines are in agreement about their environmental benefits. To what extent, if any, can and should the environmental benefit of the wind turbines affect their aesthetics? Is the aesthetic value limited to what we experience through the senses?

The third example is one of the most mundane activities of our daily lives: laundry. Despite its usual characterization as a dreary chore dominated by practical concerns, laundry provides a surprisingly rich array of aesthetic issues, ranging from the concept of 'cleanliness' and neat personal appearance to the bodily engagement in doing laundry and controversies surrounding laundry hanging in some communities in the United States. Laundry exemplifies how the dimension of our lives that does not receive academic attention in fact offers a treasure trove of aesthetic issues.

The controversies surrounding the aesthetics of wind turbines and laundry hanging provide a segue into Part III: consequences of everyday aesthetics. One of the persistent charges against everyday aesthetics discourse is its alleged triviality and insignificance, particularly in comparison with the established aesthetic paradigm consisting of great works of art and beautiful or sublime aspects of natural environment that have profound significance in people's lives. Based upon the conceptual analysis in Part I and exploration of examples in Part II, Part III develops the role of everyday aesthetics in determining the quality of life and the state of the world. My main thesis is that the seeming insignificance and triviality of everyday aesthetics conceals the considerable power everyday aesthetics wields on humanity's ongoing project of world-making.

The benefit of more attentive and mindful living through the lens of everyday aesthetics is rather familiar to its advocates, as well as to the practitioners in different fields, such as art, psychology, and religion. While I agree with them on the importance of such benefit to the individuals, I emphasize the moral, social, political, and environmental ramifications of everyday aesthetics, whether regarding interpersonal relationships, consumerism, civil and humane society, or a sustainable future. Here, we have to be careful not to subsume aesthetics under these other considerations; we need to keep focusing on the sensuous quality experienced with sensibility. At the same time, we should avoid disconnecting aesthetics from the concerns of the rest of life, a stance favored by some critics of everyday aesthetics, because doing so does disservice to its indispensable place in people's lives and marginalizes its role in society. It is vital that we remain cognizant of the fact that everyday aesthetics determines the quality of society, and ultimately the state of the world, for better or worse.

This book thus challenges the model and assumptions derived from the philosophy of art and beauty that still dominate Anglo-American aesthetics. They include object-, spectator-, and judgment-oriented discourse; the exclusion of proximal senses and bodily engagement from aesthetics proper; and the reluctance to connect aesthetics to other realms of life. I would characterize my challenge, however, to be constructive, rather than destructive, by expanding and enriching the existing discourse. It is ultimately a call for restoring aesthetics' important connection to the other aspects of our lived experiences and a plea to take its social responsibility seriously.

Notes

1. Liu Yuedi, "'Living Aesthetics' from the Perspective of the Intercultural Turn," included in *Aesthetics of Everyday Life: East and West*, eds. Liu Yuedi and Curtis L. Carter (Newcastle upon Tyne: Cambridge Scholars Publishing, 2014), p. 15.

2. John Dewey points out, "we have no word in the English language that unambiguously includes what is signified by the two words 'artistic' and 'esthetic.'" *Art as Experience* (New York: Capricorn Press, 1958), p. 46.

3. Ben Highmore, *Ordinary Lives: Studies in the Everyday* (Oxon: Routledge, 2011), p. x. Highmore also points out that "the successful colonization of aesthetics by the artwork and the institutional structures of value that surround it" derailed the project of aesthetics which originated with Baumgarten to analyze the realm of perception by distinguishing it from the realm of rationality and cognition. He thus declares that "the initial project of aesthetics . . . has yet to be fulfilled, at least in the academic realm of aesthetics." ("Homework: Routine, Social Aesthetics and the Ambiguity of Everyday Life," *Cultural Studies* 18.2/3 (2004), p. 314.)

4. Hans Ulrich Gumbrecht, "Aesthetic Experience in Everyday Worlds: Reclaiming an Unredeemed Utopian Motif," *New Literary History* 37 (2006), p. 314, p. 315. So as not to increase the number of notes, throughout the book, the page number of all the quoted passages from the same work cited in the same paragraph will be consolidated in one note, as it is done here.

5. Katya Mandoki, *Everyday Aesthetics: Prosaics, the Play of Culture and Social Identities* (Aldershot: Ashgate, 2007), p. 30.

PART I

Concepts

Everyday Aesthetics as an Essentially Contested Field

Everyday aesthetics, as I explained in the Introduction, is not a new field of aesthetics, and its recent 'emergence' should be understood primarily in the context of twentieth-century Anglo-American aesthetics. At the same time, within this context, there has been an increasingly lively debate over the conceptual framework of everyday aesthetics. Part I joins this ongoing discussion on the contested notions of 'everyday' and 'aesthetics' by asking what these concepts include and exclude. Specifically, Chapter 1 discusses two trajectories for developing the aesthetics of the ordinary and familiar, namely the experience of the extraordinary through defamiliarization and the experience of the ordinary as ordinary. Chapter 2 responds to the prevailing criticism of everyday aesthetics that its triviality and extreme subjectivity call into question its legitimacy and credentials as an academic discourse.

1

The Aesthetics of the Ordinary and Familiar

1.1 'Everyday' as an Essentially Contested Concept

Because everyday aesthetics was initially proposed as a way of overcoming modern Western aesthetics' limitation on people's aesthetic life as its subject matter, its scope has not been clearly defined. For example, my initial impetus for writing *Everyday Aesthetics* was to address aesthetic issues regarding objects and activities not covered by fine arts, nature, and popular arts. Kevin Melchionne is correct in observing that everyday aesthetics deals with "a default third basket for what is not comfortably categorized as fine art or natural beauty."[1] He thus questions what constitutes 'everyday' in everyday aesthetics.

It turns out that 'everyday' is an elusive, as well as a highly contested, concept. Many of us feel as if we know what it is, but articulating it is another matter. The difficulty here reminds us of the famous statement by Justice Potter Stewart of The United States Supreme Court regarding obscenity: "I know it when I see it."[2] One problem is that I think I know more or less what *my* 'everyday' consists of, but it applies only to me—a married Japanese woman with two grown children and a college professor living in a typical American suburb. But what counts as 'everyday' differs from person to person depending upon gender, age, cultural background, lifestyle, home and work environment, occupation, hobby, and the like. For example, working on a farm constitutes a farmer's everyday life while it is a rare experience that may actively be sought out by a city dweller who chooses to participate in a tour that incorporates work experience, such as a day working in a vineyard. For those residents in a densely populated urban area with a developed network of public transportation, as well as for those living in different parts of the world, riding in a car may be a rare occasion, while it is a daily routine for many living in typical American suburbs. Furthermore, as pointed out by Ossi Naukkarinen, it also changes within the course of one's life, so that what constituted 'everyday' for a child, mostly play, inevitably changes as one matures and enters adulthood.[3] There is also a great variation among different cultural practices, rendering one culture's rather routine practice a rare and special occasion for another culture.[4]

The notion of 'everyday' thus becomes hopelessly unwieldy and it is impossible to come up with a list of objects and activities that belong to it. However, I propose that what is most important for the purpose of everyday aesthetics is not so much an inventory of objects and activities but rather the mode of experience based upon an attitude we take toward them. We tend to experience 'everyday' objects and activities, whatever they may be, mostly with pragmatic considerations. Preoccupation with accomplishing a certain task often eclipses the aesthetic potentials of these 'everyday' objects and activities.[5] These experiences are generally regarded as ordinary, commonplace, and routine. Such characterization may be the best way to characterize 'everyday,' allowing different ingredients according to diverse occupation, lifestyles, and living environments. I agree with Naukkarinen's characterization: "The everyday attitude is colored with routines, familiarity, continuity, normalcy, habits, the slow process of acclimatization, even superficiality and a sort of half-consciousness and not with creative experiments, exceptions, constant questioning and change, analyses, and deep reflections."[6] Locating the defining characteristics of 'everyday' in the attitude and experience rather than a specific kind of objects and activities has the advantage of accounting for how works of art, such as paintings, could be an ingredient of somebody's everyday experience if his job is to wrap, package, and ship them.

Another problem regarding what constitutes 'everyday' is that there are those events and occasions in one's life that happen only occasionally or even rarely: a party, holiday celebration, wedding, funeral, sporting event, and the like. Not only do these events not take place on a daily basis for most people (except for professionals for whom their work is to orchestrate these events) but also they are often permeated with specific aesthetic considerations: interior decoration, table setting, music, incense, flower arrangements, food and drinks, and many others. We are predisposed to attend to aesthetic dimensions of these events, whether as a host or as a guest. Does this mean that these experiences should be excluded from the scope of everyday aesthetics because of their infrequent occurrence and the predominance of aesthetic considerations guiding their experience? Kevin Melchionne would exclude these experiences from the domain of everyday aesthetics because for him regular and frequent occurrence is one of the conditions necessary for 'everyday.'[7]

However, I agree with Thomas Leddy's "expansionist" account and include all of these experiences under the purview of everyday aesthetics.[8] Some aspects of our everyday life are more art-like in the sense of intentional attention to aesthetics, while other aspects are primarily experienced without conscious aesthetic attention. Though I believe the core of everyday aesthetics resides in the latter, there is no reason to exclude the former. For example, some of our daily activities lend themselves to requiring aesthetic attention: choosing which clothes and jewelry to wear and putting them on in a certain way, picking flowers and making an arrangement in a vase just to brighten up the living room though not for any special occasion, and the like. As Naukkarinen suggests, one could imagine a spectrum with two contrasting extremes, one end indicating those rare occurrences most of which involve intentional inclusion of aesthetic planning and expectation, as well as those daily activities that are predominated by aesthetic considerations (as in choosing the clothes), and the other end occupied by other objects and activities, such as household chores and preparing work-related documents, toward which we normally take a non-aesthetic attitude for pragmatic purposes.[9] Our lives consist of diverse experiences, some more aesthetically oriented than others, some more contemplative while others more physical in nature, some experienced literally daily while others only occasionally. I think it is a mistake to limit what counts as the legitimate ingredients of everyday life for everyday aesthetics discourse: life does not come in neat packages of different experiences and everyday aesthetics should embrace its complexities with all the messiness created by them.

1.2 Everyday Aesthetics as Defamiliarization of the Familiar

1.2.1 Defamiliarization of the familiar

I just stated that 'everyday' relevant to everyday aesthetics should embrace diverse contents, including those rare events permeated by specific aesthetic considerations like weddings and holiday celebrations. These literally out-of-the-ordinary events and occurrences may have an advantage over the run-of-the-mill mundane events in terms of producing aesthetic responses. However, the literal out-of-ordinariness is not a necessary requirement for everyday aesthetics. The most challenging, and what I would argue forms the core of everyday aesthetic, is those aspects of our lives that are familiar, routine, and ordinary. The commonly given narrative regarding them goes like this. Everyday life is so familiar, so ordinary, and so routine-like that it forms a kind of background. In order for this aspect of our life to be fore-grounded as the object of aesthetics, it has to be illuminated in some way to render it out-of-the-ordinary, unfamiliar, or strange: it needs to be defamiliarized.

In this regard, one could characterize the notion of adventure proposed by Self-Taught man in Jean-Paul Sartre's *Nausea* as naïve. For him, adventure is "an event out of the ordinary without being necessarily extraordinary," such as "getting on the wrong train. Stopping in an unknown city. Losing your briefcase, being arrested by mistake, spending the night in prison."[10] Everyday aesthetics advocates who call for defamiliarization of the ordinary would instead focus on the nature of our attitude and experience rather than the kind of events and occurrences. All we need to do is to break out of the habitual way of experiencing all-too-familiar objects, environments, and events that prevents us from gaining aesthetic appreciation of them.

There are many examples to characterize this mode of experiencing 'everyday' aesthetically, and they together weave a familiar narrative of everyday aesthetics. First, consider Edmund Burke's discussion of novelty fueled by curiosity:

Curiosity from its nature is a very active principle; it quickly runs over the greatest part of its objects, and soon exhausts the variety which is commonly to be met with in nature; the same things make frequent returns, and they return with less and less of any agreeable effect. In short, the occurrences of life, by the time we come to know it a little, would be incapable of affecting the mind with any other sensations than those of loathing and weariness.[11]

Burke concludes by declaring that "a daily and vulgar use" will bring things into "a stale unaffecting familiarity." Things will recede into the background of our experience composed of familiar things that do not arouse any curiosity or excitement.

Rita Felski gives a similar description, although she argues against the commonly held view of defamiliarization as a condition of aesthetics:

habit is excoriated as the enemy of an authentic life, an insidious, invisible, corroding away of the soul. Routine reconciles us to the irreconcilable even as it transforms what was once magical into the drab and commonplace. The all-too-familiar numbs and pacifies us, lulling us into a trance-like forgetfulness; unable to experience the vivid, clamoring there-ness of the world and to be fully immersed in the moment, it is as if we had never truly lived.[12]

In the face of this drab, unenlightened routine, the popular narrative holds that "aesthetic experience promotes a radically sensitized acuity of perception that is the antithesis of everyday inattentiveness," and "the everyday must be rescued from oblivion by being transformed; the all too prosaic must be made to reveal its hidden subversive poetry. The name for this form of aesthetic distancing is of course defamiliarization."

This move toward defamiliarizing the all-too-familiar for enriching everyday life, in particular work life, is the strategy encouraged by 'artification' advocates who see benefits of applying art-like practice in those areas of life normally not associated with art. For example, advocates of arts in industry encourage us to adopt the "I-want-to-just-experience-life-to-the-maximum mindset."[13] Particularly because "in an office environment, experiencing life to the maximum is not always easy," they recommend bringing "the same intensity (of experiencing art) in one's job." Referring specifically to organizational life, another commentator makes a similar observation: "The ordinary . . . is easily strange enough" but it is eclipsed by "the atypical" which "can fend for itself," so we need to make an extra effort to illuminate "the ordinary" to make it "strange."[14] Artification strategy fully recognizes and utilizes art's power for sharpening one's perception. Referring to the workplace participants in photography sessions who testified that their visual experience became fuller, richer, and more intense, one commentator remarks that "when life is full of activity and information, we tend to switch on the 'automatic pilot,' which means that we do not really take in the world with our senses. Life becomes dull, but actually it is not life that is to blame, but rather our outlook on life that is poor."[15]

There are indeed plenty of accounts which testify to the aesthetic richness normally hidden behind the mundane façade of the everyday that becomes illuminated with different attitudes and approaches. They come from a variety of sources, ranging from artistic vision and drug experience to philosophical worldview and spiritual discipline. I shall give some examples here.

1.2.2 Defamiliarization as alienation

The narrative favored by many everyday aesthetics advocates is how defamiliarizing the familiar lifts the otherwise humdrum dreariness up to something marvelous. However, I will start with another kind of situation in which one finds oneself as an alienated stranger in a defamiliarized world. In this account, the resulting experience is one of anxiety and alienation, not a positive, enjoyable one.

In Sartre's *Nausea*, in contrast to The Self-Taught Man's yearning for out-of-the-ordinary events, Roquentin explains: "I had imagined that at certain times my life could take on a rare and precious quality. There was no need for extraordinary circumstances."[16] Roquentin's experience of the defamiliarized familiar, however, turns out to be negative because he loses the usual control of existence through conceptualization. His "nausea" is partly caused by the failure to experience ordinary objects in their benign everyday aspect: "I told myself forcibly: this is a gaslight, this is a drinking fountain, and I tried to reduce them to *their everyday aspect* by the power of my gaze."[17] However, he starts to realize that such non-threatening everyday-ness of the world owes its ordinariness to bad faith.[18] His increasing sense of alienation from the familiar world culminates in his encounter with the chestnut tree in a park:

> And then all of a sudden, there it was, clear as day: existence had suddenly unveiled itself. It had lost the harmless look of an abstract category: it was the very paste of things, this root was kneaded into existence. Or rather the root, the park gates, the bench, the sparse grass, all that had vanished: the diversity of things, their individuality, were only an appearance, a veneer. This veneer had melted, leaving soft, monstrous masses, all in disorder–naked, in a frightful, obscene nakedness.[19]

A similar feeling of discomfort is described by Sartre's contemporary existentialist writer, Albert Camus, who characterizes this sense of alienation as "the absurd."

> A world that can be explained even with bad reasons is a *familiar* world. But, on the other hand, in a universe suddenly divested of illusions and lights, man feels an alien, a stranger. His exile is without remedy since he is deprived of the memory of a lost home or the hope of a promised land. This divorce between man and his life, the actor and his setting, is properly the feeling of absurdity.[20]

Consider also Hans Ulrich Gumbrecht's account of when things that have been familiar all of a sudden take on unfamiliar qualities:

> It happens to me, about once every week, that while I am shaving in the morning, my ears turn into an odd addition to the shape of my face as it appears in the mirror. Their form becomes strange, almost grotesque, they look superfluous and obsolete in relation to what I know about their function....Clearly, these moments of estrangement impose themselves upon the flow of my everyday experience and my activities.[21]

While Gumbrecht is not committed, like Sartre, to considering that every sudden occurrence of defamiliarization causes uneasy estrangement, he does seem to regard such defamiliarization as a requirement for everyday aesthetic experience.

Although his concern is with regard to experiencing nature, Stan Godlovitch characterizes the most appropriate appreciation of nature as "mystery, ineffability, and miraculous," resulting in "aesthetic aloofness and a sense of insignificance."[22] He argues against one of the most dominant theories in nature aesthetics today, scientific cognitivism, developed by Allen Carlson, for its presumed anthropocentric attitude. Science organizes, interprets, and analyzes nature by means of our all-too-human conceptual scheme and vocabulary; as such, science does not tell us nature's story; rather, it tells *our* story, in the sense that scientific endeavor is a kind of humanization and (conceptual) appropriation of nature to suit our needs. According to Godlovitch, in science "the object is still *ours* in a way; a complex artefact hewn out of the cryptic morass"; in short, "science...offers us only a gallery of *our own* articulated images."[23] Nature appreciated appropriately, that is, non-anthropocentrically, evades our capture and leaves us with a sense of alienation. We no longer have a grasp or control, and we feel insecure and uncomfortable.

What underlies these descriptions of experiencing ordinary things as alienation (in Godlovitch's case, nature in particular) is that the most comfortable mode of our interaction with things around us requires an act of intellectual knowing that gives us a power to control them by organizing, categorizing, and classifying them. We construct a familiar world with a scheme most useful to us and we feel secure and comfortable in it because we can command it through our rationality. This narrative will be justified *if* we assume that the act of knowing is exclusively intellectual by imposing various categories and concepts to order and organize the world. But a question can be raised as to whether this is the only kind of knowing our world. Sartrean nausea, Camus' absurd, Gumbrecht's estrangement, and Godlovitch's aloof nature all result from our presumed *inability* to contain, frame, and order the world. While Godlovitch maintains that a respectful attitude toward nature requires us to accept this inability, Sartre and Camus in particular seem to lament this inability by presupposing our never requited desire and expectation to be able to tame and exert some control, both cognitive and aesthetic, over our everyday life, environment, and nature.

1.2.3 Defamiliarization as a prerequisite for everyday aesthetics

More importantly for our discussion here, however, there are many more thinkers and writers who provide positive accounts of defamiliarization of the familiar. Iris Murdoch, for example, asks, quoting Gabriel Marcel, "Why...does Sartre find the contingent overabundance of the world nauseating rather than glorious?"[24] and similarly states that "the rich overabundance of reality, the phantasmagoria of 'disordered' sensation, seem to the author of *La Nausée* a horrifying rather than a releasing spectacle, a threat to the possibility of meaning and truth." She contrasts Roquentin's "metaphysical torment" caused by the "grey undulations" of flux with a "rose-coloured" view in Virginia Woolf's works.

Consider also another literary account that positively describes the experience of ordinary objects unmediated by concepts, hence rendered unfamiliar. In her essay on "Seeing," Annie Dillard delineates both the challenge and splendor of "seeing" without the ordinary perceptual and conceptual editing, akin to an infant's visual experience or a blind person's experience of seeing the world for the first time after his sight is restored. She describes it as "pure sensation *unencumbered by meaning*," which is difficult to achieve, because "form is condemned to an eternal dance macabre with meaning: I couldn't unpeach the peaches." Only "a discipline requiring a lifetime of dedicated struggle" to "gag the commentator, to hush the noise of useless interior babble that keeps me from seeing" and "letting go" would enable this kind of seeing. When successful, she claims, the experience provides, "even to the most practiced and adept, *a gift* and *a total surprise*."[25]

In his discussion of the "social creation" of nature, Neil Evernden points out that "to return to things themselves is to observe them *before* they were 'nature,' that is, before they were captured and explained, in which transaction they ceased to be themselves and became instead functionaries in the world of social discourse."[26] Nature humanized is not "itself," but "ours" and we are alienated from experiencing nature as the "source itself." However, Evernden characterizes the direct encounter with non-humanized nature in itself as "wonder," "sacred," and "astonishment."

Although induced by mescaline, Aldous Huxley describes the altered perception of familiar things in *The Doors of Perception*. The drug eliminates the portal through which we normally gain experience of daily life consisting of familiar objects, rendering them mere names given for utilitarian purposes. Drug-induced experience instead "raises all colors to a higher power and makes the percipient aware of innumerable fine shades of difference, to which, at ordinary times, he is completely blind." He compares this experience to an artistic way of experience of things: "What the rest of us see only under the influence of mescaline, the artist is congenitally equipped to see all the time. His perception is not limited to what is biologically or socially useful. . . . It is a knowledge of the intrinsic significance of every existent."[27]

Zen-enlightened experience also describes this phenomenon of transcending the ordinary experience of things leading to a positive apprehension of them. I will focus on Zen Buddhism of Dōgen (道元), the thirteenth-century founder of the Sōtō (曹洞) sect of Zen Buddhism in Japan, arguably the most important thinker in this tradition. According to him, Zen enlightenment can be experienced through successful overcoming of self. Any experience gained "with the burden of oneself," he claims, is "delusion," because "one's" self-interest, whether as an individual or as a species, determines the content of our experience of the world.[28]

Seeing mountains and waters has differences depending on the species. That is to say, there are those who see water as jewel necklaces . . . their jewel necklaces we see as water. There are those who see water as beautiful flowers . . . Ghosts see water as raging fire, as pus and blood. Dragons and fish see palaces and pavilions. Some may see water as precious substances and jewels, or as forests and walls . . .[29]

Hence, Zen enlightenment requires that we "not ignorantly assume that what you perceive and know as water is used as water by all other species too." Until we "learn to penetrate freely beyond these bounds," that is, bounds created by the burden of self, we "have not been liberated from the body and mind of ordinary people."

Once we transcend various categorizations and conceptualizations motivated by our self- or species-interest, we can directly experience the true reality of everything referred to as Buddha nature. The raw immediacy of the phenomenon can be felt with our whole body and mind but defies verbalization. It is describable only as "suchness," "thusness," or "here of the immediate present."[30] While Zen Buddhism challenges our all-too-human everyday life experiences, it also gives an alternative to experiencing our everyday world as nauseating and alienating. Rather than experiencing the world's aloofness or lack of rapprochement, with Zen enlightenment we 'enter into' or 'become one with' the object with our entire being. This enlightened way in which to experience the world renders any kind of objects and activities worthy of appreciation. Indeed, various Zen-inspired arts in Japan highlight the aesthetics of anything, including mundane objects and activities normally not targets of aesthetic appreciation, without any discrimination.[31]

Thomas Leddy's discussion of everyday aesthetics is the most thoroughgoing treatment of engaging in experiencing everyday life with an artistic lens, rendering the ordinary extraordinary, as the title of his recent book, *The Extraordinary in the Ordinary*, indicates.[32] The primary thesis of his everyday aesthetics is that artists are gifted in experiencing and presenting the aesthetic dimensions of everyday life, illuminating a slice of everyday life with an "aura." We in turn can gain insight into the aesthetic aspects of everyday life, usually unnoticed or hidden, by being inspired by artistic vision embodied in art.

Because we take most things for granted in our everyday dealing with them, thus paying very little attention, wearing an artistic lens often renders the familiar things strange, and we experience them as if we have never experienced them before. Such experiences are refreshing, enlightening, and exciting. One could claim that many instances of art-making consist of rendering familiar things strange and encourage the audience to attend to familiar things in a different way. I agree that this is an important dimension of everyday aesthetics and in later chapters I will discuss some of the ways in which artistic creation can help open up the world for aesthetic experience located within our everyday lives.

1.2.4 Benefits of everyday aesthetics as defamiliarization

In addition to enriching and enlivening our everyday life as well as sharpening our aesthetic sensibility, there are benefits for cultivating this kind of everyday aesthetic experience. Because aesthetic sensibility requires that we overcome our normal attitude toward the object, event, and environment, it essentially amounts to developing open-mindedness and receptivity regarding these things. We encourage ourselves to put aside preconceived ideas associated with them and allow them to speak to us and engage us. Such open-mindedness and receptivity have ethical importance. They also guide us to live mindfully by paying careful attention to things and surroundings. In short, our aesthetic horizons become widened and our lives enriched. For example, Sherri Irvin claims:

> An experience that one has every day, like drinking a cup of coffee, can become quietly exquisite and even strangely foreign when done with full attention to the feel of the cup in one's hands, the rim of the cup touching one's lower lip, and the sensation of the coffee in the mouth and going down the throat. Such commonplace moments of everyday experience are richly replete with qualities that we tend to neglect as we physically or psychologically multitask, giving our full attention to nothing.[33]

Irvin seems to implicitly endorse Zen-like stance in maximizing everyday aesthetic experience: "Indeed, for most of us who are not Zen masters, much of our experience is like this: we receive and respond to all sorts of sensory information, but without having much conscious awareness of this process."[34]

Irvin also points out that cultivating everyday aesthetic sensibility encourages us to gain gratification without incurring moral cost, such as over-consumption. She points out that "many people are fundamentally dissatisfied with their lives, and are perpetually seeking after some outside stimulus, often a consumer product, to complete them."[35] The multifaceted problems of over-consumption among affluent nations, particularly in the United States, are well-known: environmental harm associated with resource extraction, energy consumption, factory production, and disposal of goods, as well as human rights violation and environmental injustice.[36] In light of these concerns, Irvin proposes that everyday aesthetics can encourage us to derive satisfaction from our existing surroundings and possessions without seeking new sources of gratification.[37] Thus, "if we can learn to discover and appreciate the aesthetic character of experiences that are already available to us, perhaps we will be less inclined to think that we must acquire new goods that make different experiences available." Instead of discarding a piece of still-functioning furniture for looking shabby and out-of-style, we can learn to take pleasure in its aged appearance through the aesthetic value of *wabi* and *sabi* or we can gain an aesthetic pleasure from engaging in a DIY project of upholstering and repairing. We can derive a quiet satisfaction from sipping a cup of tea and petting a cat instead of getting caught up in the frenzy of 'perceived obsolescence' which compels us to go out looking for the most fashionable clothes or up-to-date gadgets that feature merely cosmetic changes without any functional improvement.[38]

There is another way in which cultivating this everyday aesthetic sensibility can be considered beneficial. This happens when one's everyday life and environment are so desperate and it is beyond one's power to literally change one's predicament, such as living in a battle-scarred zone. Consider the case of living in the Gaza Strip, which offers very few resources to create an ideal living environment for its residents. In his "Reinventing Aesthetic Values of Minimalist Architecture in the Gaza Strip, Palestine," an architect Salem Arafat Al Qudwa illustrates how its everyday environment scarred by destruction and constrained by limited resources can still offer aesthetic inspirations that should inform its architectural practice and planning. For example, he illustrates how the way in which concrete bricks are piled up has the same geometrical appeal as Donald Judd's construction and how a window pane of an apartment can be appreciated for the 2-D pattern similar to Mondrian's paintings. In making flat round-shaped breads,

similar to the basics of minimal art shapes, women are laying dough with clean flat surfaces and repeating them in rows and columns. The natural light coming through the frame of aluminum windows at each empty room and actual space of the house; and their metal protection show another sign of this simplicity, order and abstraction attitude.[39]

Given that the political situation unfortunately cannot be resolved by individual effort, everyday aesthetic experience can help its residents retain a sense of humanity, dignity, and resilience. Ultimately, according to his observation, "the prominent note is resourcefulness, not hopelessness." In such a case, everyday aesthetics' contribution to their lives can be considerable.

Thus, one way of facilitating everyday aesthetics is to focus on these moments or pockets of pleasurable experience that otherwise do not get attention because they become absorbed into the background of our life. The assumption underlying all of these claims is that once we adopt an appropriate mindset and cultivate a sharper aesthetic sensibility, whether it be through an artistic lens or a Zen-like stance, positive aesthetic values can be found, or constructed, in almost every aspect of everyday life. This move to turn the mundane, everyday, humdrum into an aesthetic treasure trove is an attempt to extend the time-honored aesthetic attitude theory to everyday life. This understanding of everyday aesthetics confirms the claims made by predecessors that "anything at all, whether sensed or perceived, whether it is the product of imagination or conceptual thought, can become the objects of aesthetic attention" and "anything that can be viewed is a fit objet for aesthetic attention," including "a gator basking in a mound of dried dung."[40] This sharpened aesthetic sensibility deployed for enriching our everyday aesthetic experience works as a corrective to one writer's observation that "this catholicity in the denotation of 'aesthetic object'...has gone strangely unremarked," as well as Leddy's assessment that, "although many aestheticians insist that aesthetic qualities are not limited to the arts, even *those* thinkers generally take the arts as the primary focus of their discussion."[41] Interpreted this way, the strategy to extend the applicability of aesthetics to everyday life is restorative; it is returning the notion of 'aesthetic' to its original meaning and giving a more faithful account of our aesthetic lives.

1.3 Limitations of Everyday Aesthetics as Defamiliarization

Various accounts of everyday aesthetics so far help expand the domain of aesthetics by including the ingredients of everyday life, ranging from objects, environments, to activities and social relationships. I do not deny the importance of this expanded scope, the role art plays in facilitating such experience, and their value and benefit in our life. However, there are several problems with this understanding of everyday aesthetics *if* it is presented as its exhaustive account. I believe that this defamiliarization account is only one part of everyday aesthetics, and something distinctively everyday about everyday aesthetics, I fear, is not captured by this mode of thinking. I do believe that there are other important dimensions of everyday aesthetics that this account does not address. Describing these other aspects of everyday aesthetics is challenging, however, because of their elusive and paradoxical nature. At the same time, I believe that they form the core issues of everyday aesthetics and they are worth exploring.

1.3.1 Problem of indiscriminate defamiliarization

First, this kind of aesthetic experience brought forth through defamiliarization is possible only against the background of the everyday which remains familiar, ordinary, and mundane. The appreciation of the defamiliarized familiar makes sense only in contrast to the familiar experienced as familiar. Furthermore, if every moment of our life and every object surrounding us are made special, their specialness gets compromised or even disappears.

For example, consider employing strategies for "experiencing life to the maximum" in the work environment, advocated by the artification proponents.[42] Dillard, Zen practitioners, and others who recommend cultivating such artistic perception do not necessarily advocate adopting this mode of experiencing all the time. First, it is not clear how this intense art-like contemplative experience can coexist with the practical matters at hand if the former is to dominate our daily life. One can have a fascinating art-like experience of a paper clip, for example, but a report needs to be written and the desk top needs to be organized, even in an artified work environment. Huxley indeed worries that "if one always saw like this, one would never want to do anything else" and "this participation in the manifest glory of things left no room . . . for the ordinary, the necessary concerns of human existence, above all for concerns involving persons."[43]

Second, even if it were possible for every aspect of our life to become art-like, the potency of "strangeness" that artistic vision entails becomes diluted. To put it differently, if our life becomes a continuous series of "an experience," in Dewey's sense, can we even make sense of the notion of "an experience"? While increasing the occasions for having "an experience" may enrich our lives, this notion has significance *precisely because* it stands out against the background of the humdrum. Dewey's characterization of the humdrum is rather negative, just as artification advocates describe a typical, un-artified working life as mechanical and dehydrated. However, it is not clear whether Dewey would advocate turning every humdrum aspect of our lives into "an experience." Indiscriminately increasing art-like experience will end up diluting the very intensity and special-ness we seek. Instead, I think what needs to be pursued is a balance between such intense experience and the mundane.

1.3.2 Paradox of defamiliarization

Another, and perhaps more crucial, issue with accounting for everyday aesthetics by defamiliarization is its inherent paradox—to experience and appreciate the everyday as something standing out is to negate the very everydayness that needs to be captured and appreciated. This paradox has been pointed out by those who engage in everyday studies as well as advocates of everyday aesthetics.

For example, Rita Felski claims that the defamiliarization strategy comprom-ises the exploration of everyday life in its very "everydayness."[44] Everyday life offers "the stubborn resistance . . . to critical theories of defamiliarization and demystification" that may attempt to counter the association of the everyday with "habit, repetition, convention, the unthinking performance of routine activities."[45] She observes that even cultural studies dedicated to capturing the mundane and humdrum nature of quotidian life seldom succeeds.

Some thinkers on everyday studies actually do question this tendency to identify everyday aesthetics with art-like experience. For example, Ben Highmore formulates the particular difficulty of studying the everyday such as domestic chores: "how . . . would we call attention to such 'non-events', without betraying them, without disloyalty to the particularity of their experience, without simply turning them into 'events'?"[46] That is,

If . . . the everyday is seen as a 'flow,' then any attempt to arrest it, to apprehend it, to scrutinize it, will be problematic. Simply by extracting some elements from the continuum of the everyday, attention would have transformed the most characteristic aspect of everyday life: its ceaseless-ness.[47]

Attempts to appreciate everyday life with the artist's eye and musician's ear, Highmore claims, "ultimately provide little with which to recover *routine* for aesthetic attention."[48]

It is clear that the familiar and the ordinary can generate an aesthetic experience when we render them unfamiliar and extraordinary by isolating them from their everyday context and shedding a different light on them. However, are the ordinary and the everyday *as ordinary and everyday* always incompatible with the aesthetic? Do they always have to be put "out of gear" or "distanced" from the normal flow of experience in order for its aesthetic potential to be actualized, as Edward Bullough seems to claim with his fog-at-sea example whereby the aesthetic experience happens only when a passenger succeeds in distancing himself from the possible danger posed by the situation? Is experiencing and appreciating the familiar as familiar, the ordinary as ordinary an oxymoron? Although Leddy's recent work seems to deny this possibility, his earlier writing articulates the challenge posed by this possibility:

> It would seem that we need to make some sort of distinction between the aesthetics of everyday life ordinarily experienced and the aesthetics of everyday life extraordinarily experienced. However, any attempt to increase the aesthetic intensity of our ordinary everyday life-experiences will tend to push those experiences in the direction of the extraordinary. One can only conclude that there is a tension within the very concept of the aesthetics of everyday life.[49]

The most systematic examination of this problem is given by Allen Carlson in his recent work on "the dilemma of everyday aesthetics."[50] He argues that both a formalist and aestheticization approaches to everyday aesthetics create, rather than resolve, this dilemma because both lift the ordinary out of the ordinary. Carlson also concludes, and I agree, that Leddy's view developed in his *Extraordinary in the Ordinary* based upon the notion of the "aura" does not solve the dilemma, either. Finding satisfaction in simple and mundane slices of life, such as the example of drinking coffee and petting a cat given by Sherri Irvin, is more promising in solving the dilemma, but Carlson raises skepticism regarding what Christopher Dowling calls the "aesthetic credential" of such satisfactions, particularly if they are derived from proximate senses.[51] Carlson finds Arnold Berleant's engagement account of aesthetic experience most promising in solving the dilemma because "there is nothing in the concept of engagement itself that requires the items with which one is engaged to be other than ordinary, mundane, common, routine, humdrum, banal, and even just downright uninteresting."[52]

However, he finds that in solving the dilemma, the engagement model creates a new problem: "when we turn our aesthetic appreciation away from that which is itself special and extraordinary, such as great art and magnificent nature, and toward that which is truly ordinary in itself, such as everyday life, there is little or nothing to motivate, maintain and ultimately sustain aesthetic appreciation."

Carlson's own solution to the dilemma is to invoke cognitivism that was initially developed for his theory of nature aesthetics. By involving the basic knowledge regarding everyday affairs and objects, we can sustain our appreciation of mundane objects and activities in their very ordinariness: "it is that knowledge of the workings of the everyday world makes it interesting and, moreover, interesting enough to both motivate and sustain aesthetic appreciation."[53] He is correct about the necessity of some knowledge about the everyday objects and activities for aesthetically appreciating them in their ordinariness, but it does not get us too far because the notions of the ordinary and the familiar already imply some cognitive understanding of what they are, how they function, what their cultural significance is, and so on. Otherwise, they are simply unfamiliar to us and we cannot experience or appreciate them as familiar or ordinary.

Furthermore, as Carlson himself does point out, cognitive understanding, while necessary, does not provide a sufficient condition for having an aesthetic experience of the ordinary ordinarily experienced.[54] I can think of the following scenario where our basic cognitive understanding of a familiar object is necessary but leads to an out-of-the-ordinary appreciation. Consider, for example, the particular thrill of watching a juggler managing several knives in the air or a circus performer swallowing a sword. The excitement we feel is precisely because of our knowledge of what a knife or a sword does. The performance of such a feat provides a rather out-of-the-ordinary aesthetic experience of watching someone handling a knife, different from watching my mother skillfully chop vegetables as part of her domestic routine, though both experiences require my understanding of what a knife does. Thus, I believe that solving the dilemma of experiencing the ordinary as ordinary needs to include something more than basic cognitive understanding of the items.

1.4 Aesthetics of the Familiar as Familiar

1.4.1 Experiencing the ordinary in the familiar

How, then, is it possible to have an aesthetic experience of the ordinary and the familiar without making them stand out as extraordinary and unfamiliar?

What would be the content of such an experience beyond the basic cognitive understanding? One could claim that as soon as we pay attention to the humdrum and the familiar of everyday life, we take it out of the ordinary context; hence, experiencing the ordinary as ordinary is theoretically impossible.

I do believe, however, that experiencing the ordinary as ordinary is possible *and* it offers the core of everyday aesthetic experience. My argument is this: paying attention and bringing background to the foreground is simply making something invisible visible and is necessary for any kind of aesthetic experience, whether of the extraordinary or of the ordinary. Bringing background to the foreground through paying attention contrasts with conducting everyday life on autopilot, which puts the ingredients of everyday life beyond capture by our conscious radar. But putting something on our conscious radar and making something visible does not necessarily render our experience extraordinary.

There are two sets of contrast we need to consider here. One set is being aware and attentive, contrasted with going through motions on autopilot, although it is not an unconscious state. This latter state can be compared to Dewey's description of our usual way of operating: "it is possible to be efficient in action and yet not have a conscious experience. The activity is too automatic to permit of a sense of what it is about and where it is going. It comes to an end but not to a close or consummation in consciousness. Obstacles are overcome by shrewd skill, but they do not feed experience."[55] For example, I usually chop vegetables quite mindlessly, only concerned with the outcome so that I can finish making salad.

The other contrast is between experiencing the familiar quality of the everyday and experiencing its defamiliarized strangeness. That is, I can attend to the appearance of the vegetables, their feel against my fingers and the knife, the kinetic sensation of using the knife and the staccato sound it makes, all of which are all-too-familiar, *or* I can experience all of these familiar things as if I am encountering them for the first time. Both of these experiences require awareness, attention, and mindfulness and contrast with chopping vegetables on autopilot. It seems to me that the contrast that is important here is not the first set between being aware and sleep-walking on autopilot, but rather the second set regarding the different characters of the experience we become aware of when we get roused out of sleep-walking on autopilot.

Mindful attention can either lead to focus on the familiar quality of the everyday or instead highlight the defamiliarized strangeness of the everyday. Being aware and paying attention is simply a prerequisite of any kind of aesthetic experience, whatever the content. To paraphrase Annie Dillard's observation, with mindful attention, I may experience an unpeached peach or a peach in its very peach-ness.

Although proposed with a different purpose, we can apply here George Dickie's criticism of the examples that are given to support the aesthetic attitude theory. If the proper aesthetic appreciation of a stage production of *Othello* requires that one "attend to" the theatrical performance without the distraction of thinking about one's personal situation or wondering how the stagehand managed to move the stage scenery, Dickie claims that there is no need to introduce a special concept like "disinterestedness" or "aesthetic attitude." He asks: "Why not ask me straight out if I paid attention?"[56] The important distinction, therefore, is between paying attention and not paying attention due to "the occurrence of irrelevant associations which distract the viewer."

It may be the case, as William James observed, that our everyday life is permeated with habit, and "habit diminishes the conscious attention with which our acts are performed" to the point that we cannot explain how we do things literally every day, such as "certain daily offices connected with the toilet, with the opening and shutting of familiar cupboards"; neither can people "tell off-hand which sock, shoe, or trousers-leg they put on first" or answer "which valve of my double door opens first" and "which way does my door swing."[57] Until or unless something is changed, askew, or awry, "our higher thought-centres" hardly know matters that can be easily performed by "our lower centres."[58] Although putting on shoes and trousers results from our conscious will and we are not unconscious, it is as if there is no volitional will involved in the action. If such habitual actions make up the bulk of the humdrum aspects of everyday life, we can exclude them from everyday aesthetics, but the reason is the lack of attention, which places them under the conscious radar, rather than their routine and humdrum quality.[59] Dewey declares that "the enemies of the esthetic are neither the practical nor the intellectual. They are the humdrum."[60] I would instead hold that the enemies of the aesthetic are inattentiveness and mindlessness.

What happens, then, when we pay attention to the humdrum and place it within the reach of our attention radar? The usual narrative is to emphasize the humdrum as dreary, drab, tedious, monotonous, boring, bland, banal, stale, either lacking any order or organized purely mechanically. Marx set in motion an account of the everyday experience of a worker in the capitalist system as humdrum. The proletariat's work is repetitive with no emotional satisfaction or fulfillment, and their home life is also tedious, filled with back-breaking chores yielding very little pleasure. Marx describes typical factory workers' experiences as follows: "The wearisome routine of endless drudgery in which the same mechanical process is ever repeated, is like the torture of Sisyphus; the burden of toil, like the rock, is ever falling back upon the worn-out drudge."[61]

Dewey also characterizes the humdrum as dreary, consisting of "slackness of loose ends; submission to convention in practice and intellectual procedure" in which "things happen, but they are neither definitely included nor decisively excluded; we drift. We yield according to external pressure, or evade and compromise. There are beginnings and cessations, but no genuine initiations and concluding. One thing replaces another, but does not absorb it and carry it on."[62] The bulk of our everyday lives is indeed a tedious succession of events, often performed by rote or simply to fulfill a goal: put on clothes, wash face, straighten out the house, and go grocery shopping. Nothing stands out to arrest our experience in its track, so to speak. According to Dewey again, "there is experience, but so slack and discursive that it is not *an* experience."[63] The humdrum contrasts with "an experience" for several reasons: (1) it lacks any coherent structure such as initiation, middle, and conclusion; (2) it lacks a pervasive quality that gives a unity to the experience; (3) the succession of events is mechanical, rigidly prescribed, or lacks rhyme or reason. Because of these reasons, Dewey declares that "such experiences are *anesthetic*."[64]

However, does such lack of a coherent structure and a unified expressive quality disqualify humdrum experience from the realm of aesthetics? I would argue against Dewey and insist that such experiences are not *anesthetic*. Though they may not provide us with "an" experience, they still affect us in an aesthetically relevant way. Consider Highmore's interpretation of Dewey's description of the humdrum. He points out that Dewey unwittingly provides a superb characterization of the aesthetic texture of the everyday: "there is an aspect of Dewey's approach to experience that can be used to adjust his allocation of aesthetic experience and which allows us to read certain passages within *Art as Experience* as positioning humdrum experience as aesthetic (or potentially aesthetic) experience."[65]

The idea of slack experience seems eminently suited to the diffuse consciousness of routine. Similarly the idea of 'drift', the picking up and letting go of concentration, works to point to the strange *character* of routine, humdrum life.... It should also be noted that 'slackness' and 'drift' are themselves descriptions of forms, albeit more formless forms than those more self-contained entities that Dewey wants to privilege. It is this sense of the opening up of humdrum experience to aesthetic expression which will also constitute new forms of experience that is being performed by Dewey, against his own intentions but in a way that partially proves his thesis.[66]

It seems to me that insofar as we experience the humdrum as dreary, tedious, bland, disorderly, incoherent, disorganized, monotonous, boring, and so on, it is charged with *its own* aesthetic (though not positive, enjoyable, and appreciative) character. It may be the case that we normally don't pay attention because of its relative invisibility and background-like nature, which makes the standout experience, what many would call the aesthetic experience par excellence, possible. At the same time, I don't think that, by paying attention to the monotonous and tedious aspects of our everyday life, we can necessarily transform them into extraordinary experiences, nor provide an occasion for having "an experience." It may not be enjoyable, memorable, or special, but such quotidian ordinariness does provide an aesthetic (understood in a classificatory sense) texture of everyday life. It *characterizes* the texture and rhythm of everyday life; it does not render everyday life character-less.

1.4.2 Honorific and classificatory uses of 'aesthetic'

Many advocates of everyday aesthetics, however, adhere to the honorific use of the term 'aesthetic' and maintain that the lack of a positive aesthetic quality in the humdrum disqualifies it from the realm of aesthetics. They share Dewey's notion of the aesthetic as "perception and *enjoyment*."[67]

Contemporary advocates of everyday aesthetics also identify the aesthetic as enjoyable and pleasurable. For example, Arto Haapala states that "we should simply become more aware of the *pleasurable* aspects of the everyday," although he argues against making them "strange" and "unfamiliar," in short, extraordinary, and advocates appreciating the ordinary in its ordinariness.[68] In her discussion of the pervasiveness of the aesthetic in ordinary experiences, including scratching an itch, Sherri Irvin also identifies aesthetics with a positive experience. She claims that "insofar as we are led to ignore it [everyday experience] or regard it as unworthy of attention, we deprive ourselves of a source of gratification," and "if we attend to the aesthetic aspects of everyday experience, our lives can come to seem more satisfying to us, even more profound."[69]

Thomas Leddy is most clear in claiming that "aesthetics has more to do with positive than with negative qualities" and "many kinds of 'making special'...are important aspects of everyday life."[70] According to him, "the goal of aesthetic experience is pleasure" and everyday aesthetics should work on "encouraging more aesthetic experiences in the everyday realm, and promoting the conditions that support those experiences."[71] Thus, Leddy claims that "there are...terms that denote purely *non-aesthetic* experience, for example 'dull,' 'boring,' and 'ordinary'" and "the ordinary qua ordinary is uninteresting or boring and only becomes *aesthetic* when transformed."[72]

However, I question these accounts of the aesthetic. That is, why must the term 'aesthetic' be defined honorifically? It is true that in common usage the term 'aesthetic' is generally understood in an honorific sense identified with beautiful, aesthetically positive, or artistically good, instead of a classificatory sense which simply indicates relevance to the aesthetic realm. But, as D. W. Prall points out, "the surface of all of our experience is aesthetic," retaining the root meaning of the term.[73] At the same time, in academic discourses other than philosophical aesthetics, the term is often used in the classificatory sense. For example, as I discuss in Chapter 6, the 'aesthetics' of manner and etiquette refers to bodily gestures, facial expression, and tone of voice, whether they are polite or rude. Such is the notion of "*aesthetic* of character" or the "aesthetic of morals," as used by Nancy Sherman in her discussion of manners and morals.[74] Furthermore, the role of aesthetics is a contested issue in art education. Against Kevin Tavin's claim that incorporating aesthetics into art education implicitly endorses its hidden socially and politically determined power structure, Paul Duncum points out that aesthetics simply has to do with sensibility-mediated responses to various cultural sites and activities and it is in itself value-neutral. He sees "aesthetics in morally neutral terms, as amoral, as neither inherently commendable nor damnable" and it should not be "constricted to either the entirely pleasurable or the morally commendable."[75] Referring back to the Greek term, *aesthesis*, Duncum points out that "aesthetics as *aesthesis* allows us to address agreeable experience but also disagreeable experience, the pleasant but also the unpleasant."[76] Finally, in design discourse, aesthetics simply refers to aesthetic considerations, such as the use of certain colors, texture of the material, the style and size of font, some giving rise to effective result while others not.

It is particularly crucial in everyday aesthetics that we keep the classificatory sense of 'aesthetic' as its primary meaning—that which is relevant to the aesthetic sphere. Regarding aesthetics in this value-neutral way is important precisely because the power of the aesthetic can affect us positively or negatively, and in certain contexts, it becomes extremely important that we remain vigilant about the way in which we are thus affected. Such contexts include detecting negative aesthetics in our life and environment, as well as intentional orchestration of aesthetic factors to manipulate people for commercial or political purposes. This issue will be the subject of Chapter 7 on the power and use of aesthetics. The conclusion I want to draw here is that, if the humdrum nature of daily life is a dreary drudgery, it does not render it anesthetic; rather, it is still an aesthetic texture of everyday life, though negatively experienced.

1.4.3 *Positive characterization of the ordinary*

However, is the ordinary of everyday life always or necessarily a drab drudgery, hence aesthetically negative? I think it is a mistake to label everyday ordinariness always in the negative manner. Just as defamiliarizing the ordinary can yield positive and negative experiences as I argued before, I believe that the everyday life as familiar and ordinary *can* be a source of positive experience, though perhaps not as intense or powerful as experiencing it as extraordinary. The qualities such as familiarity, comfort, stability, intimacy, homey, warmth, reassurance, and safety are often used to characterize this experience. Arto Haapala, for example, maintains that the familiar provides us with a sense of comfort, stability, safety, and at-home-ness and such qualities do provide a different kind of positive aesthetic experience. Such an experience, according to him, is:

more subjective than the aesthetics of unfamiliar surroundings. . . . This does not make the aesthetics of the everyday less satisfying than the aesthetics of the strange. Ordinary everyday objects lack the surprise element or freshness of the strange, nevertheless they give us pleasure through a kind of comforting stability, through the feeling of being at home and taking pleasure in carrying our normal routines in a setting that is 'safe.'[77]

He points out, and I agree, that "art is presented in contexts that create strangeness, and the tendency in aesthetics has been to maximize strangeness and to minimize familiarity" and "in the context of art the everyday loses its everydayness: it becomes something extraordinary." The point is not to deny the place for the extraordinary in everyday aesthetics but to deny its exclusivity.

Another set of positive characterizations of everyday life can be found in Yi-Fu Tuan's discussion. He recognizes that familiarity and routine are unlikely candidates for aesthetic appreciation: "At first we are likely to think that nothing is more contrary to the aesthetic, for whatever becomes routine fades from consciousness. Moreover, the necessities of life, which routine and order serve, tend to be viewed as outside the aesthetic realm."[78] However, one needs some degree of familiar environment, usually provided by 'home':

familiarity breeds affection when it does not breed contempt. . . . Beyond clothing, a person in the process of time invests bits of his emotional life in his home, and beyond the home in his neighborhood. To be forcibly evicted from one's home and neighborhood is to be stripped of a sheathing, which in its familiarity protects the human being from the bewilderments of the outside world. As some people are reluctant to part with their shapeless old coat for a new one, so some people—especially older people—are reluctant to abandon their old neighborhood for the new housing development.[79]

One's attachment and affection for 'home,' whether it be literal family home or hometown, is not based upon any requirement that it be "beautiful by artbook standards." Rather, it is derived from other values, such as "comfort and security, a haven of human warmth."[80] These qualities underlie people's intimate relationship with a specific place that Tuan terms "Topophilia."

Tuan admits that home's "informal characters of the order there and the typically diffuse multisensory ambience"[81] tend to dissociate it from the aesthetic as commonly understood. Indeed, many aestheticians are reluctant to include a sense of comfort, diffused multisensory ambience, and primarily subjective and personal response under aesthetic purview. In Chapter 2 I will argue against their reasons for excluding them from the aesthetics discourse.

Another characterization of the everyday experienced in its familiar mode may include qualities such as 'intimacy' and 'flow.' Ben Highmore points out that everyday life is permeated by both physical intimacy and psychological closeness. Everyday life concerns "that arena of life that is materially closest to us" as well as "emotional, sexual and psychological closeness."[82] A similar point is made by Dan Moller in his discussion of 'the boring.' While the quality of boringness in a work of art generally affects our experience negatively, particularly if such quality is not justified by the overall theme, he points out that the boring in our everyday life can indicate intimacy.

Unlike art, where sitting through a boring performance means only that the artist has to some degree failed and that we must suffer, the fact that we let ourselves be bored together says something about our attitudes toward one another, since we do not let just anyone bore us. Running the risk of boring one another takes courage. It would be easier, perhaps, to keep up a running patter during those long silences, but this would prevent us from realizing some of the benefits of mutual boredom.[83]

I don't think we need to settle whether the everyday ordinariness designates dreary tedium or familiar comfort. Most people, I believe, experience everyday life in both ways, depending upon contexts and circumstances. I also believe that most people at times experience aspects of everyday life as unfamiliar. Various characterizations I compiled in this chapter so far testify to the diverse ways in which we experience everyday life aesthetically (in the classificatory sense). I believe that what we need is a balance between these diverse kinds of experience to maintain a healthy life. If one is condemned, whether by choice or by circumstance, to experience everyday life exclusively as tedious monotony, life is going to feel meaningless. In such a case, a concerted effort to maximize aesthetic potentials from hidden crevices of life goes a long way to improve the quality of life. On the other hand, if one is always experiencing everything as unfamiliar, such as a perpetual traveler by choice, or an unfortunate person who is forced to uproot herself constantly, one's stability and attachment to some sense of 'home' will be damaged. Many of us experience a sense of relief when coming home after a vacation or a journey, even if it was full of excitement.

Although it complicates things, therefore, I opt for embracing the wide swath of everyday aesthetics in all its rich variety so as to be faithful to our experience. If there is an error involved, I prefer to err on the side of over-inclusiveness than under-inclusiveness. Simplifying the discourse by limiting the aesthetic to only one kind, whether it be the unfamiliar or the tedious or the homey, does not do justice to the rich tapestry of experiences life offers. I agree with Highmore that routines, in particular work and chore, "are often likely to become...emotionally draining" although they can also be "peppered with moments of tenderness and affection." And "it is the *simultaneity* of this that strikes me as both interesting and centrally important to the study of daily life, the way that routine can be experienced simultaneously as joyous and tedious, tender and frustrating."[84]

I would go even further and argue that the critical challenge of everyday aesthetics is not to determine the exact aesthetic character of the everyday (dreary tedium or reassuring familiarity?) or to strategize how to enliven the routine. I would argue that the most important issue is rather to discriminate between when and in what context it is appropriate and desirable to transform the ordinary into the extraordinary and when it is better to recognize negative aesthetic experiences as negative so that we can work on changing them in the literal sense. I believe that one of the challenges everyday aesthetics poses is to practice art of living and negotiate daily life by sometimes developing its extra-ordinary aesthetic potentials, other times savoring the very ordinariness of the familiar, yet some other times sharpening a critical perception of the aesthetically negative aspects of our lives with an eye toward improving them.

∗   ∗   ∗

This chapter has explored different ways in which the aesthetic experience of everyday life can happen. Sometimes, defamiliarization of the familiar and ordinary aspects of everyday life gives rise to an intense extraordinary experience. Some other times, the familiar and ordinary is experienced as such, comprising the aesthetic texture of mundane life. The resultant experience can be positive, but not always. But negative experience is also aesthetic in the classificatory sense. What is common to these diverse modes of aesthetic experience is mindful attention, perceptual engagement, and employment of sensibility toward everyday life.

Notes

1. Kevin Melchionne, "The Definition of Everyday Aesthetics," *Contemporary Aesthetics* 11 (2013), 1. Introduction http://www.contempaesthetics.org/newvolume/pages/article.php?articleID=663.
2. *Jacobellis v. Ohio* (1964).
3. Ossi Naukkarinen, "What Is 'Everyday' in Everyday Aesthetics?" *Contemporary Aesthetics* 11 (2013) http://www.contempaesthetics.org/newvolume/pages/article.php?articleID=675.

4. For example, giving a gift that is meticulously wrapped is a common, if not daily, occurrence in a gift-giving culture like Japan, while in the United States such a practice may be limited to special occasions like a birthday, holiday, and wedding.
5. The classic formulation of this view can be found in Edward Bullough, "'Psychical Distance' as a Factor in Art and an Aesthetic Principle," *The British Journal of Psychology* 5 (1912–13), pp. 87–118; Jerome Stolnitz, "The Aesthetic Attitude," in *Introductory Readings in Aesthetics*, ed. John Hospers (New York: The Free Press, 1969), pp. 17–27; and Paul Ziff, "Anything Viewed," in *Oxford Readers: Aesthetics*, eds. Susan L. Feagin and Patrick Maynard (Oxford: Oxford University Press, 1997), pp. 23–30.
6. Naukkarinen, "What Is 'Everyday' in Everyday Aesthetics?," Sec. 2.
7. "Everyday aesthetics concerns our recurring, daily routines rather than episodic events or projects." Melchionne, "The Definition of Everyday Aesthetics," Sec. 2a.
8. Thomas Leddy, "The Experience of Awe: An Expansive Approach to Everyday Aesthetics," *Contemporary Aesthetics* 13 (2015) http://www.contempaesthetics.org/newvolume/pages/article.php?articleID=727.
9. See Naukkarinen's chart in Sec. 1 of "What Is 'Everyday' in Everyday Aesthetics?"
10. Jean-Paul Sartre, *Nausea*, tr. Lloyd Alexander (New York: New Directions Publishing, 1964), pp. 35–6 and p. 36.
11. Edmund Burke, *A Philosophical Enquiry into the Origin of Our Ideas of the Sublime and Beautiful* (Oxford: Oxford University Press, 1990), p. 29. The following reference to "vulgar use" and "unaffecting familiarity" is also from p. 29.
12. Rita Felski, "Introduction," *New Literary History* 33/4 (2002), p. 608, p. 608, and p. 609.
13. Lotte Darsø, *Artful Creation: Learning-Tales of Arts-in-Business* (Frederiksberg, Denmark: samfundslitteratur, 2004), p. 14. The passages in the next sentence are also from p. 14.
14. R. Winder and N. Baker cited by David Silverman, "Routine Pleasures: The Aesthetics of the Mundane," included in *The Aesthetics of Organization*, eds. Stephen Linstead and Heather Höpfl (London: SAGE Publications, 2000), p. 137.
15. Darsø, *Artful Creation*, p. 120.
16. Sartre, *Nausea*, p. 37.
17. Sartre, *Nausea*, p. 78, emphasis added.
18. Iris Murdoch characterizes Roquentin's experience thus: "The things which surround us, usually quiet, domesticated and invisible, are seen suddenly as strange, seen as if for the first time." *Sartre: Romantic Rationalist* (New Haven: Yale University Press, 1969), p. 10.
19. Sartre, *Nausea*, p. 127.
20. Albert Camus, *The Myth of Sisyphus and Other Essays*, tr. Justin O'Brien (New York: Vintage Books, 1955), p. 5, emphasis added. He continues on p. 11: "The world evades us because it becomes itself again. That stage scenery masked by *habit* becomes again what it is.... that denseness and that strangeness of the world is the absurd." (emphasis added).
21. Hans Ulrich Gumbrecht, "Aesthetic Experience in Everyday Worlds: Reclaiming an Unredeemed Utopian Motif," *New Literary History* 37 (2006), p. 308. Sartre also gives

a similar account of Roquentin experiencing his face in the mirror as an alien entity (pp. 16–18 of *Nausea*).

22. Stan Godlovitch, "Ice Breakers: Environmentalism and Natural Aesthetics," *Journal of Applied Philosophy* 11/1 (1994), p. 23, p. 26.
23. Godlovitch, "Ice Breakers," p. 23, emphasis added.
24. Murdoch, *Sartre*, p. 12, p. 42, p. 37.
25. Annie Dillard, "Seeing," originally in *Pilgrim at Tinker Creek* (1974), included in *Environmental Ethics: Divergence and Convergence*, eds. Richard G. Botzler and Susan J. Armstrong (Boston: McGraw-Hill, 1998), pp. 118, 119, 121, 120, 121, emphases added.
26. Neil Evernden, *The Social Creation of Nature* (Baltimore: The Johns Hopkins University Press, 1992), p. 110. The subsequent passage is also from the same page.
27. Aldous Huxley, *The Doors of Perception* (New York: Harper & Row, 1954), p. 53, p. 27, p. 33.
28. Dōgen, "The Issue at Hand," in *Shōbōgenzō (The Storehouse of True Knowledge): Zen Essays by Dōgen*, tr. Thomas Clearly (Honolulu: University of Hawaii Press, 1986), p. 32.
29. Dōgen, "Scripture of Mountains and Waters," p. 93. The following three passages are from p. 96.
30. Dōgen, "The Issue at Hand," "The Nature of Things," and "Scripture of Mountains and Waters," respectively.
31. I explored this point in "The Japanese Aesthetics of Imperfection and Insufficiency," *The Journal of Aesthetics and Art Criticism* 55/4 (1997), pp. 377–85.
32. Thomas Leddy, *The Extraordinary in the Ordinary: The Aesthetics of Everyday Life* (Peterborough: Broadview Press, 2012).
33. Sherri Irvin, "Scratching an Itch," *The Journal of Aesthetics and Art Criticism* 66/1 (2008), p. 31. D. W. Prall also discusses the pleasure of drinking coffee, though in his discussion the experience is a respite from the busy work day. He characterizes the experience as "a directly satisfactory sensuous content, simply good to have in itself, a moment of directly felt pleasure, taken in isolation from the hurried business of a long day, and dwelt on fondly" and "one of the satisfying features of the surface of the world we live in." *Aesthetic Judgment*, first published in 1929 (New York: Thomas Y. Crowell Company, 1967), p. 39.
34. Sherri Irvin, "The Pervasiveness of the Aesthetic in Ordinary Experience," *British Journal of Aesthetics* 48/1 (2008), p. 35. Leddy, in contrast, has some issues with characterizing maximization of everyday aesthetic experience as Zen-like. See pp. 199–201 of his *Extraordinary*.
35. Irvin, "Pervasiveness," p. 41.
36. A good and easily accessible overview of various problems associated with today's industrial production can be seen in "The Story of Stuff" (2007) http://storyofstuff.org/movies/story-of-stuff/. I will take up the issues of consumer aesthetics in Chapter 6.
37. Irvin, "Pervasiveness," p. 41, p. 42.
38. Another example illustrating the benefit here is cultivating the taste for vegetarian food, as Sherri Irvin points out:

Vegetarianism is construed as a simple case of sacrifice, of adopting a certain kind of asceticism which may seem both aesthetically distasteful and motivationally

unsustainable. Attention to the aesthetic character of everyday experience may substantially alleviate this problem.... Rather than viewing vegetarianism as a matter of
giving things up, we can view it as a matter of finding different ways to indulge the
tastes that were once satisfied by meat consumption. (p. 43 of "Pervasiveness")

39. Salem Y. Arafat Al Qudwa, "Reinventing Aesthetic Values of Minimalist Architecture in
the Gaza Strip, Palestine," presented at The First Jordanian and International Conference
on Architecture and Design, 2014, p. 3 and p. 3 (text courtesy of the author).
40. The first passage is by Stolnitz, "The Aesthetic Attitude," p. 27. The second passage is
from Ziff, "Anything Viewed," pp. 29 and 23. Although both passages invoke
"aesthetic attention," which can be interpreted either in a classificatory or in an
honorific sense, it is clear from their overall discussion that both are using it in the
honorific sense: aesthetically positive.
41. Jerome Stolnitz, "On the Origins of 'Aesthetic Disinterestedness'," originally published
in *The Journal of Aesthetics and Art Criticism* (1961), included in *Aesthetics: A Critical
Anthology*, eds. George Dickie and R. J. Sclafani (New York: St. Martin's Press, 1977),
p. 624. Thomas Leddy, "Everyday Surface Aesthetic Qualities: 'Neat,' 'Messy,' 'Clean,'
'Dirty,'" *The Journal of Aesthetics and Art Criticism* 53/3 (1995), p. 259.
42. Darsø, *Artful Creation*, p. 14.
43. Huxley, *The Doors of Perception*, pp. 34–5.
44. Felski, "Introduction," p. 610.
45. Felski, "Everyday Aesthetics," *The Minnesota Review* 71–2 (2009), p. 3.
46. Highmore, "Homework: Routine, Social Aesthetics and the Ambiguity of Everyday
Life," *Cultural Studies* 18.2/3 (2004), p. 307.
47. Ben Highmore, *Everyday Life and Cultural Theory: An Introduction* (Oxon:
Routledge, 2010), p. 21.
48. Highmore, "Homework," p. 313.
49. Thomas Leddy, "The Nature of Everyday Aesthetics," in *The Aesthetics of Everyday
Life*, eds. Andrew Light and Jonathan M. Smith (New York: Columbia University
Press, 2005), p. 18.
50. Allen Carlson, "The Dilemma of Everyday Aesthetics," in *Aesthetics of Everyday Life
East and West*, eds. Liu Yuedi and Curtis L. Carter (Newcastle upon Tyne: Cambridge
Scholars Publishing, 2014), pp. 48–64.
51. Carlson, "The Dilemma of Everyday Aesthetics," pp. 56–7. Christopher Dowling,
"The Aesthetics of Daily Life," *British Journal of Aesthetics* 50/3 (2010), pp. 225–42.
I will examine this issue in Chapter 2.
52. Carlson, "The Dilemma of Everyday Aesthetics," p. 60, p. 61.
53. Carlson, "The Dilemma of Everyday Aesthetics," p. 63.
54. Regarding an example of a baseball game and the necessity of having some knowledge
of baseball in sustaining one's appreciation, Carlson states: "this is only to claim that
knowledge, such as this is typically necessary for motivating and maintaining the
aesthetic experience of many of the events, activities and objects of everyday life, not
that it is sufficient for doing so" (Carlson, "The Dilemma of Everyday Aesthetics,"
p. 64).
55. John Dewey, *Art as Experience* (New York: Capricorn Press, 1958), p. 38.

56. George Dickie, "The Myth of the Aesthetic Attitude," in *Introductory Readings in Aesthetics*, ed. John Hospers (New York: The Free Press, 1969), p. 30, p. 32.

57. William James, *The Principles of Psychology*, Vol. 1 (New York: Dover Publications, 1950), p. 114 (original all in italics, eliminated here to minimize distraction), p. 115.

58. James, *The Principles of Psychology*, p. 115. James, however, also points out the virtue of habit by describing a man without any habit: "there is no more miserable human being than one in whom nothing is habitual but indecision, and for whom the lighting of every cigar, the drinking of every cup, the time of rising and going to bed every day, and the beginning of every bit of work, are subjects of express volitional deliberations" (p. 124). For James, the importance of habit-forming spills over to the moral sphere in that it is not sufficient for one to figure out the morally right course of action and to have an inclination or sentiment to execute it; one has to take "advantage of every concrete opportunity to *act*" and "a tendency to act only becomes effectively ingrained in us in proportion to the uninterrupted frequency with which the actions actually occur, and the brain 'grow' to their use" (p. 125). A similar claim is made by the advocates of the ethic of care as well as Confucianism. I will explore this point in Chapter 7.

59. I shall return to what lurks under the conscious radar in Chapter 6, as we are often affected by the sensory experiences without being aware, let alone without consent, which is increasingly becoming the hallmark of contemporary capitalism.

60. Dewey, *Art as Experience*, p. 40.

61. Cited by Highmore, *Everyday Life*, pp. 6–7. This class-based narrative of the routine of everyday life partly underlies Jacques Rancière's "distribution of the sensible." According to him, those aspects of people's lives that are rendered 'invisible' represent the experiences of the socially and politically oppressed who do not have a 'voice' and cannot come to the aesthetic table (understood as sensible rather than with the usual connotation of beautiful or artistic). Jacques Rancière, *Aesthetics and its Discontents*, tr. Steven Corcoran (Cambridge: Polity Press, 2009). Early forms of artistic activism that attempt at redistributing the sensible are Situationist International and Surrealism, as documented by Highmore in *Everyday Life*.

62. Dewey, *Art as Experience*, p. 40. There is a remarkable similarity between this characterization of humdrum by Dewey and Roquentin's description: "The scenery changes, people come in and go out, that's all. There are no beginnings. Days are tacked onto days without rhyme or reason, an interminable, monotonous addition" (*Nausea*, p. 39).

63. Dewey, *Art as Experience*, p. 40.

64. Dewey, *Art as Experience*, p. 40, emphasis added.

65. Highmore, *Ordinary Lives*, p. 40.

66. Highmore, *Ordinary Lives*, p. 44, emphasis added. Highmore also characterizes "slackness, formlessness, drift" as "themselves descriptions of forms" ("Homework," p. 316).

67. Dewey, *Art as Experience*, p. 46, emphasis added. Similarly, he states that "the word 'esthetic' refers...to experience as appreciative, perceiving, and *enjoying*" (p. 47, emphasis added).

68. Arto Haapala, "On the Aesthetics of the Everyday: Familiarity, Strangeness, and the Meaning of Place," in Light and Smith, *The Aesthetics of Everyday Life*, p. 52, emphasis added.
69. Irvin, "Pervasiveness," p. 41. For example, an otherwise boring meeting has a potential for a positive aesthetic experience because "there is a texture of experience in those moments that it is possible to appreciate aesthetically, to gain a real satisfaction from" ("Scratching," p. 32).
70. Leddy, *Extraordinary*, p. 64, p. 76.
71. Leddy, *Extraordinary*, p. 114, p. 116. He points out that contemporary art, in particular painting and photography, helps to cultivate an aesthetic sensibility which renders experience of things like a junkyard, suburban malls, telephone poles, commercial strips, and the like aesthetically positive (p. 96). More examples can be found in his "The Aesthetics of Junkyards and Roadside Clutter," *Contemporary Aesthetics* 6 (2008) http://www.contempaesthetics.org/newvolume/pages/article.php?articleID=511.
72. Leddy, *Extraordinary*, pp. 151–2 and p. 112, both emphases added. The same assumption underlies the following passage: "seeing something peeling as ugly and then wanting to repaint it is *not aesthetic* unless it is part of an overall experience characterized by a kind of pleasure. Also, one should distinguish between ugliness that simply invites its elimination and ugliness that invites its contemplation: *only the latter is aesthetic*" (p. 115, both emphases added).
73. Prall, *Aesthetic Judgment*, p. 31.
74. Nancy Sherman, "Of Manners and Morals," *British Journal of Educational Studies* 53/3 (2005), p. 272, p. 281.
75. Paul Duncum, "Reasons for the Continuing Use of an Aesthetics Discourse in Art Education," *Art Education* 60/2 (March 2007), p. 47. Duncum is responding to Kevin Tavin's criticism of the use of aesthetics in art education discussed in "Eyes Wide Shut: The Use and Uselessness of the Discourse of Aesthetics in Art Education," *Art Education* 60/2 (March 2007), pp. 40–5.
76. Paul Duncum, "Aesthetics, Popular Visual Culture, and Designer Capitalism," *Journal of Art and Design Education* 26/3 (2007), p. 287.
77. Haapala, "On the Aesthetics of the Everyday," p. 50. The following passages are from p. 51.
78. Yi-Fu Tuan, *Passing Strange and Wonderful: Aesthetics, Nature, and Culture* (Washington, D.C.: Island Press, 1993), p. 113.
79. Yi-Fu Tuan, *Topophilia: A Study of Environmental Perception, Attitudes, and Values* (Englewood Cliffs: Prentice-Hall, 1974), p. 99.
80. Tuan points out: "Home offers warmth, familiarity, and comfort" (*Passing*, p. 118).
81. Tuan, *Passing*, p. 113.
82. Highmore, *Ordinary*, p. 15.
83. Dan Mollar, "The Boring," *The Journal of Aesthetics and Art Criticism* 72/2 (2014), pp. 189–90.
84. Highmore, "Homework," p. 311.

2

Challenges and Responses to Everyday Aesthetics

In the last chapter I argued for diverse modes of everyday aesthetics, in particular by making a case for the ordinary and familiar of everyday life experienced as ordinary and familiar, whether its content be positive or negative. In this chapter, I will continue to lay the conceptual foundation for everyday aesthetics by presenting and responding to commonly raised criticisms.

The general thrust of the criticisms is derived from the typical trajectory of modern Western aesthetics that is primarily concerned with the objectivity of aesthetic judgments. This objectivity-driven discourse gives rise to a number of implications, namely the distinction between the aesthetic value proper and the merely pleasurable, the requirement of framing an aesthetic object, and a spectator-focused approach. These implications of prevailing Western aesthetic discourse have given rise to a number of criticisms of everyday aesthetics. By arguing against these criticisms, I hope to show in this chapter how this objective judgment-driven discourse is not always appropriate for everyday aesthetics.

2.1 Objectivity-Seeking and Judgment-Oriented Aesthetics Discourse

2.1.1 Everyday aesthetics' lack of aesthetic credentials

First, let me examine a commonly held criticism of everyday aesthetics that it trivializes aesthetics by including pleasures derived from proximal senses. This distinction underlies Christopher Dowling's recent challenge to everyday aesthetics. Taking an example of scratching an itch provided by Sherri Irvin, Dowling worries that "while these experiences seem to have a pleasurable or enjoyable character, it is not clear what is achieved by appropriating the term 'aesthetic' here."[1] By unduly equivocating the aesthetic and the pleasurable, he is concerned that everyday aesthetics trivializes the discourse and loses sight of "the core concept of the aesthetic." As is often the case when distinguishing aesthetic pleasure proper from mere bodily pleasure, Dowling appeals to Kant's distinction between the beautiful and the agreeable. The beautiful (representing the aesthetic value), according to Kant and Dowling, allows intersubjectivity, making dispute possible, while the agreeable is merely subjective and there is no sense in which we can engage in a dispute. Dowling encourages that "one should...acknowledge the distinction between purely subjective and idiosyncratic avowals on the one hand, and, on the other, judgments with the kind of 'normative aspect' Kant associates with beauty." He also urges one to "recognize that the 'aesthetic' judgments that are typically of interest in discussions of art are those possessing such a normative aspect such that judgers will...demand agreement from apparent dissenters." The merely agreeable pleasures lack "aesthetic credentials," according to him, because they generate only "mere first-person reports that are of little interest to others because others can never share them."

Glenn Parsons and Allen Carlson give a similar challenge against inclusion of bodily pleasures in the aesthetic arena. They claim that inclusion of purely bodily pleasures, such as "the pleasures of exercising, taking a bath, drinking lemonade, or engaging in sexual activity," will make the domain of aesthetics too broad and lead to *reductio ad absurdum*.[2] They give several reasons for this claim. First, they appeal to the time-honored distinction between the distal and proximal senses: "traditional aesthetic theories are almost univocal in insisting upon a fundamental difference in kind between aesthetic pleasures and pleasures that are merely 'bodily', such as the pleasure of a warm bath, the pleasure of eating an apple, or sexual gratification." But it is not only in aesthetic theories but also common linguistic usage that, according to them, testifies to the distinction.

Second, again appealing to "the current linguistic usage," they point out that we do not "classify bodily pleasures, such as those due to warm baths and sexual intercourse, even when those pleasures are complex, specifiable, and meaningful, with the pleasures of listening to Bach or gazing on the *Mona Lisa*."[3] Third, the experiences gained through proximal senses are localized, while those gained through distal senses are not. Finally, a bodily, multisensory engagement with objects by including touch, taste, and smell, allows "less of a place for knowledge and criticism in the appreciation of the everyday," leading to relativism which they, like many other aestheticians, seek to avoid. They conclude that the most we can say about proximal sensory experiences is that they are "adjuncts or admixtures to aesthetic appreciation," but "not elements of it, strictly speaking."

Echoing Parsons and Carlson, Jane Forsey, in her discussion on the aesthetics of design, also gives the same challenge regarding everyday aesthetics advocates' inclusion of bodily pleasure. Doing so, according to her, "threatens to collapse aesthetic experience into bodily pleasure in general, a distinction that...is important to maintain."[4] She asks regarding the pleasure of drinking lemonade: "is it in any way beautiful or aesthetically great, meaningful or profound?"

I will argue against their criticism of everyday aesthetics in sections 2.1.2, 2.1.3, and 2.1.4. But at first it is important to remind ourselves that the distinction between distal and proximal senses is derived from the Western mind–body dualism that privileges mind and distal senses. It is by no means a universally shared view, and the appeal to "the traditional distinction" needs to be qualified. Even within the Western philosophical discourse, there have been increasing challenges to this hierarchical dualism, ranging from feminism and environmental ethics to comparative philosophy. As I mentioned in the Introduction, a number of issues debated in everyday aesthetics discourse, indeed the necessity of its very existence, may be a non-issue in other cultural and intellectual traditions. However, given that the debate is taking place in the context of everyday aesthetics situated in the Western aesthetic tradition, I will continue my response to the above challenges.[5]

Specifically, I will address the following three points: (1) the charge that bodily sensations do not lead to meaningful, profound experiences typically provided by distal sensory experiences, such as appreciation of Bach or the *Mona Lisa*; (2) the presumed impossibility of shareability and communicability of experiences gained by proximal senses; (3) the lack of frame for an aesthetic object that leads to relativism of judgment.

2.1.2 Everyday aesthetics' lack of seriousness and profundity

First, let me examine the claim that if an experience does not generate a profound, meaningful appreciation typically afforded by works of art and magnificent nature, it lacks aesthetic credential. The problem of this stance is that such a strict requirement would exclude many experiences and judgments regarding art, as some art objects fail to provide profound experiences. That is, even within the realm of art, such experiences are rarified. We gain a variety of experiences from diverse art objects, some unforgettably powerful while others mediocre. So, unless we want to commit to limiting *bona fide* aesthetic experience to only those derived from appreciation of Bach or the *Mona Lisa*, we cannot count the lack of similar experiences in everyday life gained from proximal senses against their inclusion in the aesthetics discourse.

The issue, however, is larger than the status of proximal senses. It regards whether the aesthetic inquiry should be restricted to the traditional issues dealing with beauty and sublimity that often afford us a profound and meaningful experience. What about other qualities we often experience, such as pretty, cute, sweet, glamorous, exuberant, vibrant, peaceful, subtle, calm, cozy, comfortable, and the like? There are also negative qualities such as drab, dowdy, nondescript, gaudy, garish, offensive, unsightly, repulsive, and so on. Let us put aside for the moment those negative qualities, as I will devote section 7.4 in the final chapter to the importance of negative aesthetics.

Thomas Leddy provides a thorough discussion of "a bestiary of aesthetic terms" and concludes that "a fruitful way to explore the aesthetics of everyday life is through discussion of aesthetic terms."[6] He reviews and argues against the support of various predecessors for excluding many of these terms from the aesthetic realm because they are considered not serious enough. The upshot of his view, which I share, is that there is no inconsistency in including a variety of these terms in the aesthetic arena without committing to considering their value to be equal. He argues that "aesthetics has levels: 'fun,' 'pretty,' 'clean,' and 'ordered' are relatively simple, surface-oriented aesthetic concepts, whereas 'beautiful,' 'sublime,' 'elegant,' are more complex and multi-layered." As he puts it, some aesthetic qualities belong to "major league" while others to "minor league."

I find Leddy's speculation for the possible reason behind this hierarchy to be very interesting. His previous work on qualities such as "sparkle" and "shine" sheds light on how these qualities immediately attract the young and the unsophisticated. He observes that the attraction to these qualities is often associated with the aesthetic values of the working class, the poor, children, folk customs and pre-industrial societies.[7] In a more recent discussion in his book, Leddy offers the same explanation: "It is possible that the concept of the pretty has, in part, been downgraded in our society for sexist and homophobic reasons. Adultist (only children care about the pretty) and classist (concern about the pretty is low-class) reasons may also play a role."[8] If we follow the view that the aesthetic proper needs to be limited to the beautiful, the meaningful, and the profound, does it mean that those whose experiences consist primarily of the pretty, the shiny, the glittering, the cute, and so on, have no aesthetic life to speak of? It may be the case that their aesthetic lives are missing something and thereby impoverished, compared to those whose aesthetic lives consist of appreciating the works of Bach or the *Mona Lisa*. But that is different from denying the aesthetic status of those "minor league" aesthetic qualities.

Although experience of these qualities may not require a sophisticated sensibility or sharpened perceptive power, they are not unmediated knee-jerk reactions, either. For example, the quality of being dirty and messy presupposes a certain framework and cultural practice, and it is the placement of a substance within it that makes something dirty, not the substance itself. Mary Douglas points out that what is considered dirty is displacement of an object, such as

"shoes . . . on the dining-table; . . . cooking utensils in the bedroom, or food bespat-
tered on clothing; . . . outdoors things indoors . . . "⁹ Arthur Danto also points out
that "there is nothing disgusting in the sight of a baby with food all over its face,
though, depending on circumstances, we may find it disgusting that a grown
man's face should be smeared with *marinara* sauce."[10]

Furthermore, in discussing everyday aesthetics, it is particularly important to
include those 'minor league' aesthetic qualities in its purview. It is because our
daily lives are more often guided by our responses to those qualities than to the
profound experience of beauty. I buy a dress because it is pretty, put a crystal
ornament near a window so that it will sparkle, have a heart-warming moment
seeing an online video clip of cute puppies, settle into a chair near the fireplace to
enjoy the cozy feeling, and the like. It is true that none of these experiences
normally elevate my soul, enlighten my worldview, or lead to an existential
awakening like a great work of art or magnificent nature. But one could claim
that what they lack in profundity and intensity is made up by their prevalence in
our life. In addition, as I will explore in Part III, in our daily lives, our responses to
these qualities often lead us to a certain action, such as purchasing or discarding
the object, or supporting a certain cause. Commercial enterprise and political
campaigning also often make use of these qualities that are easily recognizable
and have the power to affect people's thinking and resultant actions. For these
reasons, I believe that it is a mistake to disregard qualities like pretty and cute
from the aesthetic realm.[11]

2.1.3 Proximal senses' lack of claim to universality

But what about the aesthetic credential of bodily pleasures gained through the
proximal senses of touch, smell, taste, and proprioception? First, it should be
noted that there have been an increasing number of contemporary writings that
support the aesthetic credential of proximate senses. The reasons range from the
possibility of ordering and arranging such experiences, equivalent to compositions facilitated by distal senses, the proximal senses' capability of embodying
meaning and providing knowledge, the ever-increasing popularity of practices
like wine-tasting, perfumery, and food criticism with distinct vocabulary and
criteria, and the recent proliferation of art projects that feature experiences
gained through proximal senses.

In spite of these recent developments, however, as we have seen, there continues to be a reluctance to include proximal senses in the aesthetics discourse,
because they are usually considered quintessential knee-jerk reactions with no
mediating reflection or contemplation. Pleasures of touching a piece of silk, eating
a strawberry, and smelling a rose are immediate; we don't need the particular

training or sophisticated sensibility that is required when listening to Bach or looking at the *Mona Lisa*.

However, is this a fair comparison? I think the problem here is that the experience gained through proximal senses in these criticisms is often character-ized as an isolated singular occurrence. Kant's discussion is instructive here, although I disagree with his overall view of excluding proximal senses from the realm of the aesthetic proper. If we were to follow Kant, not only do we need to exclude proximate senses but also the Lockean secondary qualities from consti-tuting the beautiful. For the former, he lists examples such as the taste of Canary wine and the smell of a flower. Even within the experience gained through distal senses, he excludes secondary qualities such as the color violet, the green of a grass plot, and the sound of an instrument.[12] The beauty of a painting, thus according to him, consists of delineation:

In painting, sculpture and in all the formative arts—in architecture and horticulture, so far as they are beautiful arts—the *delineation* is the essential thing; and here it is not what gratifies in sensation but what pleases by means of its form that is fundamental for taste. The colors which light up the sketch belong to the charm; they may indeed enliven the object for sensation, but they cannot make it worthy of contemplation and beautiful.... The *charm* of colors or of the pleasant tones of an instrument may be added, but the *delineation* in the first case and the composition in the second constitute the proper object of the pure judgment of taste.[13]

If we highlight his admission here that the charm of colors or of the pleasant tones of an instrument may be added to the beauty of the object, and if we follow his definition of the beautiful as purposiveness without a purpose, then it seems to me that a case can be made that bodily sensations and Lockean secondary qualities can be constitutive of beauty. Color, tone, and other bodily sensations should be able to contribute to the beautiful insofar as they form a relationship with the delineation, beauty proper in his theory, or amongst themselves.[14]

The pleasure derived from scratching an itch can be used as an example of a pleasurable feeling that is merely an agreeable sensation without aesthetic rele-vance *if* it is taken in isolation from the context in which it occurs and without regard to its place in the flow of everyday experience. However, once that sensation is integrated into the rest of the experience, I believe it can play a role in constituting part of our aesthetic life, as explained by Irvin:

Once we see the particular phenomena as embedded within a more complex structure of experience...the reluctance to apply aesthetic concepts should diminish. Though one might resist speaking of a color or simple auditory tone, *perceived on its own*, as aesthetic, it is clear that such simple elements contribute to the aesthetic character of the more complex structure of which they are a part. And, when we think of them as part of a complex structure, it becomes appropriate to speak of the elements themselves as having an aesthetic character.[15]

Understood this way, seemingly purely physiological response like getting a relief from scratching an itch cannot be automatically dismissed from the realm of the aesthetic. Irvin continues: "Itches and scratches have their own place in human experience that is hardly exhausted by an understanding of their physiological functions and roles: perhaps we can appreciate them aesthetically by acknowledging such things as how they call attention to our somatic experience and how they color that experience in certain ways."[16] Overall, "when a basic somatic experience such as an itch takes its place in a larger structure of experience that we may attend to and appreciate, it clearly is appropriate to see it as having an aesthetic character."

Kevin Melchionne's response to Dowling's critique of everyday aesthetics' presumed lack of aesthetic credentials is also helpful here. What defines everyday life, Melchionne argues, is its place in "the pattern of everyday life."[17] What we do in everyday life is not isolated from the flow of life. Instead, "ordinary experiences typically derive significance from their role in a pattern of daily life" and

slices of experience, by themselves, cannot tell us much about aesthetic value in everyday life. Part of the problem in the debate is that we are treating thin trenches of everyday life as autonomous objects, as if moments of daily life come before us one after the next, each to be considered on its own terms, like paintings in a gallery.

So, "by focusing on discrete moments, we have mistaken the very ontology of everyday aesthetic life. What matters is the routine, habit, or practice, the cumulative rather than individual effect." Thus, the experience of scratching an itch *in isolation* and *by itself* may not carry any aesthetic credential, just as the color red itself divorced from what it is red of (e.g., sunset) and the circumstance surrounding the experience, but when it is experienced as a part of the whole or within the flow of one's life, we cannot automatically dismiss it for being a purely bodily, hence trivial, sensation.

A good example to illustrate the integral role an uncomfortable itch can play in providing an overall aesthetic experience is Baird Callicott's description of wading into a bog. In addition to seeing not-so-spectacular plants, he narrates that the experience is not particularly pleasant; indeed, it can be uncomfortable: "To reach the bog I must wade across its mucky moat, penetrate a dense thicket of alders and in summer fight off mosquitoes, black and deer flies. My shoes and trousers get wet; my skin gets scratched and bitten. The experience is not particularly pleasant or, for that matter, spectacular; but it is always somehow *satisfying aesthetically*."[18] But why is it aesthetically satisfying when there is so much bodily discomfort, including the itches from mosquito and fly bites? It is because of the sense of the place, in this case a bog, felt by the unified combination of various elements, including bodily discomfort. Callicott identifies the beauty of a bog as "the palpable unity and closure of the interconnected living components" and he argues that such a unity can be experienced only with the conceptual understanding of a bog as an ecological unit: "it is this conceptual act that completes the sensory experience and causes it to be *distinctly aesthetic, instead of merely uncomfortable*."

Although going through a bog is not a typical everyday activity for many (unless one is a nature lover, a cranberry farmer, or possibly a surveyor working in boggy and marshy areas), his account of experiencing a bog with all its dimensions helps provide a case where the physiological response *can* become an indispensable part of an aesthetic experience. Of course, one can have a similar experience minus the annoyance of pesky insects and resultant bites and welts by, for example, enclosing oneself in a glass container. Then the experience gained will not be a full-fledged experience *of the bog*, though it can still be an aesthetic experience. The difference will be comparable to climbing a mountain which makes one exhausted and breathless instead of taking a ropeway to reach the summit. The bodily sensations, such as aching muscles, sore feet, sweaty skin, breathlessness, thirst, and the increasingly heavy weight of the backpack, may not belong to the aesthetic realm *if taken by themselves in isolation*, even if such a surgical maneuver were to be possible. But *taken together*, they are integral to the experience of mountain-climbing. The point here is simply to establish that the physiological response cannot be automatically excluded from the realm of the aesthetic.

Wading through a bog and mountain climbing present cases in which an unpleasant bodily sensation like an itch and a sore muscle can contribute positively toward an overall aesthetic experience. But what about the more familiar cases where an itch is experienced simply as an unpleasant annoyance? Does its negative quality take this sensation outside of the aesthetic realm? I don't think that is necessarily the case, either. I admit that there probably is not much that is aesthetically relevant if I itch due to an allergic reaction to a medication. If the itchiness is severe, that discomfort will overtake my attention. But consider a case I believe is familiar to many of us where we are bothered by an itchy feeling caused by a fabric label sewn into the shirt collar. It is a minor everyday annoyance but it can be a part of reflection on the bad design of the label, in terms of its material and placement. My annoyance can be developed into a critique of the poor design of the shirt, despite its otherwise aesthetically attractive appearance, because I detect that there was not sufficient consideration given to the user experience of wearing it. One could claim that my negative response to the itchy feeling is simply a pragmatic concern and does not belong to the aesthetic realm. Although it certainly is a trivial matter and it lacks the profundity of a typical aesthetic experience, I do believe that my negative reaction to the shirt's design does belong to the aesthetic realm insofar as it is instigated by my perceptual interaction with the object that leads me to reflect upon the (de)merit of the specific design.

These examples demonstrate that what appears to be a purely physiological response is not necessarily irrelevant to aesthetics. What makes it an integral part of an aesthetic experience, whether positive or negative, is that it is not experienced as a singular sensation in isolation from the rest of experiences. This point is instructive when we consider its implications to other bodily-oriented sensations. It explains why I believe that the aesthetics of taste cannot be treated in isolation from other sensory involvement, and why we have to follow a very artificial, unnatural, and often awkward steps when doing wine tasting and similar taste tests. Eliminating all kinds of distractions so that the testers can focus on the wine's taste is designed to help ensure the objectivity of their judgments, and this isolation strategy is modeled after appreciation of paradigmatic art—in a museum, a concert hall, or a theater.

However, *in our everyday life*, when we eat food and drink wine, their taste is never experienced in isolation. We eat and drink in a certain context and situation, such as with friends, a supervisor, or strangers, in a fancy restaurant, fast food joint, or at home, with or without background music, using elegant glassware and a plate or in a plastic cup and a paper plate. Does the taste of expensive champagne stay the same if we drink it out of a paper cup? Does a homey meatloaf change its taste if it is beautifully presented on a fancy plate with exquisite garnishes? The champagne and meatloaf stay the same, but our *experience* is greatly affected by these contextual changes.

David Howes and Constance Classen make a similar observation regarding the taste test to determine which tastes better, Coke or Pepsi. Regardless of the fact that testers often cannot distinguish the two tastes, they insist that Coke (or Pepsi) tastes better. Here, "clearly, non-gustatory factors are playing a role" and "while the sensuality of perception should not be forgotten in the search for sensory meaning, it is important to keep in mind that the experience of that sensuality is itself shaped by diverse personal and cultural associations."[19] Consider another example of drinking the same wine under different ambient lights. Howes cites a research result that red lighting suggested 50 percent more sweetness to the subjects.[20]

In one sense, our judgment of the taste regarding these things should not change according to a different context and association, because the wine itself stays the same. The usual conclusion of these experiments is how easily people are fooled by factors other than the taste itself. However, when we are dealing with everyday aesthetics, we are dealing with *our experience in the ordinary context*. The criticisms that we fail to uphold objectivity, we are too easily swayed by different contexts, or we are incorrect in our appraisal, do not have much relevance because we can never err in having a certain experience. For the purpose of everyday aesthetics, instead of concluding the unreliability of those sensory experiences, what we need to conclude is that our ordinary experience is seldom obtained through a single sensory source.

The recent development in sensory studies sheds light on the way in which we normally experience the world, often identified as synaesthesia, understood not as an anomaly whereby a certain sound is associated with a color, for example, but rather as how we normally engage with the world through all the senses that are integrated. For example, Howes and Classen argue:

With the exception of the purified audiovisual worlds of modern media, touches and smells and savours are experienced together with sights and sounds. Sensations reinforce each, play off each other and, at times, contradict each other...they are part of an interactive web of experience, rather than each being slotted into a separate sensory box.[21]

They also point out that the assumption that vision and sound can be objectified and experienced in common while the other bodily sensations are private, personal, and subjective, is not shared universally or throughout history. They attribute the modern Western reliance on vision and hearing to the development and accessibility of writing as a form of disseminating knowledge. According to them, "one reason why modern Westerners do not feel compelled to make more collective sensory associations, ... may be precisely because we rely on our collective knowledge being stored outside of human bodies and minds in written texts," in comparison with the pre-modern period when "speech, intermingled ... with smells and sights, and even touches, made communicating a multisensory experience."[22]

Contemporary Western aesthetic sensibility, cultured in its artistic convention, such as listening to music in a concert hall, appreciating a drama on the theater stage, and looking at paintings in a museum, is premised upon isolating the specific distal sense experience from the rest of the environment and flow of life constituted by experiences gained by proximate senses and other distal senses. For example, as Jim Drobnick observes, typical art museums are white anosmic cubes with no touch allowed. Besides the need to protect and preserve the art objects, such denial of sensory engagement except for vision helps the viewers to isolate the painting or sculptural piece from the rest of our experiential field and concentrate on appreciating what the object has to offer.[23] All the distractions are eliminated in favor of our focused experience in isolation. We normally disregard the painting's relationship to the wall, the cough of the audience, and the stuffiness of the air in the theater space, and we do so for a good reason. Such is a necessary strategy to fully experience the intensity and integrity of the art object.

However, this mode of isolation most appropriate in art appreciation is not readily applicable to everyday experiences except for those cases in which we intentionally isolate a specific object for focused aesthetic attention as if it were a work of art. Instead, typically, a painting on the living room wall is experienced in its relationship to the rest of the room and furniture, the family drama over Thanksgiving dinner is orchestrated not only by the actions of each family member but also by the aroma of roasted turkey, clanking of the wine glass, and the centerpiece of arrangement of flowers and fruits. The music played by the high school marching band is appreciated alongside the excitement of the forthcoming football game, cheering of the people on the bleachers, and crisp autumn air tinged with the smoky smell of fallen leaves. We certainly *can* isolate one element from these multisensory experiences, but doing so takes away the usual, ordinary, everydayness of those experiences.

In this regard, the following anecdote related by a contemporary Japanese aesthetician, Takashina Shūji, is instructive. He cites a story shared by a professor of agriculture who conducted research on people's attitude toward non-human animals. In response to the question regarding what is the most beautiful non-human animal, American respondents immediately gave responses such as horse, lion, and so on, while the same question was met with puzzlement by Japanese respondents. What the Japanese respondents came up with was an answer like: "little birds scattering and flying against the sky lit with sunset."[24] Takashina derives from this story the difference between regarding beauty as a quality of an object (like a horse) and regarding beauty as generated by a situation.

Although Takashina's discussion is geared toward explaining the Japanese sense of beauty, I do not consider these two different approaches to beauty to be culturally specific, although the Japanese aesthetic sensibility is indeed weighted toward appreciating what may be called circumstantial beauty. It is because such an approach is not lacking in the Western aesthetic discourse, though admittedly not mainstreamed. For example, Archibald Alison is one of the few Western aestheticians whose aesthetic theory based upon association addresses this very issue. He points out how 'the same sound' of an eagle or an owl changes its character depending upon the time of the day (morning or night) and location (in captivity or in the wild).[25] As I will discuss in section 2.1.4,

Gernot Böhme's aesthetics of atmosphere also moves aesthetics away from being focused on an object in isolation from its surroundings.

2.1.4 Lack of frame

These considerations give rise to another challenge to everyday aesthetics' presumed lack of objectivity and impossibility of a discourse. Inclusion of bodily sensations as an integral part of an overall aesthetic experience, according to the critics, renders the object of aesthetic experience frameless. One can throw in random ingredients as its constituents, thereby making an objective account of experience impossible. This is in contrast to a paradigmatic example of art that is governed by conventional agreements that determine what is/is not enclosed within its frame. For example, the shiny reflection of the gallery lighting on a painted canvas is usually not a part of the painting; neither is a distant traffic noise heard in the midst of an orchestra playing a symphony. Though not without controversy, there is more or less an agreement on the frame surrounding art.

The argument for the necessity of a more or less determinate frame for aesthetic appreciation is given by Parsons, Carlson, and Forsey. Regarding my example of appreciating a baseball game in which I included not only the drama and players' movements on the field but also the cheers of the fans, the smell of hot dogs, and the heat of the sun beating down on our necks, Parsons and Carlson claim:

> Saito's conception of appreciators creating the object of their aesthetic experience,… renders a normative dimension for such appreciation elusive: it becomes difficult to see how aesthetic responses to the everyday might be critiqued as more or less appropriate, or how any meaningful critical discourse might be developed in regard to it.[26]

Forsey joins their criticism by also claiming that "framelessness and indeterminacy bring with them the problems of subjectivity and aesthetic relativism."[27]

There are several responses to the above challenge. I agree that *if* the aim of everyday aesthetics is to make a judgment on the aesthetic merit/demerit of an object, there needs to be agreement on what constitutes the object of judgment. Otherwise, we discuss and debate cross-purposely. I may be making a judgment on the aesthetic value of a couch itself while my husband may be concerned with its fittingness with the rest of our living room décor. My friend may be interested in the Boston Red Sox game *as a baseball game* while I may be more interested in the Sunday outing in Fenway Park. My view is that all of these should belong to everyday aesthetics. The first of these pairs is more familiar to us from art aesthetics premised upon the isolation strategy explained before, which provides a better platform for a determinate frame. This mode of experience expects an object to be of a determinate kind, such as a couch or a baseball game. I don't deny that we do experience everyday objects and events this way and make appropriate judgments—that the couch is exquisite, that the ball game was lackluster, and so on. Appreciating the Red Sox game *as a baseball game* would be the same whether one is watching it from the bleacher or from inside an air-conditioned VIP box seat. Comparing the notes and judgments between and among fans, whatever the circumstance of their viewing vantage point, should be possible.

However, I do not want to limit the scope of everyday aesthetics to only such a judgment-oriented discourse. Though it is meant as a criticism of my discussion of a baseball game, Parsons' and Carlson's comments are actually helpful in clarifying my view. They point out that my discussion shifts "between the phrase 'aesthetic appreciation,' with its connotation of an object possessing a more or less determinate aesthetic character that we may succeed or fail in appreciation, and the less committal 'aesthetic experience,' with more emphasis on the latter phrase."[28] I agree that my discussion equivocates the aesthetic appreciation of the baseball game as a baseball game and the aesthetic experience surrounding the game that is constituted by ingredients that do not belong to the game itself, including proximal sensations. My view is that such an aesthetic experience should be included in the purview of everyday aesthetics.

In this regard, it will be helpful to consider Gernot Böhme's proposal for "atmosphere as the fundamental concept of a new aesthetics." He points out that "the old aesthetics is essentially a judgmental aesthetics, that is, it is concerned not so much with experience, especially sensuous experience...as with judgments, discussion, conversation."[29] He presents his "new aesthetics" as a way of going beyond or overcoming the limitations of the aesthetics discourse dedicated to judgment-making by suggesting that "atmosphere" is neither a purely objective feature of the world nor a mere subjective psychical state projected onto the world.

Atmospheres are neither something objective, that is, qualities possessed by things, and yet they are something thinglike, belonging to the thing in that things articulate their presence through qualities...Nor are atmospheres something subjective,...determinations of a psychic state. And yet they are subjectlike, belong to subjects in that they are sensed in bodily presence by human beings and this sensing is at the same time a bodily state of being of subjects in space.[30]

Examples he gives are: "a strained atmosphere in a room, of an oppressive thundery atmosphere, or of the serene atmosphere of a garden" and there are many ways in which atmospheres are characterized: "serene, serious, terrifying, oppressive, the atmosphere of dread, of power, of the saint and the reprobate."

And apprehension of these atmospheres will "give us insight into the connexion between the concrete properties of objects (everyday objects, art works, natural elements) and the atmosphere which they radiate" which facilitates creation of a certain atmosphere found in "design, stage sets, advertising, the production of musical atmospheres, cosmetics, interior design."[31] A stage set designer can manipulate a number of elements to generate a melancholy atmosphere, where the feeling of melancholy works as the unifying principle for all the ingredients, although there is no instruction manual for creating a melancholy stage set, such as what color to use as the background, what sort of stage props should be used and how they are to be arranged, and so on. All the elements come together *as if* they are orchestrated to give rise to a melancholic ambience. One can put a Kantian spin on this by characterizing the craft of a stage set designer as creating purposiveness without a purpose.

While Böhme's interest seems to be weighted toward those activities that specifically aim at creating a certain atmosphere, I would expand the field even wider to include human interactions with each other as well as with the physical environment, which give rise to a certain atmosphere created spontaneously and surreptitiously without any conductor or organizer behind the scene. As I will discuss in Chapter 6, the nature of human interactions is constituted not only by what is said or done but perhaps more importantly by *how* it is said or done. The manner in which the conversation and action are carried out belongs to the realm of aesthetics insofar as they are sensuous qualities of the speech and action. For example, gentle and thoughtful demeanor among people in a communal gathering expressed through elegant body movements and softly and gently spoken words with a smile give rise to an affable, convivial ambience that goes beyond the content of the conversation. The aesthetics of the physical environment consisting of things such as its spatial configuration, the kind of arrangement of furniture and the background sound also adds to or detracts from the overall atmosphere.

Particularly when the atmosphere of conviviality and gaiety emerges spontaneously among strangers, it gives rise to a pleasant surprise. Such an air results from the lucky combination of the people's movements and actions, the weather condition, the particular contribution of piped-in music to the space, the street vendors' carts, and the aroma of what they are cooking, and so on.[32] By calling for a "new" aesthetics centered around the notion of atmosphere instead of a clearly definable and bounded object, it is not clear whether Böhme proposes to *replace* the traditional, object-centered aesthetics with this new aesthetics or *expand* its realm.[33] My view on everyday aesthetics is that the realm of aesthetics needs to be *expanded* to include those aspects of our aesthetic life heretofore not adequately captured by object-centered aesthetics that requires a clear and definable framing boundary.

2.2 Spectator Aesthetics vs Activist Aesthetics

2.2.1 Creator-oriented aesthetics

There is another reason why I believe it is a mistake to limit the aesthetic membership to judgment-oriented experiences. Traditional Western aesthetics is heavily weighted toward characterizing the experiencing agent as a spectator, similar to the way in which the experience of art is commonly characterized. The typical focus is on how a spectator 'receives' and 'responds to' an aesthetic object, such as a work of art or a natural object. The limitation of this focus can be revealed by examining alternative views.[34]

Friedrich Nietzsche observed this dominant mode of the Western aesthetic tradition, arguing that "our aesthetics have hitherto...only formulated the experiences of what is beautiful, from the point of view of the *receivers* in art. In the whole of philosophy hitherto the artist has been lacking."[35] He specifically mentions Kant in this regard: "Kant, like all philosophers, instead of envisaging the aesthetic problem from the point of view of the artist (the creator), considered art and the beautiful purely from that of the '*spectator*'."[36]

His own aesthetics instead focuses on the way in which we act as an artist of our own life by giving it "an aesthetic justification."[37] One can fashion one's self and life as a work of art by affirming every ingredient as contributing to an artistic whole, similar to the way in which a tragic event is necessary for a Greek tragedy or dissonance for classical music. That is, "even the ugly and disharmonic are part of an artistic game" and "it is only as an aesthetic phenomenon that existence and the world are eternally justified."[38] If successful, every contingency in life will be considered an inevitable and necessary part of an artistic whole:

...whatever it is, bad weather or good, the loss of a friend, sickness, slander, the failure of some letter to arrive, the spraining of an ankle, a glance into a shop, a counter-argument, the opening of a book, a dream, a fraud—either immediately or very soon after it proves to be something that "must not be missing."[39]

The same artistic justification underlies what he calls "a great and rare art": "to 'give style' to one's character," which is "practiced by one who surveys everything his nature offers in the way of weaknesses and strengths, and then fits it into an artistic plan until each element appears as artistic and reasonable and even the weaknesses delight the eye."[40] As such, "in man *creature* and *creator* are united" and the man who fancies that "he is a *spectator* and *listener* who has been placed before the great visual and acoustic spectacle that is life...overlooks that he himself is really the poet who keeps creating this life."[41]

Western aesthetics' almost exclusive attention to the appreciators' experience can be highlighted by comparing it to other traditions that emphasize the aesthetics involved in the creative act. The Japanese aesthetic tradition, for example, is dominated by writings by the *practitioners* of various arts, such as painting, tea ceremony, flower arrangement, haiku, linked verse, Noh theater, and martial arts. While discussion of the aesthetic experience of the *receiver* of art is not absent, their writings largely address the issues involved in the creative acts. As one commentator of Japanese aesthetics observes, "Japanese aestheticians... have generally very little to say about the relationship between the work and the audience, or about the nature of literary and art criticism."[42] Furthermore, what may at first appear to be training manuals for artistic practices are ultimately treatises on what constitutes a good life and how to live such a life. There is no separation between and among the aesthetic (via artistic activities), the moral, the spiritual, and the practical.

Even within a typical 'spectator's' experience, some writers in the Western aesthetic discourse have pointed out that it is never a passive, receptive experience and that it involves the 'spectator' in actively creating the aesthetic experience. Dewey, for example, points out that the aesthetic should not be interpreted solely as characterizing the receiving end of perception. A common assumption, according to Dewey, is that the perceiver or appreciator "merely takes in what is there in finished form."[43] However, he stresses that "perception is an act of the going-out of energy in order to receive, not a withholding of energy. To steep ourselves in a subject-matter we have first to plunge into it." The role of a perceiver thus includes that of a creator because "to perceive, a beholder must *create* his own experience. And his creation must include relations comparable to those which the original producer underwent."[44] Thus, for him, in aesthetically experiencing something, "doing" and "making" are inseparable from "undergoing" and "receiving." These observations lead him to complain about "a certain verbal awkwardness" regarding the term 'esthetic' because "we are compelled sometimes...to cover the entire field and sometimes to limit it to the receiving perceptual aspect of the whole operation."[45]

Similarly, Arnold Berleant's long-held theory of aesthetic experience as "engagement" also stresses the importance of the active engagement of the viewer, listener, reader; in short, the presumed 'receiver' of aesthetic experience. Aesthetic experience, even when characterized as 'contemplative,' it is possible only with the investment and creative activity of the experiencing agent through the operation of sharpened sensibility, imaginative power, and associative involvement. Dewey's and Berleant's discussions are useful in reminding us that, even as a 'spectator' or 'receiver,' we are never a sitting duck, so to speak, but rather an active agent of creative engagement with what we are perceiving. In short, we are never passive and inactive when it comes to aesthetic experience.

My concern with the limitation of the commonly held 'spectator' account goes one step further when considering everyday aesthetics. I am particularly interested in the way in which everyday aesthetics involves those dimensions of our lives where we are literally doing things to/with/for objects, environments, other humans and creatures, and so on.

While Nietzsche's account of us acting as the artist of our lives does not necessarily exclude us from literally doing things, our creative act in his view is still largely dependent upon what happens to us, such as sickness, failure of a letter to arrive, loss of a friend mentioned in the above cited passage, and his challenge is to see whether we are courageous enough to say "yes" to them, thereby rendering them indispensable ingredients of our lives. As such, the active engagement of our artistic activity is weighted more toward a conceptual, attitudinal stance rather than actually performing various acts.

The Japanese tradition, on the other hand, focuses on the literal activities of the artists, and since many Japanese art activities, such as tea ceremony, flower arrangement, haiku making, and martial arts are indeed commonly practiced by amateurs, it may come close to accounting for the aesthetic involved in the actual 'doing' of something. However, even by the amateurs, these activities are specifically practiced as art, somewhat separate from everyday activities such as cooking, cleaning, working, and the like.

2.2.2 Aesthetics of 'doing'

Appreciating an object, environment, event, and so on as spectators certainly constitutes one aspect of everyday aesthetic experience. I enjoy the functional beauty of my chair, savor the crisp air of the morning after the first snowfall, and relish the smell of coffee coming out of a neighborhood café.[46] At the same time, various activities that make everyday life for everyone can be appreciated from the perspective of the one engaged in the act: cooking, cleaning, gardening, laundering and ironing, mowing the lawn, repairing and painting, and so on. I can be someone admiring my neighbor's pretty garden or I can be the one deriving pleasure from planting flowers and caring for them; I can appreciate the fresh and crisp smoothness of a shirt laundered and ironed by somebody else or I can be aesthetically engaged with hanging laundry outdoors taking advantage of a sunny and windy day; I can enjoy the shiny surface of a doorknob restored by a handyman or I can make it my Sunday hobby to restore old furnishings while enjoying the quiet bodily engagement with the tool and the material. The first of these pairs is easily recognizable as belonging to the domain of aesthetics in the sense that my judgment (that my neighbor's garden is pretty, for example) can be shared, discussed, and sometimes disputed. But what about the second of these pairs where we are active agents engaged with doing things?

Just as Dewey and Berleant remind us that the typical aesthetic experience of a spectator is never passively receiving but rather results from both undergoing and doing, or receiving and creating, the activities we undertake, the second of the aforementioned pairs, also involve both operations. When I plant flowers, I think about the most aesthetically pleasing arrangement; when I hang laundry, I try to make the resultant appearance as inoffensive, orderly, and organized as possible. My 'doing' things is informed by spectator-like aesthetic judgments.

However, the experience involved in 'doing' things tends to fall outside of the traditional aesthetic radar for three reasons. First, doing things almost always involves physical activities, thus involving bodily engagement, and we have already seen that the Western philosophical tradition has tended to neglect issues related to body. Second, doing things in everyday life often involves chores, such as cooking, cleaning, laundering, taking care of the yard, and the like, which also get neglected as worthy subjects for philosophical examination. Recent developments in philosophy, particularly in aesthetics and feminism, as well as in art, help challenge this neglect of the body and the daily chores; they highlight the significance of these neglected aspects of our life. Third, such experience involved in 'doing' is not recognized as part of aesthetics because it is difficult to subject one's experience of engaging in an activity to an evaluative aesthetic judgment. There is no clear 'object' of experience which makes it possible to form an aesthetic judgment. For example, Forsey points out that "cleaning, chopping, and repairing are clearly quotidian *but not clearly objects of any kind*."[47] We can dispute whether a garden is pretty, but can we dispute whether or not the experience I am having while gardening qualifies as a Deweyan experience? Is it rather a trivial and purely subjective feeling that lacks "aesthetic credentials"? And is it appropriate to apply the judgment-oriented mode of aesthetic inquiry to such an experience?

Let's consider several accounts associated with food as a testing site. The quintessential candidate for aesthetics regarding food is, of course, the judgment we make on what we eat. Is this apple pie a good one? Is the pad thai at the new Thai restaurant delicious? Is the new recipe I tried for meatball better or worse than my usual one? Does sushi made by Jiro deserve three Michelin stars? What is overlooked is that there are many other dimensions of experiencing food besides tasting and making an aesthetic judgment on it. Let me compile some accounts given for the activities (in the most literal sense) associated with food.

Buffalo Bird Woman describes planting and caring for corn in great details. The experience includes a careful observation of nature to determine the best time for planting, bodily movements required in planting, pattern for planting the seeds, the care that goes into protecting it from crows, treating corn as children by singing to them, and communal reciprocity and support. Some of the descriptions are as follows:

I cultivated each hill carefully with my hoe as I came to it; and if the plants were small, I would comb the soil of the hill lightly with my fingers, loosening the earth and tearing out young weeds.

We cared for our corn in those days as we would care for a child, for we Indian people loved our gardens, just as a mother loves her children, and we thought that our growing corn liked to hear us sing, just as children like to hear their mother sing to them.[48]

Can't these series of activities belong to her aesthetic life? Although we ourselves may lack similar experience (like singing to the plants in our garden), can't we empathize with her expression of care embodied in her interaction with the soil, seeds, and singing?

As for the activity of cooking, let us hear from women writing about their everyday home cooking. Consider Luce Giard's "Doing Cooking" in which the title itself is indicative of her interest in and attention to the activity, separate from the joy of eating.

... the everyday work in kitchens remains a way of unifying matter and memory, life and tenderness, the present moment and the abolished past, invention and necessity, imagination and tradition—tastes, smells, colors, flavors, shapes, consistencies, actions, gestures, movements, people and things, heat, savoring, spices, and condiments. Good cooks are never sad or idle—they work at fashioning the world, at giving birth to the joy of the ephemeral; they are never finished celebrating festivals for the adults and the kids, the wise and the foolish, the marvelous reunions of men and women who share room (in the world) and board (around the table). Women's gesture and women's voices that make the earth livable.[49]

Audre Lorde also recounts her experience of helping her mother grind spices in a mortar, which includes rhythmic body movement punctuated by the muted sound of thump and the tactile sensation of pressing around the carved side of the mortar. All these sensory experiences "transported me into a world of scent and rhythm and movement and sound that grew more and more exciting as the ingredients liquefied."[50] Verta Mae Smart-Grosvenor's account of her so-called "vibration cooking" explicitly relates the daily home cooking to aesthetics. "I'm talking about being able to turn the daily ritual of cooking for your family into a *beautiful everyday happening*."[51]

Aesthetic experience regarding food also includes the bodily activity of eating. Richard Shusterman's account of his training at a Zen monastery is instructive here. He characterizes the practice as a challenge of cultivating "graceful, mindful elegance."[52] It requires a careful attention to "the aesthetically proper way to pick up and put down one's chopsticks and to hold one's rice bowl and cup" and "how we chewed and swallowed our food, how we passed food to our eating companions." The reward of such an arduous practice is described as follows: "Not only did my attention to savoring, chewing, and swallowing enhance the sensory pleasures of these activities, but also my focused awareness on the hand and body movements involved in taking and passing the food made these movements more enjoyable and graceful." He offers this example of eating as "aesthetic transformation of everyday life," what I called defamiliarization of the familiar, rather than the familiar experienced as familiar, which I consider to be the core of everyday aesthetics. But the point I want to derive from these examples is that food aesthetics is not limited to making a judgment on the taste of food, the issue that currently dominates the discourse.

What can be noted in all of these descriptions of engaging in activities is that the experience narrated is synaesthetic based upon bodily engagement (body movement, tactile sensation of dealing with soil, handling a mortar, feeling the heat, holding chopsticks, and the like, in addition to sound, smell, taste, as well as vision) and it is imbued with memory and associations. It is also inseparable from other values permeating our everyday life such as fellowship, reciprocity, care, and love. If one were to follow a typical trajectory of the aesthetics discourse, these features tend to disqualify these experiences from entering into the realm of aesthetics. As discussed before, bodily engagement is not a typical subject matter for spectator-oriented aesthetics, there is no resultant aesthetic judgment to speak of, and bodily sensations and memory are too subjective and personal to be readily shareable. I can do my best to describe my childhood memory of helping my mother in the kitchen and how my current activity of cooking in my own kitchen conjures up all the sweet memories associated with it and how the tactile sensation and the crisp staccato of chopping vegetables give me a pleasure. However, others can only proximate my feeling but cannot share in with my very personal and private experience, unlike the way we can all share our experience of watching a film and debate its artistic merit. Ultimately, therefore, are such experiences simply pleasurable and enjoyable without being specifically aesthetic?

It may be the case, as Dowling points out, that "mere first-person reports . . . are of little interest of others because others can never share them," hence lacking aesthetic credentials.[53] But does that mean that a substantial part of our everyday life falls outside of the aesthetic purview? Does the experience of the pleasure, often bodily engaged, we derive from daily activities lack aesthetic credentials because we do not, nor do we expect to, make a judgment about it?

2.2.3 Alternative to judgment-oriented aesthetics

It is true that we do not engage in making any 'judgment' regarding these accounts by examining whether the acting agents should be deriving pleasure from these activities or whether their experience is accurately described. We don't criticize them for being incorrect or wrong and engage them in a debate, unlike the way in which my husband and I disagree about the aesthetic value of the couch we are considering purchasing and try to convince the other. When I engage in an everyday activity like cooking, ironing a shirt, and cleaning the bathroom and if I derive pleasure doing these things, my experience is private and personal—I don't announce it and encourage my family to engage in a discussion about the value or veracity of my experience.

However, it is not clear whether it is impossible to invite others to share in, if not literally then vicariously, those experiences. The accounts related to food production and consumption I provided above resonate with us (perhaps more of us women?), even without the specific experience of planting the corn or grinding spices in a mortar. Theoretically, my private experience of cooking can be shareable if only I had a talent for articulating it in writing, speaking, or even communicating it artistically. Also, note that Shusterman characterizes his attempt to coordinate his eating experience with those of his companions "added a meaningful dimension of collaborative communal interaction that further enriched the dining experience."[54] The value of reading other people's accounts of their activities is that it encourages us to be mindful of our own experience and enriches the quality of our daily life, as I will argue in Chapter 5 on the aesthetics of laundry hanging.

I will end this part of the discussion with one of the examples given by Parsons and Carlson for a purely subjective experience: taking a bath. This may be a quintessential private activity in today's Anglo-American world. However, for many other cultures, this exemplifies a communal, social activity. Hence, if it is an example of purely subjective, non-shareable private experience, it is not clear whether it is due to a specific cultural practice or rather something intrinsic to this activity. When I grew up in Japan, regular bathing took place in a neighborhood public bath, and most vacation destinations there still continue to be hot spring resorts. Many other cultures also engage in communal bathing or sauna. Although bathing in Japan can be a solitary experience just as in the West, communal bathing is still a large part of Japanese people's experience.

Co-bathers, whether family, friends, or total strangers, can share enjoying the experience by taking into consideration a number of elements: being enveloped by the hot water and steam; the fragrance of the wood if the paneling and/or tub is made of Japanese cypress or cedar, and sometimes the fragrance of a seasonal flower or fruit added to the water; the view of a distant landscape if the resort hot spring is located with a large window overlooking the landscape; the texture of rocks and feeling of cool breeze if the bath is located outdoor, and the list goes on. Except for the landscape view, these are all bodily sensations, gained through proximal senses. But in what way are these not shareable? We can share comments with each other about the sense of relaxation, well-being, and the like, and compare notes with each other. In fact, there are guidebooks to various hot springs in Japan that describe the quality of water beyond its health benefits, such as its temperature (ranging from lukewarm to scaldingly hot), the sharp sensation due to acidity, soft feeling on the skin due to hydrogen carbonate, foaming texture due to its CO_2 content, smell of sulfur, soothing for itchy skin, and so on. There are several websites, with ranking either voted by the visitors or organized by travel professionals.[55]

I do not see any good reasons to follow Kant's treatment of these bodily experiences as merely adding "charms" to the experience composed of sight and sound, or dismissing the entire experience for lacking aesthetic credentials due to the subjective nature of the experience. The judgment-oriented aesthetics that is appropriate for the traditional aesthetics modeled on experience of art is not appropriate for accounting for the aesthetics involved in 'doing' things. A phenomenological description rather than a critical discourse is more suited for this dimension of our everyday aesthetic life. This view is shared by other advocates of everyday aesthetics. For example, Melchionne claims that "the promotion of discourse as a philosophical value leads us to miss huge swathes of our everyday lives. One of the virtues of a stronger version of the aesthetics of everyday life is that it offers a path to a richer phenomenology of aesthetic experience."[56] This view is echoed in Böhme's proposal of aesthetics of atmosphere and ambience. He points out that "the aesthetics of atmospheres shifts attention away from the 'what' something represents to the 'how' something is present. In this way, sensory perception *as opposed to judgment* is rehabilitated in aesthetics and the term 'aesthetic' is restored to its original meaning, namely the theory of perception."[57] Finally, Ben Highmore proposes to return aesthetics to its origin as formulated by Baumgarten: it is to "fashion 'reverse-images' out of aesthetic theories that are anchored in regimes of valorized art and beauty, but can be redirected in reverse to accommodate the ambiguity of routine" and it will also mean that "the first task of aesthetics . . . will not be *judgment* but *description*."[58]

One may wonder what is the value or purpose of phenomenological descriptions of one's aesthetic experience of doing things. Doesn't it ultimately encourage self-absorption and self-indulgence? What difference does it make if I derive pleasure from scratching an itch, drinking tea, hanging laundry, and cooking dinner? I think the benefit is several-fold. First, as I discussed previously, attending to and cultivating an aesthetic appreciation for these activities help us develop a mindful way of living. In particular, it facilitates leading a good life without the usual trappings of requiring material abundance accompanied by various moral, social, and environmental problems. Second, by being particularly attentive to the literal bodily engagement with the world, we can restore our mode of being-in-the-world that tends to be compromised particularly today where bodily engagement with the world becomes less and less due to increasingly electronically mediated communication and relationships.

Restoring our physical engagement with the world, whether through active involvement of proximate senses or through physical activities, has further important existential implications. Though his concern is specifically with the increasingly visual primacy of experiencing architecture, Juhani Pallasmaa's following comments are helpful here:

The hegemonic eye seeks domination over all fields of cultural production, and it seems to weaken our capacity for empathy, compassion, and participation with the world. . . . [T]he nihilistic eye deliberately advances sensory and mental detachment and alienation. Instead of reinforcing one's body-centered and integrated experience of the world, nihilistic architecture disengages and isolates the body, and instead of attempting to reconstruct cultural order, it makes a reading of collective signification impossible.[59]

Finally, a phenomenological description faithful to our everyday aesthetic life unencumbered by the traditional spectator-centered and judgment-oriented aesthetics reminds us that the aesthetic dimension of our lives is not separate from the other aspects and neither are we a disembodied existence isolated from the world.

*   *   *

I devoted Part I to arguing that everyday aesthetics discourse expands the scope of aesthetics to appropriately account for the rich and diverse content of everyday life. I specifically demonstrated how the commonly accepted narrative of defamiliarizing the familiar, emphasis on positive aesthetic experience, and the judgment-oriented mode of aesthetics place an undue limitation on everyday aesthetics. My intent is not to deny or invalidate these mainstream strategies of aesthetics; rather, I am expanding what belongs to the aesthetic realm, not replacing the tradition account.

As such, my account is a challenge to the existing aesthetics discourse. However, I disagree with Forsey's characterization of this challenge as "dismissing the tradition so completely," "almost total dismissal…of the traditions of the aesthetic discipline," "the repudiation of the discipline," and "a wholesale rejection of work in the discipline to date."[60] It may be a matter of different emphasis, but I am not sure whether a proposal for expansion and addition would count as a total dismissal of the existing discourse. I would rather characterize everyday aesthetics' challenge to the existing aesthetics discourse as a proposal for enrichment. I would compare my proposal to Arthur Danto's account of how new works of art expand the definition of art by calling attention to features that were not thought about before. If an artist declares a new predicate H to be relevant for his work to gain a membership to the artworld,

> both H and non-H become artistically relevant for *all* painting, and if his is the first and only painting that is H, every other painting in existence becomes non-H, and the entire community of paintings is enriched, together with a doubling of the available style opportunities. It is this retroactive enrichment of the entities in the artworld that makes it possible to discuss Raphael and De Kooning together, or Lichtenstein and Michelangelo.[61]

Introduction or addition of H put forward as a challenge to all the previous paintings lacking H does neither dismiss nor invalidate the art status of the previous paintings, nor the relevance of artistic qualities $A \sim G$ that guided interpretation and appreciation previously. Rather, it calls attention to the fact that the previous works do not possess H, thereby enriching the artistic discourse.

In a similar vein, when everyday aesthetics includes the familiar experienced as familiar whether negatively or positively, atmosphere and bodily activities that lack clear object-hood, and experience gained through proximal senses, it enriches the aesthetics discourse. For example, it calls attention to the fact that the appreciation of a baseball game *as a baseball game* is based upon a circumscribed set of constituents excluding smell and taste. Thus, I do not dismiss or repudiate aesthetics discourse modeled after art aesthetics. I do insist, however, that such a mode, *if taken as the exhaustive account of everyday aesthetics*, does not do justice to all the rich and diverse dimensions of everyday aesthetic life.

As Böhme points out, with the expansion of the scope of aesthetics, "we can now add with equal right the aesthetics of everyday life, the aesthetics of commodities and a political aesthetics."[62] Although I argued for the importance of phenomenological description as a viable and necessary operative of everyday aesthetics, in later chapters I will also be arguing for the necessity of a normative discourse, though different from the judgment-based, art-oriented sense. It is because, as I shall demonstrate, the power of everyday aesthetics to direct our actions is considerable. Particularly regarding the aesthetics of commodities and political aesthetics, we have to cultivate aesthetic literacy and vigilance because, as Böhme points out, these spheres of aesthetics involve "aesthetic manipulation." Precisely because of the considerable, but often unrecognized, role that everyday aesthetic plays in the collective and cumulative project of world-making, it behooves everyday aesthetics discourse to direct it toward better world-making.

Notes

1. Christopher Dowling, "The Aesthetics of Daily Life," *British Journal of Aesthetics* 50/3 (2010), p. 226, p. 226, p. 228, p. 238.
2. Glenn Parsons and Allen Carlson, *Functional Beauty* (Oxford: Oxford University Press, 2008), p. 178, p. 177.
3. Parsons and Carlson, *Functional Beauty*, p. 180, p. 194, p. 194.
4. Jane Forsey, *The Aesthetics of Design* (Oxford: Oxford University Press, 2013), p. 209, pp. 209–10.
5. Parsons and Carlson do acknowledge that their criticism is based upon a Western-centric view and try to argue against it (pp. 182–9) by pointing out that similar linguistic distinction between the beautiful and the bodily pleasure exists in Turkish and Chinese languages.
6. Thomas Leddy, *The Extraordinary in the Ordinary: The Aesthetics of Everyday Life* (Peterborough: Broadview Press, 2012), p. 185, p. 155, p. 175. He also makes the same point in "Defending Everyday Aesthetics and the Concept of 'Pretty,'" *Contemporary Aesthetics* 10 (2012) http://www.contempaesthetics.org/newvolume/pages/article.php?articleID=654.
7. Thomas Leddy, "Sparkle and Shine," *British Journal of Aesthetics* 37/3 (1997), p. 260.
8. Leddy, *Extraordinary*, p. 162.
9. Mary Douglas, *Purity and Danger: An Analysis of Concept of Pollution and Taboo* (London: Routledge, 2002), pp. 44–5.
10. Arthur Danto, *The Abuse of Beauty: Aesthetics and the Concept of Art* (Chicago: Open Court, 2004), p. 53. Kendall Walton also suggests that the attribution of aesthetic qualities not only to art but also to other objects often requires a consideration of the category they belong to. For example, "a small elephant...might impress us as charming, cute, delicate, or puny." "Categories of Art," in *Philosophy Looks at the Arts*, ed. Joseph Margolis (Philadelphia: Temple University Press, 1978), p. 99.
11. For discussion of some of these 'minor league' aesthetic terms and their commercial appeal, see Daniel Harris' *Cute, Quaint, Hungry and Romantic: The Aesthetics of Consumerism* (Cambridge: Da Capo Press, 2000).
12. Immanuel Kant, *Critique of Judgment*, tr. J. H. Bernard (New York: Hafner Press, 1974). The reference to wine is on p. 46, smell of a flower on p. 123, color violet on p. 47, green of grass on p. 59, tone of a wind instrument on p. 47 and that of violin on p. 59.

13. Kant, *Critique of Judgment*, p. 61. Also refer to his discussion of geometrical figures on p. 78, p. 13, and p. 168.

14. However, Kant still would not regard the purposive relationship between and among proximal senses as constituting beauty, as he remarks on "a man who knows how to entertain his guests with pleasures (of enjoyment for all the senses), so that they are all pleased." Kant seems to treat such a pleasant experience not as a bona fide experience of beauty because, according to him, "the universality is only taken comparatively; and there emerge rules which are only *general* (like all empirical ones), and not *universal*, which latter the judgment of taste upon the beautiful undertakes or lays claim to. It is a judgment in reference to sociability, so far as this rests on empirical rules" (pp. 47–8). The reason may be that proximal senses, in particular taste and smell, invite a physiological reaction, hence purely subjective with no possibility of intersubjectivity, such as the same smell enjoyed by one giving another a headache (p. 123).

15. Irvin, "Scratching an Itch," *The Journal of Aesthetics and Art Criticism* 66/1 (2008), pp. 29–30, emphasis added.

16. Irvin, "Scratching an Itch," p. 30, p. 33.

17. Kevin Melchionne, "Aesthetic Experience in Everyday Life: A Reply to Dowling," *British Journal of Aesthetics* 51/4 (2011), p. 438, p. 439, p. 439.

18. J. Baird Callicott, "The Land Aesthetic," *Orion Nature Quarterly* 3 (1984), p. 20, p. 21, both emphases added.

19. David Howes and Constance Classen, *Ways of Sensing: Understanding the Senses in Society* (London: Routledge, 2014), p. 8.

20. David Howes, "Selling Sensation," *New Scientist* 219/2934 (2013), p. 29.

21. Howes and Classen, *Ways of Sensing*, p. 5. Without using the term 'synaesthesia,' Japanese designer Kenya Hara makes the same point regarding color. Color is always of something like "the rich golden yellow of the yoke from a broken egg, or the color of tea brimming in a teacup" and as such they are not merely colors. Instead, "they are perceived at a deeper level through their texture and their taste, attributes inherent in their material nature" and "color is not understood through our visual sense alone, but through all the senses." *White*, tr. Jooyeon Rhee (Baden: Lars Müller Publishers, 2010), p. 3.

22. Howes and Classen, *Ways of Sensing*, pp. 170–1.

23. Jim Drobnick, "Volatile Effects: Olfactory Dimensions of Art and Architecture," in *Empire of the Senses: The Sensual Culture Reader*, ed. David Howes (Oxford: Berg, 2005): 265–80.

24. Takashina Shūji, *Nihonjin ni totte Utsukushisa to wa Nanika* (*What is Beauty to the Japanese?*) (Tokyo: Chikuma Shobō, 2015), p. 164, my translation. Hara Kenya also points out that medieval Japanese aesthetics, given rise to by arts such as the tea ceremony, Noh theater, flower arrangement, garden design, and the like, emphasizes the aesthetics of "*koto*" (roughly equivalent to situation) rather than of "*mono*" (object). *Nihon no Dezain—Biishiki ga Tsukuru Mirai* (*Japanese Design—Future Created by Aesthetic Sensibility*) (Tokyo: Iwanami Shoten, 2012), p. 74. Throughout this book, for contemporary Japanese authors whose work was published in Japanese,

I will follow the Japanese custom and put their last name first. For their work published in English, I will keep their first name first.

25. I explored Alison's discussion on this point in *Everyday Aesthetics* (Oxford: Oxford University Press, 2007), pp. 121–2.
26. Parsons and Carlson, *Functional Beauty*, p. 55.
27. Forsey, *Aesthetics of Design*, p. 213.
28. Parsons and Carlson, *Functional Beauty*, p. 56.
29. Gernot Böhme, "Atmosphere as the Fundamental Concept of a New Aesthetics," tr. David Roberts, *Thesis Eleven* 36 (1993), p. 114.
30. Böhme, "Atmosphere as the Fundamental Concept," p. 122.
31. Böhme, "Atmosphere as the Fundamental Concept," p. 119, p. 123, p. 123, p. 123.
32. Such a creation of an ambience resulting from many factors spontaneously congealing is explored, with case studies informed by fieldwork, by Miyahara Kōjirō and Fujisaka Shingo in *Shakai Bigaku e no Shōtai* (*Invitation to Social Aesthetics*) (Kyoto: Minerva Shobō, 2012). A shorter English version is "Exploring Social Aesthetics: Aesthetic Appreciation as a Method for Qualitative Sociology and Social Research," *International Journal of Japanese Sociology* 23 (2014), pp. 63–79.
33. Böhme, "Atmosphere as the Fundamental Concept," p. 125. In the preface to *Nichijōsei no Kankyō Bigaku* (*Aesthetics of Ordinary Environment*), the editor Nishimura Kiyokazu points out that the traditional art-centered aesthetics is focused on "thing," but such an approach is not appropriate for inquiring the aesthetics of place for living (biotope) and environment for living (Tokyo: Keisō Shobō, 2012), p. i.
34. I name such alternatives to the spectator-oriented aesthetics "activist" aesthetics. I borrow this term from Arnold Berleant's characterization of Henry David Thoreau's nature aesthetics from his "Thoreau's Aesthetics of Nature" presented at the 71st Annual Meeting of the American Society for Aesthetics, 2013.
35. Friedrich Nietzsche, *The Will to Power*, trans. Walter Kaufmann and R. J. Hollingdale, ed. Walter Kaufmann (New York: Vintage Books, 1968), p. 429, emphasis added.
36. Friedrich Nietzsche, *On the Genealogy of Morals* in *Basic Writings of Nietzsche*, trans. and ed. Walter Kaufmann (New York: The Modern Library, 1968), p. 539, emphasis added.
37. Friedrich Nietzsche, *The Gay Science*, trans. Walter Kaufmann (New York: Vintage Books, 1974), p. 164, emphasis added. Similarly, "it is only as an *aesthetic phenomenon* that existence and the world are eternally justified" and "existence and the world seem justified only as an *aesthetic phenomenon*" (*The Birth of Tragedy* in *Basic Writings of Nietzsche*, trans. and ed. Walter Kaufmann (New York: The Modern Library, 1968), p. 52 and p. 141, the last emphasis added).
38. Friedrich Nietzsche, *The Birth of Tragedy*, p. 141, p. 52.
39. Nietzsche, *Gay Science*, p. 224, emphasis added.
40. Nietzsche, *Gay Science*, p. 232.
41. Friedrich Nietzsche, *Beyond Good and Evil* in *Basic Writings of Nietzsche*, trans. and ed. Walter Kaufmann (New York: The Modern Library, 1968), p. 344 and *Gay Science*, p. 241. Richard Shusterman also points out the importance of aesthetics to

include artists' experience by citing Nietzsche in "Aesthetic Experience: From Analysis to Eros," *The Journal of Aesthetics and Art Criticism* 64/2 (2006), pp. 217–29.

42. Makoto Ueda, *Literary and Art Theories in Japan* (Cleveland: Press of Case Western Reserve University, 1967), p. 226.

43. John Dewey, *Art as Experience* (New York: Capricorn Press, 1958), p. 52, p. 53.

44. Dewey, *Art as Experience*, p. 54. Similar passages include: "instead of realizing that this taking in involves activities that are comparable to those of the creator"; "receptivity is not passivity" (p. 52).

45. Dewey, *Art as Experience*, p. 46.

46. As mentioned before, these bodily sensations are never experienced in isolation from the rest of experience. In our daily life, it is experienced in a particular context and as a part of the flow of life.

47. Forsey, *Aesthetics of Design*, p. 237, emphasis added.

48. Buffalo Bird Woman, "from *Buffalo Bird Woman's Garden*," in *Cooking, Eating, Thinking: Transformative Philosophies of Food*, eds. Deane W. Curtin and Lisa M. Heldke (Bloomington: Indiana University Press, 1992), p. 274, p. 275.

49. Luce Giard, "Doing Cooking," in *The Practice of Everyday Life*. Volume 2: Living & Cooking, ed. Luce Giard, trans. Timothy J. Tomasik (Minneapolis: University of Minnesota Press, 1998), p. 222.

50. Audre Lorde, "from *Zami: A New Spelling of My Name*," in Curtin and Heldke, *Cooking, Eating, Thinking*, p. 288.

51. Verta Mae Smart-Grosvenor, "from *Vibration Cooking: or the Travel Notes of a Geechee Girl*," in Curtin and Heldke, *Cooking, Eating, Thinking*, p. 294, emphasis added.

52. Richard Shusterman "Everyday Aesthetics of Embodiment," in *Rethinking Aesthetics: The Role of Body in Design*, ed. Ritu Bhatt (New York: Routledge, 2013), p. 30, p. 31, p. 30, p. 31, p. 30. This issue will be explored more in Chapter 6.

53. Dowling, "The Aesthetics of Daily Life," p. 238.

54. Shusterman, "Everyday Aesthetics of Embodiment," p. 31.

55. A good discussion of the various aesthetics related to Japanese bath is Peter Grilli's *Pleasures of the Japanese Bath* (New York: Weatherhill, 1992).

56. Melchionne, "Aesthetic Experience," p. 442.

57. Gernot Böhme, "Atmosphere as an Aesthetic Concept," *Daidallos* 68 (1998), p. 114.

58. Ben Highmore, "Homework: Routine, Social Aesthetics and the Ambiguity of Everyday Life," *Cultural Studies* 18.2/3 (2004), pp. 314–15.

59. Juhani Pallasmaa, *The Eyes of the Skin: Architecture and the Senses* (Chichester: John Wiley & Sons, 2007), p. 22. Pallasmaa even goes so far as to criticize singling out vision in isolation from the rest of sensory input, especially today where many of us are immersed in vision-dominated culture.

The perception of sight as our most important sense is well grounded in physiological perceptual and psychological facts. The problems arise from the isolation of the eye outside its natural interaction with other sense modalities, and from the limitation and suppression of other senses, which increasingly reduce and restrict the experience of the world into the sphere of vision. This separation and reduction fragments the

innate complexity, comprehensiveness and plasticity of the perceptual system, reinforcing a sense of detachment and alienation.   (p. 39)

60. Forsey, *Aesthetics of Design*, p. 203, p. 219, p. 221, p. 220.
61. Arthur Danto, "The Artworld," in *Philosophy Looks at the Arts*, ed. Joseph Margolis
(Philadelphia: Temple University Press, 1978), pp. 143–4.
62. Böhme, "Atmosphere as the Fundamental Concept," p. 125. The reference to aesthetic manipulation also is on p. 125.

PART II

Cases

From Sky to Earth

Part I was devoted to exploring conceptual issues regarding everyday aesthetics. My aim was to respond to questions raised about the legitimacy of this discourse by expanding the scope of aesthetics to capture rich and diverse contents of our aesthetic lives. Sometimes we gain aesthetic experience of mundane objects comprising our daily lives through defamiliarization, often with insight and inspiration provided by art. Other times we derive aesthetic pleasure from savoring the very ordinariness of daily lives, giving rise to a sense of comfort, security, and stability. Yet some other times we are aesthetically charged in doing things and managing daily life.

If Part I can be characterized as 'talking about' everyday aesthetics, I would characterize the next three chapters comprising Part II as 'doing' aesthetics. By exploring three specific cases starting with the sky and bringing the discussion down to earth, I want to demonstrate how mundane objects, environments, and activities can affect our aesthetic lives in different ways, sometimes with serious consequences for the quality of life and the state of the world.

3

The Aesthetics of Emptiness
Sky Art

I argued in Chapter 1 that one value of cultivating everyday aesthetic sensibility is to sharpen one's awareness toward what otherwise escapes our attention due to habitual experience and to nurture open-mindedness which contributes to a more mindful way of living. Although I also argued that it is equally, if not more, important to experience the ordinary in its very ordinariness, there is no question that one important role of everyday aesthetics is to encourage illuminating and defamiliarizing the ordinary in our lives. As many everyday aesthetics advocates have argued, in particular Thomas Leddy, art has an indispensable role to play in this regard. In this chapter, I will join them by providing one example in which art helps us attend to and have an aesthetic experience of something we take for granted that surrounds us all the time: sky and the objects and phenomena within it.

Sunny sky, clouds, stars, and the like have historically evoked aesthetic appreciation and inspired poetic imagination. For example, many myths and folk tales are associated with various celestial objects and phenomena, such as constellation of stars, lightning, and formation of rain clouds. However, in our contemporary (and increasingly urban) living, they are often experienced primarily for pragmatic reasons—whether we can count on sunny weather the next day, whether we should bring an umbrella when going out, whether air pollution has worsened, and so on. In our fast-paced lives, we seldom pause and take note of the *aesthetics* of celestial phenomena.[1] As if to remind us of the rich reservoir of the aesthetic potentials of celestial phenomena, there has been a recent trend for art projects that aim at highlighting the aesthetic dimensions of the sky and its environment. I shall call them 'sky art' and I would like to explore their significance in this chapter.

The sky and celestial objects and phenomena have provided subject matters for representational art in the past, such as paintings, photographs, and program music pieces (Gustav Holst's *The Planets* being the best known). More recently, they have also inspired installations with various mechanisms to record the movements of celestial bodies and phenomena.[2] My focus here, however, will be those art pieces that *appropriate* the actual sky and celestial events themselves in the direct manner, either as a big canvas or as the main feature.

The examples of sky art I discuss in this chapter raise a number of important issues: the aesthetics of the sublime, their changeable nature, outdoor locations (some urban and some remote), and their often large scale that is sometimes criticized as being a masculine gesture. However, my discussion will concentrate on the different ways in which these artworks *incorporate* the sky and celestial phenomena, which in turn determine the roles played by the artists and their creations that are different from such roles played in conventional art. With respect to these art projects, the relationship between art-making and their role in facilitating a richer aesthetic experience of the sky and celestial objects and events is rather complicated. As such, they offer a fertile ground for us to explore the ways in which art helps us cultivate everyday aesthetic sensibility, in this case of the sky. Furthermore, they have important implications for aesthetic theory by centering the focus on perceptual experience rather than on objects.[3] I found it helpful to make use of the Buddhist notion of 'emptiness' in analyzing sky art because of its particular relationship to the sky in Chinese and Japanese languages. Despite the lack of evidence that any of the artists I discuss were aware of this linguistic fact, I will develop my discussion by utilizing this association between sky and emptiness.

3.1 Sky and Emptiness

Let me first begin by noting an important connection between 'sky' and the notion of 'emptiness,' at least according to both Chinese and Japanese traditions, as well as in Buddhism. The Chinese character for 'sky,' 空, also adopted by the Japanese, consists of two parts, the top part 穴 meaning 'hole' and the bottom part 工 meaning 'artifice' or 'construction' in the shape of a ruler. This word origin indicates that the sky was considered by the ancient Chinese people to be a hole, the depth of which could not be fathomed by a ruler or the view of which needs an artifice such as a window frame. This character for 'sky' is also used for 'emptiness.' This double usage reflects our common experience in which the sky is perceived as an empty void in and under which various objects exist, lacking the same kind of object-hood we normally assign to objects like rocks and trees.

When we examine Buddhism, we find that the most important foundation of Mahayana Buddhism is the doctrine of emptiness, or *śūnyatā* in the original

Sanskrit. It is the view that everything in this world is empty of absolute, independent identity and permanence. In contrast to the Western philosophical tradition that privileges Being, an independent, discrete, and permanent substance, as the ultimate reality, Buddhism characterizes reality as Becoming or phenomena that are mutually dependent and inter-related. As explained by the Dalai Lama:

One of the most important philosophical insights in Buddhism comes from what is known as the theory of emptiness. At its heart is the deep recognition that there is a fundamental disparity between the way we perceive the world, including our own experience in it, and the way things actually are ... According to the theory of emptiness, any belief in an objective reality grounded in the assumption of intrinsic, independent existence is simply untenable. All things and events, whether material, mental, or even abstract concepts like time, are devoid of objective, independent existence.[4]

A similar account is given by Thomas Cleary in his commentary on the Zen writings by Dōgen, a thirteenth-century Japanese priest:

Emptiness means that things in themselves are indefinable; being dependent on relations, things are said to have no individual or absolute nature of their own. It is this nonabsoluteness which is called emptiness. Another way of expressing it is in terms of inconceivability. The descriptions by which things are defined, and even the experience of things, depend on the mind, and are not the supposed things in themselves. Thus the nature of things in themselves is said to be inconceivable, beyond description, or 'empty.'[5]

This Buddhist ontology that denies the independent and permanent existence of things, including the self, leads to an existential revelation and heuristic strategy for enlightenment that also invokes the notion of 'emptiness.'[6] Variously characterized as not clinging, overcoming, transcending, shedding, or forgetting, Buddhism teaches us to empty ourselves of our usual way of experiencing the world and commonly held desires regarding the self and the world, as it is inane to develop an attachment to things whose presumed permanence is illusory. In fact, such clinging based upon illusion is believed to cause misery and suffering. The Dalai Lama thus characterizes the view that has not been enlightened by the notion of emptiness not only "a fundamental error," but also "the basis for attachment, clinging and the development of our numerous prejudices."[7] Indeed, Dōgen reminds his students that neither physical materials like hair, skin, and blood, nor mental entities like mind, thought, awareness, and knowledge constitute the self, and he instructs them to "just forget yourself for now and practice inwardly—this is one with the thought of enlightenment."[8] Enlightenment, according to him, means being free from attachment to things and so-called self, with "no abiding, no attaching, no standing still, and no stagnating."

In light of this Buddhist theory of emptiness, it is instructive that the Chinese character for emptiness is the same one for the sky. Indeed, both Chinese and Japanese Buddhist texts use the character for sky when referring to the notion of emptiness. It is true that, according to Buddhism, even a typical 'object' such as a tree or a mountain also lacks an underlying substance—just like the sky. However, in our ordinary experience, the sky represents this notion of emptiness most effectively, due to its apparent lack of solidity and permanent stability, the two factors that typically compel us toward the commonly held belief in the object-hood of material existence. Thus, though referring primarily to Tibetan Buddhist art, Philip Rawson points out that "one potent metaphor for the void...is the sky."[9]

I find it illuminating to apply this affinity between the sky and the Buddhist notion of emptiness when exploring various examples of contemporary sky art. Despite the absence of direct references to the Buddhist notion of emptiness, some of the artists and their commentators often invoke 'emptiness' and 'void' when explaining and interpreting the works. I believe that this reference lends support to analyzing sky art by making use of these notions. Furthermore, this lack of object-hood in the ordinary sense helps highlight the importance of perceptual experience, rather than the object itself, as the locus of aesthetics.

3.2 Emptiness of Reality Exemplified by Sky Art

3.2.1 Sky as a blank canvas

Let me first explore how the Buddhist ontological claim about emptiness could be useful in interpreting sky art. There are at least two ways in which appropriation of the sky in sky art can be interpreted as providing illustrations of the Buddhist notion of emptiness as the nature of ultimate reality. One is the use of sky as a big canvas. Perhaps the most prominent contemporary examples are those by a Chinese artist, Cai Guo-Qiang, whose commissioned work entitled *Footprints of History* was part of the opening ceremony of the 2008 Beijing Olympic Games. One of his favored media, fireworks, was used to fire a series of twenty nine giant footprints in the sky, representing the number of previous Olympic Games. His other works also create things like mushroom clouds with gunpowder (*The Century with Mushroom Clouds: Project for the 20th Century*, New York City and Nevada, 1996), rainbows with fireworks (*Transient Rainbow*, New York City, 2002; *Black Rainbow*, Spain, 2005), and, most recently, a 500m ladder structure suspended from a helium balloon set ablaze from its base (*Sky Ladder*, Huiyu Island, China, 2015).[10] All of these works are noteworthy for their short duration, but, more importantly for my discussion here, they are created against the *background* of the sky. The sky provides a big canvas for these projects and Cai himself calls these firework projects "paintings in the cosmos."[11]

The use of the sky as a big canvas dates back to 1970s with the emergence of various earthworks. One of the pioneers, Dennis Oppenheim, created *Whirlpool: Eye of the Storm* (1973), which simulated a tornado trace by the white smoke discharged by an aircraft.[12] While this piece is an isolated example of sky art in Oppenheim's *oeuvre*, Otto Piene, a contemporary of Oppenheim, created a series of sculptural pieces that float in the sky primarily by using helium-filled rubber.[13] Piene characterizes these works of sky art as "inherently a social art"[14] because they move "away from a closed, elite enclave into a public program that sought to engage and interact with the different worlds outside and within the academy."[15] As evidenced by his attraction to kites, Piene regards sky as providing an open space suitable for public gathering around the art pieces. Furthermore, the sky in these works offers a peaceful environment instead of a background for violence such as air raids and bombing, which were familiar to Piene, who lived through World War II in Germany.[16]

Thus, although for different reasons, Cai, Oppenheim, and Piene use the sky similarly as a big canvas or an environment in which to place their art objects or events. By not occupying the central place, the sky in these art pieces can be interpreted as embodying emptiness in the sense that it recedes from asserting its own existence. Our attention is drawn more to the fireworks, white smoke, and inflatable objects, all of which exist in or against the sky, though without the space and background provided by the sky these art objects/events cannot take place. One could compare this use of the sky to Japanese Zen-related arts' expression of 'emptiness' in their use of a blank paper for brush ink painting, silence in haiku and Noh music, and the art of no action in Noh theater. Will Petersen, for example, points out that:

[T]he blank sheet of paper is perceived only as paper, and remains as paper. Only by filling the paper does it become empty ... [E]mptiness, expressed as vacant space in visual art, silence in music, time and spatial ellipses in poetry or literature, or non-movement in dance, requires aesthetic form for its creation and comprehension ... [T]he idea of emptiness is not a concept reached by analytical reasoning, but one that must be perceived in aesthetic terms.[17]

In our aesthetic experience of these works of sky art, we find a similarly interesting paradox. This paradox is created by the juxtaposition of the sky's move away from its own self-assertion and its emptiness that is highlighted by these objects and events.

3.2.2 Emptying artistic creation

If the examples of sky art so far represent the notion of emptiness by their use of the sky as a blank canvas, another way in which sky art can illuminate the notion of emptiness is more complex and possibly artistically richer. This second way is to make the artist's creation itself empty its physicality and identity in order to facilitate the viewer's appreciation of the sky and various celestial phenomena. Let me give several examples, the first half highlighting the celestial phenomena and the latter half highlighting the sky.

Piene remarked in 1970 that "a lightning rod can be considered a most fascinating piece of conceptual art."[18] Seven years later, such an idea materialized in Walter de Maria's *Lightning Field*, which consists of 400 twenty-foot-tall metal poles that act as gigantic lightning rods erected in a grid formation on a high desert in New Mexico. While its official website states that it is "a sculpture to be walked in as well as viewed" and its "full experience ... does not depend upon the occurrence of lightning,"[19] its title indicates that the lightning phenomenon *is* the focus of this work.

Another artist whose installations also operate more as a tool to facilitate experiences of the cosmic phenomena rather than as a sculptural piece is Nancy Holt. Her *Sun Tunnels*, located in Utah and completed in 1976, consists of four large concrete tubes pierced by holes of varying size that correspond to the pattern of four constellations: Draco, Perseus, Columba and Capricorn.[20] The sun's rays come through the holes and compose the light arrangement of each constellation inside the tunnels. Furthermore, the tunnels are aligned so that the sunrise and sunset at both solstices can be seen through them. Her desire to provide a setting for people to experience the cosmic events on a human scale is also evident in her partially completed project, *Sky Mound*, which is located in northern New Jersey.[21] It is both a landfill reclamation project and a public park, with metal poles to frame events such as solstices and equinoxes, an area to view the moon, and a mound from which to view the rising and setting of the brightest stars, Sirius and Vega.

A similar sculptural setting that makes our experience of the sun more notable is Baile Oakes' *Gestation*, located in Santa Monica, CA, at a park overlooking the Pacific Ocean. The full power of this piece is felt when the sunset can be seen in the narrow aperture during the winter solstice. As described by Oakes: "The Sun will appear in the top of the aperture as the day of the Solstice approaches, and will each day move gradually down the aperture until, on the day of the Solstice, the setting Sun meets the ocean. On this day it reminds those present of the important event that nurtures all of our lives on Earth—the conception of the rebirth of Spring."[22]

As for facilitating an aesthetic experience of the sky itself, consider the series of outdoor works by Anish Kapoor, which can be characterized as a large-scale modern-day Claude glass for the sky. For example, his *Sky Mirror* projects in different outdoor venues are literally round mirrors for the sky, a recent one being placed for a period of time in Rockefeller Plaza, Manhattan (2006).[23] By far the most monumental and permanently sited piece is *Cloud Gate*, which was installed in Chicago's Millennium Park in 2004. It is a gigantic, perfectly polished stainless steel structure that resembles a mercury drop or a kidney bean, which, I can testify from my firsthand experience, provides a stunning reflection of the sky, clouds, and the surrounding urban buildings. Just as Claude glass was convex, allowing for the composition of the surrounding landscape, this huge curvaceous metal surface functions as a mirror that distorts and thereby composes the skyscape (Figure 3.1).[24]

A similar attempt at bringing the sky down to the earth can be seen in Tadao Ando's architectural space at Chichū Art Museum, which is located on an island in the Seto Inland Sea, Japan. For this museum, he created an underground space

Figure 3.1 *Cloud Gate* (Chicago)

to house three canvases of Monet's water lilies, site-specific installations of Walter de Maria, and James Turrell's skyviewing room. In addition, Ando created a wall that "opens into a huge round hall reaching up to the skylight" with a round pool beneath to reflect the sky above.[25] One could liken the effect of the pool of water reflecting the infinite height of the sky to M. C. Escher's *Puddle* (1952), which depicts the skyscape reflected in the seemingly unfathomable depth of a puddle.

Among contemporary artists, James Turrell stands out for his dedication to facilitating our experience of the sky and other celestial phenomena, as well as light. His *oeuvre* has been consistently focused on the nature of our perceptual experience; as such, the emphasis is on immateriality such as of light and sky. He created many structures that help provide an aesthetic experience of the sky and celestial phenomena by changing the condition of our perception. For example, his *Skyroom* or *Skyspace*, located in different parts of the United States, Europe, and the above-mentioned Chichū Art Museum, are essentially a series of rooms with openings in the ceiling. Though simple in terms of their construction, the experience of the sky facilitated by them is anything but simple, due to their framed openings. By blocking everything else that typically becomes the center of our attention with the sky as a background, such as a surrounding cityscape, the *Skyroom* setting forces us to attend to the sky as the main focus. Specifically, the sky's changing light and color become intensified; the same is true for the movement of the clouds and the night-time appearance of the moon and stars. After visiting a *Skyroom* at P.S. 1 Museum in Long Island City, NY, I share one commentator's response that "it is as if I am suddenly being shown how to look at the sky. I have lived under it all my life, and yet I have been either too busy or too distracted to notice it."[26] Another commentator also points out that

[T]he sky is no longer the neutral background of things to be seen, but the active field of an unforeseeable visual experience ... [T]he sky is no longer vaguely 'around' or 'above' us, but *exactly there*, on top of us and against us, present because it is changing, obliging us to inhabit it, if not to rise up to meet it.... [I]t is *exactly there*, itself framed by the vibrant joint-lines that Turrell has conceived for it.[27]

Turrell's biggest and still ongoing project for the past three decades is *Roden Crater*.[28] After purchasing this dead volcano in Painted Desert, Arizona, Turrell leveled the contour of the bowl of the volcano and has been constructing a network of tunnel-like passageways and chambers within the volcano that will eventually provide different spaces from which to experience various cosmic events and phenomena with only light from the sun, moon, and stars. For example, the design of these spaces is supposed to let the viewer experience the movement of the North Star, the light from Jupiter, and camera obscura projections of the cloud, moon, and stars. It is also said that we can predict future eclipses, feel the rotation of the earth physically along its axis, and hear "the music of spheres, sounds from deep space...via a pool of water that picks up signals from quasars and distant galaxies."[29] It also provides the biggest *Skyroom* from the Eye of the Crater, a naked eye observatory "where the viewer will be able to experience the remarkable phenomenon known as 'celestial vaulting,'" because of the leveled rim of the volcanic bowl.[30]

Most of us are used to works of art that are physical objects in the traditional sense. The result is, according to one commentator on *Skyroom*, "somewhat naturally, the room or box itself becomes the first object in focus."[31] However, Turrell emphasizes that the experiences at *Roden Crater* are not of *objects*, but rather of *events*: "some...happen daily, some semiannually,...and others occur very infrequently."[32] Although there is no direct reference to the Buddhist notion of emptiness, it is illuminating that the emphasis is placed on experiencing *events*. These events constitute the Buddhist notion of reality, which negates the existence of substance that persists through time.

3.2.3 Artistic emptiness

These environmental works thus represent an alternative way in which an art object functions. Unlike traditional painting and sculpture, and even unlike early environmental art, the constructed objects, such as a room, metal poles, mirrors, and concrete cylinders are not themselves the art objects in the way a painted canvas, chiseled marble, and spiral-shaped jetty are art objects. These works are rather *facilitators* of our experience of the sky and celestial phenomena. The point of these art objects is to get us away from the preoccupation with physical objects and instead have us concentrate on the perceptual experiences made possible by these objects. They become 'empty' in the sense that their raison d'être does not reside in their physical existence itself. Of course, even for object-centered art, the most important aspect is the viewer's aesthetic experience made possible by the object's physicality. Conversely, we owe the possibility of celestial aesthetic experience to the specific physicality and features of these sky art objects. For example, the height of each pole in *Lightning Field* had to be adjusted according to the uneven ground in order to make the top of the poles uniform for attracting lightning in the widest possible scope.[33] *Cloud Gate*'s flawless mirror-like surface, a result of many trials and technical feats, is crucial in providing the utmost experience of the sky and surrounding environment. Similarly, the leveled contour of the volcano rim in *Roden Crater* is necessary for experiencing the celestial vault. However, these design decisions are guided by the best strategy for illuminating the sky and celestial phenomena, rather than a compositional consideration for the best sculptural configuration as is the case for traditional art objects.

As one commentator remarks on Turrell's sky pieces, "the real subject, and *star* of the piece, is the sky above . . . and one's own interaction with it," and *Roden Crater*, when completed, "will become a *tool* with which to experience the sky in all of its manifestations."[34] In this regard, it is instructive that Turrell admires a specific kind of Japanese gardens:

> Of all the gardens in the Japanese culture, the kind that I like very much is the kind where you do not see the hand of man. There are the traditional rock gardens with the raked sand and rock, and then there are those where you can't tell they're man-made. That is very fascinating to me, because you cannot tell where the piece of 'art' ends. This is where the ego of the artist begins to dissolve into the grand scale of things, and there's no signature. This is the kind of effort I am seeking with Roden Crater—a piece that does not end.[35]

At the same time, however, while the physicality of these art pieces thus becomes empty of their own identities, it is also crucial that we remain quite conscious of its solidity. There is a kind of dialectic generated here that enriches our aesthetic experience of these pieces. For example, Kapoor is interested in what he calls "nonobjects" and "emptiness," although he explores these phenomena by means of massive physical objects.[36] In addition to this polarity, Kapoor's works provide another layer of contrast. This contrast is represented by the constantly changing appearance of the skyscape and cityscape due to the sky's condition, cloud movements, and the viewer's physical orientation, which is highlighted by the stationary objects whose apparent permanence is accentuated by their large scale and the choice of the materials that are often associated with longevity and stability. One commentator characterizes Kapoor's pieces as addressing "universal metaphysical polarities: being and nonbeing, place and nonplace, and the solid and the intangible." He continues that Kapoor's interest in these dualities "evolved into a fascination with *voids* and *emptiness*, best exemplified by his series of concaves, spheres, and mirrored pieces" and "the theme of *emptiness* is everywhere visible in Kapoor's work."[37]

Like Kapoor's pieces, Turrell's *Skyroom* also invokes a paradox that negotiates between materiality and immateriality. On the one hand, we perceive the sky as a touchable material part of the interior space, while on the other hand we are acutely aware that it is beyond our grasp because it is literally an outer space, the reverse of a bottomless pit. By making the immaterial sky and light appear perceptually material, the experience of *Skyroom* seems to challenge us to explore their very nature. One commentator points out that "the sky that we could see was like a surface which appeared as a solid blue material, but at the same time *empty*," and "the blue sky at times looked like a painted surface, but *void* and endless and without any material quality,"[38] leading us back to the Buddhist notion of emptiness. Although there is no evidence that any Buddhist reference is intended by Turrell, this paradoxical experience of the sky afforded by *Skyroom* can be taken as an artistic illustration of the Buddhist notion of emptiness written as sky. That is, what may first appear to be a solid material object, a blue painted surface, turns out to be void of any solid substance and wholly dependent upon our perception, without thereby lacking reality. These rather complicated aesthetic experiences of sky art may actually lead us to reflect upon the nature of aesthetic experiences in general, including of more traditional art, reminding us that such experiences result from our engaged perception with the physical objects.

Thus, these examples of sky art that I have discussed in this section function as environmental art not so much for being located outdoors, but because they facilitate our encounter with (celestial) environmental conditions. As Oakes observes, unlike "past cultures [which] integrated light and shadow events into the everyday structures that sustained their communities and lives to mark the consistency of the cosmic order,"[39] in modern times we have become dissociated from cosmic order. Contemporary artists examined here "have begun to create public works that once again bring a sense of cosmic order into our lives," helping us to overcome this alienation. What is noteworthy about these art projects, however, is that we gain a direct experience of celestial conditions through indirect, artistic means. Insofar as the physicality of the objects becomes subservient to the experience of the sky that they facilitate, we can interpret these pieces as embodying the art of emptiness.

One may question whether there is any difference between these works of art and non-art structures like regular observatories. If these art pieces are primarily devices that enable us to have an experience of celestial events, are they not essentially the same as observatories in college campuses, science museums, and the like? Both are intended to facilitate a certain kind of experience, and we cannot deny that we gain scientific knowledge from our experience of sky art while we can have an aesthetic experience when looking at stars from an observatory. The similarities cannot be denied, but I believe there are important differences, keeping Turrell's *Roden Crater*, Holt's *Sky Mound*, and other observatory-like art such as Charles Ross' *Star Axis*, Robert Morris' *Observatory*, and Oakes' *Sky Center* in the realm of art.[40] First, while the scientific factors are crucial in their design, such as aligning the structure according to the earth's axis or a certain star constellation, the design is motivated by providing the optimum *aesthetic* experience for the visitor. Regular observatories, in contrast, are designed to provide the most favorable setting for *scientific* discovery. These two concerns may coincide, but the intended purposes are different.

Furthermore, this difference often translates into the structural design features. For example, some openings in *Roden Crater* are in the shape of a keyhole, which may not have any scientific value. Similarly, a sixty-meter long ascending stairway leading to the opening of Ross' *Star Axis* is meant to simulate "an astronomical ladder of time."[41] While it may have scientific significance, the importance here seems to be not simply the scientific information conveyed by those steps, but more importantly the visitor's actual experience of climbing that translates the scientific information into something that is experience-able through bodily engagement. In a regular observatory, the same information may most likely be conveyed by a chart; furthermore, such a structure may be discouraged because of the concern for accessibility. However, these details are crucial in the respective works of art in terms of orchestrating the richest aesthetic experience. In this sense, the specific physical features of each art piece become important.

At the same time, the 'emptiness' regarding the materiality of these art objects that I have been referring to cannot be applied to regular observatory structures. It is true that observatories are designed specifically and exclusively to provide a certain experience to us; in that sense, they are vehicles for experiences just as these art objects function as vehicles for the aesthetic experience of the celestial. However, the notion of 'emptiness' *relevant in the artistic sense* does not apply to observatories, although the Buddhist notion of emptiness applies to all material existence. *Roden Crater* and *Skyrooms* can be described as 'empty' in the artistic sense only in comparison to conventional art that centers viewer's attention on the physical properties of the constructed object. One could say that *Roden Crater* is empty and that *Skyroom* is empty in the way similar to what Arthur Danto terms the "*is of artistic identification.*"[42] Although Danto's "is" is proposed when discussing the definition of art, I believe I can apply this notion here to determining the artistic quality. That is, the artistically relevant 'emptiness' requires "an atmosphere of artistic theory, a knowledge of the history of art: an artworld."[43] Their *artistic* emptiness makes sense only in the context of Western art history and artworld practice. If their precedents all work in the same way as *Roden Crater* and other sky art objects do by providing an experience of something else with their specific physical characteristics, we cannot quite characterize them as being 'empty.'[44] Regular non-art observatories are not placed in the context of the artworld, and, as such, they cannot express the same kind of artistic 'emptiness' full of meaning.

At the same time, the artworld must be ready to accept a new kind of art into its membership. Early works of land art, located outdoors and exposed to natural elements allowing unplanned transformation, prepared a way for sky art to be included in the artworld. As Danto points out, just as the world has to be ready for certain things, the artworld must also be ready for certain art; he declares that *Brillo Box* "could not have been art fifty years ago."[45] In addition, minimalist works in modern American art, in particular those authored by such artists as Al Reinhardt and Mark Rothko, laid the groundwork for the artistic 'emptiness' of sky art discussed above.[46] It is necessary to be able to situate an artwork in the relevant art history and artworld, not only in order to see it as art but also to understand and appreciate its salient features (in the case of sky art, the artistic 'emptiness'). Without such knowledge, one can still have an aesthetic experience (of the sky and celestial phenomena and/or a structure of constructed space), but one will miss the 'empty' role performed by the art object. This consideration suggests another possible application of the Buddhist notion of emptiness in experiencing sky art, to which I shall now turn.

3.3 Emptying Oneself in Experiencing Sky Art

If the physical structure of these artworks can be interpreted as embodying the Buddhist concept of emptiness, a case can be made that appreciating it also requires an 'emptying' act on our part. However, I shall argue below that applying this notion of emptiness to our experience of sky art paradoxically makes clear what *not to* empty when appreciating sky art.

Buddhist teaching emphasizes the importance of 'emptying' oneself of the usual, commonsensical way of experiencing the world. What we need to empty includes not only the commonly held belief in the independent discrete existence of objects, but also the various modes of conceptualization as a way of organizing the world. Clinging to those familiar beliefs, according to Buddhism, leads us to a false view of the world, preventing us from enlightenment. Zen Buddhism in particular stresses this heuristic dimension of 'emptiness' by encouraging us to 'forget' our all-too-human perspectives and to engage in self-transcendence, whether it be overcoming our individual perspectives or anthropocentric world-views. For example, Dōgen states that "acting on and witnessing myriad things *with the burden of oneself* is 'delusion.' Acting on and witnessing oneself in the advent of myriad things is enlightenment... [S]tudying the Buddha Way is studying oneself. Studying oneself is forgetting oneself. Forgetting oneself is being enlightened by all things."[47] In short, "to learn *prajñā* (the supreme wisdom or insight) is to learn emptiness, and to learn emptiness is to learn *prajñā*."[48]

Sky art can also be interpreted as challenging us to move outside of the familiar comfort zone, whether literally in the physical sense or conceptually.

The challenge to physical comfort is posed by those examples of sky art that require our bodily engagements that are atypical of our normal experience of viewing art from an upright position. *Sun Tunnels*, *Skyroom*, and *Roden Crater* require the appreciator to crawl, crane the neck, or lie flat on the back. When an art critic, Robert Hughes, interviewed Turrell at the site of *Roden Crater*, Turrell urged Hughes to lie flat on his back against the rim of the volcano bowl. Hughes describes the experience: "framed in the arc of the rim you see the sky as a huge blue dome transparent, but somehow solid, an eyeball."[49] Such a bodily posture robs us of the usual privilege and advantage of a familiar and comfortable position of gaze afforded by our normal vantage point. As one commentator explains, *Skyspaces*

oblige us to reverse certain habitual conditions of vision brought to an artwork. For habitually...all the necessary conditions are marshaled so that our body can either dominate the work if it is small, or explore it at will...if large. Without even thinking, we adjust at our convenience the distance between our eyes and the painted or sculpted object. In short, the work allows us to master the conditions under which it is exhibited. Here...we cannot help but lean back our head—to the point of reversing the entire balance of our intentions toward the work...What we are looking at literally *hangs over* us, and in this respect *what we look at looks at us*, since these works are, all things considered, nothing other than architectural *oculi*.[50]

What this critic describes is the disturbance of our all-too-human usual stance as a subject who dominates and has control over the object through gaze. This type of art challenges us to move out of our comfort zone and submit ourselves to the direct encounter, in this case with the sky, no matter how disorienting and uncomfortable.

Furthermore, these pieces require our concentration on the subtly and slowly changing appearances on their surfaces, as well as testing our patience as we wait for a sunset or for lightning to strike in the case of other works of sky art.[51] Turrell himself is fully aware of the challenging nature of his pieces, and is unapologetic of the investment the viewer has to make in appreciating his works: "'After all we open our mouths for the dentist and sit in a waiting room for the doctor for two hours, not that visiting a 'dark space' should be like pulling teeth, but there should be an intellectual price of admission'."[52] A commentator agrees that "when entering a Turrell piece,...he is demanding the observer be involved mentally and physically."[53]

Other times, sky art challenges us to go outside of our familiar, earthly perspective by the use of imagination. For example, Piene proposed moon art, which consists of "an earth-to-moon-and-vice-versa light beam (that) could express communication as we find it when two boys flash their lights at each other from two distant trees in the night."[54] Piene's motivation behind this moon art was primarily to protect the moon from possible human abuse associated with the US space exploration that was at its heyday during his time.[55]

Cai's interest in outer space, in comparison, is to expand his canvas further, from sky to celestial space. His proposal includes *Inverted Pyramid on the Moon* and *A Certain Lunar Eclipse*, both to be practiced on the moon.[56] According to these yet-to-be-realized plans, "an inverted pyramid will be placed on the moon in juxtaposition with a pyramid on Earth," thereby creating "the continual interplay between humanity and the cosmos," and "a luminous line will appear on the obscure disk of the moon during its eclipses" in order to "awaken the conscience of the people of today who are faced with the destruction of the environment and the imbalance of life on Earth."[57] At the same time, many of Cai's completed projects on Earth are part of *Projects for Extraterrestrials*, reflecting his interest in "transmitting signals to the universe and establishing a dialogue between earth and the other planets."[58] According to Cai, such extra-terrestrial communication is more urgent than "communicating with the West," which is often expected of him because of his Chinese background and having lived many years in Japan.[59] Because of their large scale, sometimes spanning up to ten kilometers, these projects indeed lend themselves to be viewed from space. From such a cosmic perspective, Cai claims, the global perspective that includes the duality of East and West becomes less important than Earth's relationship to the rest of the universe.

These examples of cosmic art by Piene and Cai necessitate the change of our earthly stance and orientation. These pieces have to be viewed from an extrater-restrial vantage point, which may or may not be possible for most humans. Whether perceptually (if we, like astronauts, get to assume the extraterrestrial point of view in the literal sense) or conceptually (through our imagination), we as the viewers are challenged to empty ourselves of our normal terrestrial vantage points, orientation, and scale.

This shift in orientation encouraged by sky art can be compared to the Zen teaching that urges us to recognize the relativity of perceptual perspective in experiencing the world and to empty ourselves of the human conceptual frame-work. For example, Dōgen repeatedly points out that "we see and comprehend only what the power of *our* eye of contemplative study reaches"[60] and that the human experience of the world is one among many possible worlds, which today can be rephrased as denying the primacy of an anthropocentric viewpoint. He writes:

Seeing mountains and waters has differences depending on the species. That is to say, there are those who see water as jewel necklaces... There are those who see water as beautiful flowers . . . Ghosts see water as raging fire, as pus and blood. Dragons and fish see palaces and pavilions.[61]

As a result, "if we inquire into the 'familiar ways' of myriad things, the qualities of seas and mountains, beyond seeming square or round, are endlessly numerous. We should realize there exist worlds everywhere."[62]

Thus, whether physically or conceptually, these examples of sky art can be interpreted as illustrating some possible ways of emptying ourselves of our usual, commonly held experiences of the world, as well as encouraging us to step outside of our comfort zone as terrestrial beings. However, how far can we push this comparison between the Buddhist teaching of emptying our mind and the emptying of the familiar orientation in appreciating sky art? I think the answer depends upon whether our appreciation is directed toward sky art *as art* or rather toward the sky and celestial phenomena themselves, which are highlighted by sky art.

If we appreciate sky art *as art*, we have to argue *against* emptying our mind. As I pointed out at the end of the last section, we need to contextualize our experience of sky art within the framework of the artworld in order to recognize and appreciate its emptiness in terms of its being a tool or facilitator for the celestial experience, rather than asserting its own object-hood. If we transcend, forget, or overcome our knowledge that the celestial experience, whether of the sky or a sunset, is orchestrated by a specific artistic intention and extensive manipulation of physical materials, while we may still have an aesthetic experience of the celestial phenomenon, we fail to have an *artistic* appreciation. That is, with respect to many works of sky art I discussed, the particular attraction resides not only in the celestial experience made possible by them but also in the paradox experienced between their massive physicality, which has its own aesthetic qualities, and functional invisibility as tools for providing a celestial experience.[63] Appreciation of their 'emptiness' involving this paradox requires our knowledge of art history and the artworld, and calls into question the wisdom of emptying ourselves of such knowledge.

What about our experience and appreciation of the sky and other celestial phenomena facilitated by sky art for what they are, instead of as art? The Buddhist-oriented 'emptying' would require that they be experienced for simply "being such," rather than under the concept of the sky, sunset, stars, or as art. This mode of experiencing the world is not limited to Buddhism. It is also proposed by some contemporary Western philosophers and writers, with varying characterizations of what such an experience will be like. In Chapter 1, I have already discussed examples of defamiliarizing the familiar, ranging from

Jean-Paul Sartre's nausea, Albert Camus' notion of the absurd, Hans Gumbrecht's estrangement, and Stan Godlovitch's aloof nature to Iris Murdoch's
glorious richness, Annie Dillard's true seeing,[64] Neil Evernden's wonder, Aldous
Huxley's perception without filters, and, once again, Zen enlightenment.

Despite these different characterizations of what sort of experience results
from adopting the emptying attitude, all of these thinkers share in common the
view that the world as we experience it is our humanized construct and that the
emptying of the human perspective is necessary in order to have a direct
encounter with the world. With the exception of Sartre and Camus, every other
writer, as well as Zen thinkers, claims that such an approach yields an aesthetic
experience of nature. Godlovitch would further claim that such is the only
morally appropriate aesthetic appreciation of nature.

In my previous work on nature appreciation, I also argued for the moral
importance of appreciating nature on its own terms.[65] However, I also argued
that any human effort to understand nature as it is can contribute to an
appropriate appreciation of nature, which includes natural science, folk tradition,
and mythology. One of the most hotly debated topics in environmental aesthetics
is the notion of the appropriate appreciation of nature. The stage for this
debate was set by Allen Carlson, who has been consistently arguing for scientific
cognitivism in this regard.[66] Many ensuing debates are concerned with whether
or not science provides the best or the only relevant framework for appreciating
nature. However, another way of configuring the various positions on this issue is
to organize them under centric and acentric viewpoints, to borrow Godlovitch's
terms. From the acentric viewpoint, any kind of association we bring to nature
appreciation would have to be shed, as this is a way of humanizing it. This
viewpoint would reject not only the scientific cognitivism advocated by Carlson,
but also the imagination-oriented appreciation supported by Emily Brady.
Accepting this acentric view would yield an all-or-nothing stance toward our
experience, rejecting any kind of human association, regardless of content. John
Hospers has provided us with an apt characterization, arguing that such a view
would regard "a starry night...merely as an arrangement of pleasing colors,
shapes, and volumes" without appreciating it "as expressive of many things in
life, drenched with the fused association of many scenes and emotions from
memory and experience."[67]

Applied to celestial aesthetic experience, this viewpoint means that the only
appropriate aesthetic appreciation of the sky, moon, and stars happens only when
we transcend their identities as the sky, moon, and stars, as well as various facts
and associations related to them. That is, we will need to divest all of the
following cognitive considerations and associations: (1) scientific (though fairly

commonsensical) facts about them, such as the distance between where we are on Earth and the moon, the celestial bodies' movements, and the meteorological conditions that determine the color of the sky; (2) culturally significant associations, such as various myths associated with the star constellations and the cosmic creation narratives; and (3) purely capricious and trivial associations, such as a fortuitous resemblance between a cloud and a basket full of laundry.[68]

However, I do not think acentrists' call for indiscriminately rejecting all of these cognitive considerations and associations is helpful. Instead of the dichotomy between centric and acentric appreciations, or all-too-human and emptied perspectives, I believe it is more helpful to view various approaches along a continuum, with purely whimsical associations (#3 above) on the one end and the completely emptied perspective on the other end. I would place scientifically informed appreciation and other approaches that reflect human attempts to understand nature on its own terms somewhere in the middle between an acentric orientation and whimsical appreciations, although they are still reliant upon all-too-human constructs. Even those aestheticians critical of Carlson's scientific cognitivism do distinguish between "serious" and "trivial" appreciation or between "imagining well" and "imagination let loose ... for one's own pleasure seeking ends," suggesting the possibility of varied approaches ranging from the purely capricious ones to those based upon some understanding of the objects and phenomena, such as the violent turbulence of air within cumulus clouds.[69] One could even argue that the knowledge of a tremendous distance between where we are and what we see in the sky, such as the sun and moon, not to mention their size, helps us regard them with respect, because we are guided to appreciate them in light of what actually is the case.

It is true that such appreciation is guided by a human-centric viewpoint. Godlovitch is right in his claim that "if we were giants, crushing a rock monument, even a stony moon, would be no more aesthetically offensive than flattening the odd sand castle is to us now."[70] The same is true for the Zen insight that there are many possible worlds depending upon the perspective, human viewpoint being only one among numerous possibilities. However, I do not think we can escape from the fact that the aesthetic appreciation of nature, such as the sky and the moon, even with a physically or conceptually disorienting perspective facilitated by sky art, is still a primarily human experience. It is rooted in *our human* aesthetic sensibility and imaginative faculty. Even if we lose our privileged posture of gaze by having to lie flat on our backs, for example, the experience gained by assuming this unusual posture is still our human experience. Similarly, adopting an extraterrestrial viewpoint in order to comprehend Piene's moon art and Cai's cosmic project still engages our human imaginative power. Thus, while these works of sky art encourage us to empty our usual orientation, the aesthetic experience afforded by them, I believe, is still anchored in human orientation and sensibility, and insofar as aesthetic experience is concerned, I think it is inevitable. This is not to deny the possibility of a completely acentric, emptied experience, as related by many accounts of Zen enlightenment. Without denying the rich aesthetic potential of such a state, I do not think we should dismiss the very earthly and human aesthetic experience of the sky and celestial phenomena, either.

Despite the ultimate inapplicability of the Buddhist notion of emptiness to our appreciation of sky art as art and the experience of the sky and celestial phenomena themselves, I believe that such an exploration was helpful in thinking about how various conceptual considerations are relevant and indeed necessary in our experience of both art and a part of everyday life illuminated by it. Our discussion indicated that the total emptying of our minds will lead us to miss the artistic meaning of sky art altogether. Furthermore, although such a transcendent stance can be enlightening and possibly most respectful of nature, limiting our aesthetic appreciation of nature to those afforded by emptying of our minds seems to unduly compromise a rich array of other possibilities. Therefore, within the context of our aesthetic experience rooted in our all-too-human sensibility and imagination, what is most important to determine is *not* whether to empty *every* consideration when appreciating nature, but rather *which* considerations should be emptied.

*   *   *

I started this chapter with the Buddhist notion of emptiness, which is written with the Chinese character for the sky. To enable the aesthetic appreciation of emptiness, meaning the sky and celestial phenomena, the sky art objects I cited become empty by subjecting their physicality to the celestial experience they provide. The role of these art objects shifts from being the focus of aesthetic attention to facilitating an experience of the sky and celestial events, and this shift is particularly noteworthy precisely because of their massive physicality. Some act of emptying is also required of us by going outside of our usual experiential framework and submitting ourselves to what the experience affords us.

There are different ways in which art helps us become more sensitive to and appreciative of everyday life. Sometimes it frames and presents a slice of everyday life, providing a focus, illumination, and interpretation, whether as a photograph, painting, or literary piece. Some other times it constructs an artistic whole out of ingredients taken from everyday life, such as trash art and music composed of everyday sounds spliced together. Recent art projects involve 'audience' or 'viewers' as participants in the joint creation of a piece that takes place in an everyday setting, such as on a street or in a train station.

In this chapter, I presented another way in which art challenges us to forego the usual mode of experiencing an everyday environment. The resultant defamiliarized world of everyday life, in this case specifically the sky, often leads to an intense aesthetic experience. Successful art projects, such as those cited in this chapter, have the power to reveal the aesthetic gems surrounding us, though often hidden behind the veil of mundane ordinariness.

Notes

1. There is an indication that this relative neglect of sky and air as the focus of our experience is changing. For example, the 7th International Conference on Environmental Aesthetics (Finland, March 2009) was dedicated to the theme of "Celestial Aesthetics: The Aesthetics of Sky, Space, and Heaven." *Environment and Planning D: Society and Space* 29/3 (2011) features several essays on the theme of "Aerographies." This chapter originated with my presentation at the Celestial Aesthetics conference, which was substantially revised for publication in *Environment and Planning D*, which was further revised for this chapter.

2. Perhaps the most comprehensive compilation of representational art of the sky and cosmic events, though limited to the Western tradition, is Jean Clair's *Cosmos: From Romanticism to Avant-garde* (Munich: Prestel Verlag, 1999), the catalogue to accompany the 1999 exhibit at the Montreal Museum of Fine Arts. Examples of more indirect representation through installation include Joe Winter's *Xerox Astronomy and the Nebulous Object Image* (http://www.severalprojects.com), Patrick Zentz's *Heliotrope*, and Charles Ross' series of project, *Prisms and Solar Spectrum Skylights*. I thank Monica Martinez for the Winter reference. The visual images and the artists' own statements of Zentz and Ross can be found in Baile Oakes' *Sculpting with the Environment* (New York: Van Norstrand Reinhold, 1995).

3. I thank Arnold Berleant for pointing this out.

4. Dalai Lama, *The Universe in a Single Atom: The Convergence of Science and Spirituality* (New York: Morgan Road Books, 2005), pp. 46–7.

5. Thomas Cleary, *Shōbōgenzō: Zen Essays by Dōgen* (Honolulu: University of Hawaii Press, 1986), p. 36.

6. This twofold understanding of the notion of emptiness, ontological understanding of reality, and existential revelation regarding oneself, is in keeping with the definition of emptiness, *kū*, given in the Japanese Dictionary of Buddhism. There, *kū* is divided into *ninkū* (emptiness regarding self) and *hokkū* (emptiness regarding things). *Shin Bukkyō Jiten (New Dictionary of Buddhism)*, ed. Nakamura Hajime (Tokyo: Seishin Shobō, 1978), p. 125, entry on *kū*.

7. Dalai Lama, *The Universe in a Single Atom*, p. 46.

8. Dōgen, "Guidelines for Studying the Way," in *Moon in a Dewdrop: Writings of Zen Master Dōgen*, tr. Kazuaki Tanahashi (New York: North Point Press, 1995), p. 32. The next passage is from p. 41.

9. Philip Rawson, *Sacred Tibet* (London: Thames and Hudson, 1991), p. 11.

10. These examples are compiled from *Cai Guo-Qiang: on Black Fireworks* (Valencia: IVAM Institut Valencia d'Art Modern, 2005); *Cai Guo-Qiang*, ed. D. Charles (London: Thames & Hudson, 2000); *Art: 21: Art in the Twenty-First Century*, ed. Marybeth Sollins, Vol. 3 (New York: Harry N. Abrams, 2001), as well as from his website http://www.caiguoqiang.com.

11. Cited by Wu Hung, "Once Again, Painting as Model: Reflections on Cai Guo-Qiang's Gunpower Painting," *Cai Guo-Qiang: on Black Fireworks*, p. 73.

12. The visual image of this piece is available online at http://www.dennis-oppenheim.com/works/early-work/155. The description of this piece can be found in Michael Lailach's *Land Art* (Köln: Taschen, 2007), p. 82. I thank Johanna Hallsten for this reference.

13. They include *Brussels Flower* over Guggenheim (1977/78), *Iowa Star* over Anchorage, Alaska (1979), *Grand Rapids Carousel* over Grand Rapids, Michigan (1979), *Black Stack Helium Sculpture* over Mississippi River (1976), *Red Helium Sky Line* over Pittsburgh (1970), and *Sky Kiss* (1982) which features Charlotte Moorman playing cello in the air. These examples are compiled from Stephen von Wiese and Susanne Rennert (eds.), *Otto Piene: Retrospektive 1952–1996* (Köln: Wienand, 1996).

14. Otto Piene, *More Sky I* (Cambridge: Migrant Apparition, 1970), p. 49.

15. John G. Hanhardt, "A Great Experiment: Otto Piene and the Center for Advanced Visual Studies," in *Otto Piene: Retrospektive*, p. 40.

16. For Piene, "the blue sky had been a symbol of terror in the aerial war. It had meant flying weather, attacks by low-diving fighter planes and bombardments." In light of this indelible wartime association of the sky, Piene is committed to using the sky as a medium of peaceful event, rather than a battlefield: "We want to reach the sky. We want to exhibit in the sky, not in order to establish there a new art world, but rather to enter new space peacefully—that is, freely, playfully and actively, not as slaves of war technology," such as "the exploding atom bomb (which) would be the most perfect kinetic sculpture, could we observe it without trembling." All the passages are from Otto Piene, *Light Ballet* (Howard Wise Gallery: New York, 1965), no page.

17. Will Petersen, "Stone Garden," in *The World of Zen: An East-West Anthology*, ed. Nancy Wilson Ross (New York: Vintage Books, 1960), p. 107.

18. Piene, *More Sky I*, p. 54.

19. http://www.lightningfield.org.

20. The Center for Land Use Interpretation website is http://ludb.clui.org. In addition to the visual images available online through Google, there are images and discussion in John Beardsley, *Earthworks and Beyond*, expanded ed. (New York: Abbeville Press, 1989), pp. 34–6; Oakes, *Sculpting with the Environment*, pp. 56–8.

21. The visual images and discussion can be found in Oakes, *Sculpting with the Environment*, pp. 61–3, as well as in Barbara C. Matilsky's *Fragile Ecologies: Contemporary Artists' Interpretations and Solutions* (New York: Rizzoli, 1992), pp. 89–91.

22. Oakes, *Sculpting with the Environment*, p. 40.

23. See Laura Allsop, "Sky Fidelity: the World Turned Upside Down," *Art Review* 56/3 (2006), pp. 37–8 and Randy Kennedy, "A Most Public Artist Polishes a New York Image," *The New York Times* (August 20, 2006).

24. A similar use of mirrors as a vehicle to reflect the sky for our experience can be found in Juan Geuer's *Karonhia*, installed at the National Gallery of Canada in Ottawa. The difference with *Cloud Gate* is its two-dimensionality as well as the museum setting. The visual image and the artist's own statement can be found in Oakes, *Sculpting with the Environment*.

25. Kazuko Nakane, "Naoshima: Art off the Waters of Industrialized Japan," *Sculpture* 24/5 (June, 2005), pp. 10–11.

26. Richard Bright, *James Turrell Eclipse* (London: Michael Hue-Williams Fine Art, 1999), p. 10.

27. Georges Didi-Huberman, "The Fable of the Place," in *James Turrell: The Other Horizon*, ed. Peter Noever (Vienna: MAK, 2002), p. 51. Although with a totally different context and made for a practical purpose, one of the recent projects by Auburn University's Rural Studio also provides the same kind of frame for viewing the sky, though in this case from a toilet. See the discussion and the visual images of Perry Lakes Park Facilities in Andrea Oppenheimer Dean and Timothy Hursley's *Proceed and Be Bold: Rural Studio After Samuel Mockbee* (New York: Princeton Architectural Press, 2005).

28. It is still not completed, but "James Turrell Allowing Limited Visitors to Roden Crater for $6,500 a Person," according to M. H. Miller, posted on *ARTNEWS* (February 19, 2015) http://www.artnews.com/2015/02/19/james-turrell-allowing-limited-visitors-to-roden-crater-for-6500-a-person/.

29. Sollins, *Art: 21*, Vol. 1, p. 76.

30. Bright, *James Turrell Eclipse*, p. 27. Celestial vaulting is the phenomenon in which the sky is perceived as a closely fitted vault covering us from horizon to horizon rather than a limitless void extending into space. Although I am singling out *Roden Crater* in my discussion, an observatory-like work of art is by no means limited to it. One of the early "land art" or "earthwork" examples is Robert Morris' *Observatory* constructed in Oostelijk, Holland (1971–77). Charles Ross' *Star Axis* located in Chupinas Mesa, New Mexico, (since 1971) is similar to *Roden Crater* in providing a large-scale, observatory-like setting. Baile Oakes' *Silver Sands Park Sky Center* (1990–) also provides a crater-like bowl from which to observe the sky. The visual images as well as Ross' and Oakes' own statements can be found in Oakes, *Sculpting with the Environment*. The visual images and Lailach's explanation regarding Morris' and Ross' works can be found in Lailach, *Land Art*.

31. Sebastian Guinness, "James Turrell," in *Chichu Art Museum: Tadao Ando Builds for Walter de Maria, James Turrell, and Claude Monet* (Ostfildern: Hatje Cantz, 2005), p. 123.

32. James Turrell, "Roden Crater Project," *James Turrell Light & Space* (New York: Whitney Museum of American Art, 1980), p. 40.

33. The description can be found in Lailach, *Land Art*, p. 38.

34. Guinness, "James Turrell," p. 127, emphasis added.

35. Cited by Melinda Wortz, "Introduction," *James Turrell Light & Space* (New York: Whitney Museum of American Art, 1980), p. 12.

36. "Nonobjects" is cited by Kennedy, "A Most Public Artist"; "Emptiness" is cited by Mary Jane Jacob, "Being with Cloud Gate," in *Anish Kapoor: Past Present Future*, ed. Nicholas Baume (Cambridge: MIT Press, 2008), p. 131. *Cloud Gate* weighs 110 tons and its transport required reinforcement of the roads.

37. Timothy J. Gilfoyle, *Millennium Park: Creating a Chicago Landmark* (Chicago: The University of Chicago Press, 2006), p. 261 p. 265, and p. 268, emphasis added.

38. Count Giuseppe Panza di Biumo, "Artist of the Sky," in *Occluded Front: James Turrell*, ed. Julia Brown (The Museum of Contemporary Art, Los Angeles, 1985), p. 64, emphasis added.

39. Oakes, *Sculpting with the Environment*, p. 13. The next passage is also from p. 13.

40. See note 30 above for the description of the works by Morris, Ross, and Oakes.

41. Lailach, *Land Art*, p. 84.

42. Arthur Danto, "The Artworld," included in *Philosophy Looks at the Arts*, ed. Joseph Margolis (Philadelphia: Temple University Press, 1978), p. 139. Tom Leddy reminded me that, strictly speaking, Danto's "is of artistic identification" refers to the definition of art rather than the designation of artistic quality.

43. Danto, "The Artworld," p. 140.

44. Another way of putting this is, in such a fictional artworld "emptiness" may function as what Kendall Walton calls "a standard feature" and as such cannot become an expressive feature of an object. See his "Categories of Art," in *Philosophy Looks at the Arts*, ed. Joseph Margolis (Philadelphia: Temple University Press, 1978), pp. 88–116. Tom Leddy pointed out that the notion of 'emptiness' appears in different senses in Danto's work, both in "The Artworld" and *The Transfiguration of the Commonplace*. It can refer to literal emptiness, as in a canvas with nothing but a uniform color, or artistically rich emptiness, as in Shiko Munakata's woodcut print which results from splashing black ink on a plank and printing it, or a lack of artistic richness of an object created by a young artist with egalitarian attitude that is indiscernible from artistically rich objects created by established artists. See Danto's *Transfiguration of the Commonplace* (Cambridge: Harvard University Press, 1983), pp. 2–3, 51–3. The notion of emptiness is invoked by some contemporary Japanese designers, as I discuss in Chapter 6 (section 6.2.1). Given these different references to 'emptiness,' this concept may make an interesting subject matter for further aesthetic investigation.

45. Danto, "The Artworld," p. 142.

46. I thank Tom Leddy for the reference to Reinhardt and Rothko.

47. Cleary, *Shōbōgenzō*, p. 32, emphasis added.

48. Dōgen, *A Complete English Translation of Dōgen Zenji's Shōbōgenzō (The Eye and Treasury of the True Law)*, Vol. I, tr. Kōsen Nishiyama and John Stevens (Tokyo: Nakayama Shobō, 1975), p. 6. Cleary translates the original term, *kokū*, here translated as "emptiness," as "space," rendering the sentence to read: "learning wisdom is space, space is learning wisdom" (Cleary, *Shōbōgenzō*, p. 26). I prefer the Nishiyama translation of "emptiness" because the character for "ko" designates emptiness and the character for "kū" is what initiated my discussion, meaning both empty and sky.

49. BBC, *American Visions: the History of American Art and Architecture* (1996).

50. Didi-Huberman, "The Fable of the Place," p. 51.

51. Kapoor's *Cloud Gate* stands out as being a crowd-pleaser among these examples, as evidenced by its popularity including children. But, after all, it is located in an urban, civic space and as such it has to be inviting to all citizens. In this sense, this piece succeeds in fulfilling its function as a public sculpture.

52. Cited by Guinness, "James Turrell," p. 124.

53. Guinness, "James Turrell," p. 125.
54. Piene, *More Sky I*, p. 56.
55. Piene wonders "why the flag of the United Nations could not have been taken to the moon." *More Sky I*, p. 56.
56. Wu, "Once Again," p. 71.
57. Dorothée Charles, *Cai Guo-Qiang* (London: Thames & Hudson, 2000), p. 92.
58. Dawei Fei, "Amateur Recklessness: On the Work of Cai Guo-Qiang," in *Cai Guo-Qiang*, ed. D. Charles (London: Thames & Hudson, 2000), p. 9.
59. Fei, "Amateur Recklessness," p. 9.
60. Cleary, *Shōbōgenzō*, p. 34, emphasis added.
61. Cleary, *Shōbōgenzō*, p. 93. Similar passages can be found on pp. 34, 70, and 96 of the same text.
62. Cleary, *Shōbōgenzō*, p. 34.
63. It should be noted that this 'paradox' of sky art is *experiential*, referring to massive physicality and functional invisibility of physical objects *as part of the same aesthetic experience*, rather than based upon separation between the physical art object and celestial experience. I owe this point to Arnold Berleant. A wider implication of this point is that, even when we refer to the physical attributes of an object (such as massive size, surface texture, and the like), the focal point in discussing its aesthetics is our experience (the size and surface *as experienced* under a certain condition).
64. For my purpose, it is interesting to note that Dillard claims that when she succeeds in truly seeing, that is unpeaching the peach, "I sway transfixed and *emptied*." "Seeing," in *Environmental Ethics: Divergence and Convergence*, eds. Richard G. Botzler and Susan J. Armstrong (New York: McGraw-Hill, 1998), p. 120, emphasis added.
65. "Appreciating Nature on Its Own Terms," *Environmental Ethics* 20/2 (1998), pp. 135–49.
66. The list of Carlson's works will be too lengthy to give here. For the most recent list, see his *Nature and Landscape: An Introduction to Environmental Aesthetics* (New York: Columbia University Press, 2009). One of the most contentious issues in environmental aesthetics regards scientific cognitivism and I am not doing justice to the rich and complex debates surrounding it. However, I will not pursue this issue here in the interest of retaining the present focus.
67. John Hospers, *Meaning and Truth in the Arts* (Hamden: Archon Books, 1964), p. 12.
68. This example is from Ronald Hepburn, "Aesthetic Appreciation of Nature," in *Aesthetics in the Modern World*, ed. Harold Osborne (London: Thames and Hudson, 1968), p. 31.
69. Ronald Hepburn, "Trivial and Serious in the Aesthetic Appreciation of Nature," in *The Reach of the Aesthetic: Collected Essays on Art and Nature* (Hants: Ashgate, 2001) and Emily Brady, "Imagination and the Aesthetic Appreciation of Nature," in *The Aesthetics of Natural Environment*, eds. Allen Carlson and Arnold Berleant (Peterborough: Broadview Press, 2004), p. 164. The reference to the inner turbulence of the cumulus cloud comes from Hepburn's "Aesthetic Appreciation of Nature" and is contrasted with seeing the cloud formation as a basket of washing (p. 31).
70. Stan Godlovitch, "Ice Breakers: Environmentalism and Natural Aesthetics," *Journal of Applied Philosophy* 11/1 (1994), p. 18.

4

The Aesthetics of Wind Farms

In Chapter 3, I discussed the ways in which art projects facilitate our aesthetic experience of the sky and celestial objects and phenomena. These projects are specifically intended to help us focus on the celestial-scape framed or reflected by designed structures, and I argued that their physicality on the one hand becomes empty, while on the other hand, it complicates and enriches our experience. In this chapter, I want to explore a different set of structures that stand against the background of sky-scape and which are often criticized as an eyesore that ruins the surrounding landscape or seascape: the wind turbines that are becoming increasingly common sights in urban areas, farm lands, mountainous regions, and even offshore. For my discussion, I take the example close to (my) home: Cape Wind project in the Nantucket Sound off Cape Cod, Massachusetts.[1]

4.1 The Cape Wind Project

Since the beginning of its proposal filed in 2001, Cape Wind project created a storm of controversy.[2] The project that has obtained all the necessary permits has not yet started at the time of writing, as Cape Wind is still working on financing and contracting. When completed, this offshore wind farm will have 130 wind turbines, each one 260 feet, in the Nantucket Sound. It will be the first offshore wind farm in the United States and the biggest in the world. It will also become the world's eleventh largest skyline.[3]

This site was chosen based upon a review of comments and feedback solicited by the Army Corps of Engineer on its 4,000+ pages of Draft Environmental Impact Statement (DEIS) published in November 2004, which was prepared in cooperation with twelve federal agencies and seven state and local agencies, following the rules and guidelines established by the National Environmental Policy Act, Massachusetts Environmental Policy Act, and Cape Cod Commission Regional Policy Act. DEIS examines a number of issues, including needs, environmental ramifications, socio-economic impact, and comparison with alternative strategy, among others. One section dealing with alternative site analysis alone spans over 200 pages in which seventeen alternative sites were considered, eight onshore and nine offshore, based upon five criteria. Among those seventeen, four were selected for further review, with the conclusion that "Horseshoe Shoal [the site proposed by Cape Wind] was shown to be technically, environmentally and economically preferable to the other two Nantucket Sound alternatives for the proposed Project."[4] Specifically, the site's advantage over alternative sites included its constant and strong wind, sufficient open space, and relative ease of transmitting the generated electricity, as well as its easier accessibility.

Any discussion regarding a new power source needs to be prefaced by the most fundamental issue: reducing our reliance on electricity in general. Ideally there should be no need to increase power facility; instead, we should be moving toward shutting down some existing power plants without building new ones. At least some degree of reduction even in highly industrialized nations is not impossible, as indicated by the forced reduction of electricity usage in Japan after the Fukushima Daiichi nuclear power disaster when all the existing nuclear power plants were shut down. Advocates of wind power would support reducing our reliance on electricity. However, their support for wind power is in response to the unfortunate reality of having to meet the current demand and replacing old plants that need to be shut down because of their age and/or environmental harm.

Very few people dispute the environmental benefits of wind energy compared to electricity generated by coal, oil, and nuclear power, but, while they are becoming increasingly common, particularly in places like California, Texas, and throughout Europe, wind power facilities have always been met from the outset with opposition, and one study indicates that the NIMBY (Not In My Back Yard) phenomenon is greatest regarding wind farms among all utility facilities.[5] The initial problems concerning noise pollution, harm to birds, and the danger of unstable structure have since been mitigated, if not completely eliminated, by better technology. In the case of Cape Wind, the possible negative environmental impact, such as disturbance to area fish as well as to migrating birds, and interference with seafaring routes and airplane flight paths, seems to have been adequately answered.[6] So what is the source of the opposition? Aesthetics. The degree to which aesthetic considerations have played a role in this dispute is demonstrated by the fact that this Cape Wind project has generated vehement objections from Cape Cod residents, many of whom pride themselves as committed environmentalists, including Robert Kennedy, Jr.[7]

One thing that can never be changed, even with better technology, is the turbines' visibility. They cannot be hidden; nor can they be camouflaged like cell phone towers as trees and satellite dishes as giant clam shells.[8] So they are almost invariably decried as 'marring,' 'spoiling,' 'ruining,' and 'intruding on' the otherwise relatively natural landscape, such as desert, open field, mountainside, and in this case ocean, and criticized for creating an 'eyesore.' The late Walter Cronkite, a former part-time resident of Martha's Vineyard, for example, worried that "it will be most unsightly for what is now open bay. Everyone will see it, anyone who wanders on the water, who has a home that faces the water."[9] Furthermore, though environmentally benign, the turbines represent technology, which in general is regarded as incompatible with, or incongruent in, a relatively uncultivated landscape setting. But, by necessity, wind farms have to be located on open, unhindered lands, or in this case the water. As a result, they are viewed as machines intruding in a garden, to borrow Leo Marx's imagery.[10]

According to both my research and informal polling among my friends and colleagues, the aesthetic verdict is split. For each criticism of wind farm as an eyesore that spoils the pristine landscape, I find a positive aesthetic judgment of these machines for being graceful, elegant, inspirational, and dancer-like. One may be tempted to leave this aesthetic controversy as an irreconcilable 'matter of taste,' keep aesthetics out of the fray and let scientists, engineers, and environmentalists battle it out. However, unlike other 'matters of taste' that at least seem to be often without serious consequences, this issue calls for some kind of decision, simply because, while we are engaged in the issue purely as a spectator, our opinions on this issue go a long way toward shaping the future of the world in the most literal sense. A strong opposition would kill these projects, as almost happened in the Cape Wind case. This is one of the clear examples, along with other examples in the subsequent chapters, which demonstrate that aesthetics has consequences.

Are there, then, ways in which we can develop a reasoned discussion on the aesthetics of wind farms and raise it above mere matters of taste? In what follows I will explore several strategies in support of the aesthetics of wind turbines.

4.2 Strategies to Transform the Aesthetics of Wind Farms

4.2.1 Imaginative comparisons

One strategy might be to urge the opponents to imaginatively compare the wind farm in the sea with something else located at the same site but with *negative* environmental connotations. Let them imagine a series of oilrigs, or a nuclear power plant or a factory with belching toxic emission constructed on an artificial island. I would assume that there will be a consensus that those objects will be both environmentally *and* aesthetically unacceptable. Then let them compare their reaction regarding these hypothetical cases to their reaction regarding the wind farm. Even if their aesthetic response is still negative toward the wind farm, at least they will most likely admit that it is not as strong as their reaction to these hypothetical examples. Their negative aesthetic reaction here will then be *mitigated* by their positive response to the wind farm's environmental benefit. So, a case can be made that the aesthetic status of the wind farm is *less bad* than some other cases.

A similar strategy also requires an imaginative thinking of another hypothetical case. We may ask the opponents to imagine an ultimate consequence of not pursuing this kind of clean energy. Assuming that our reliance on unsustainable forms of energy continues, we will need to build more power plants and transmission lines for harvesting and transporting more oil, natural gas, and uranium, all of which would exacerbate the destruction of natural habitats and landscapes, create pollution, and increase the possibility of environmental catastrophes, such as oil spills and nuclear accidents.[11] In fact, Cape Cod residents themselves had to contend with an oil spill from a leaking barge in April 2003.[12] Even if their own water view is unaffected, other parts of their landscape would be negatively affected. So this wind farm will be a small aesthetic price to pay, in comparison with future landscape destruction on a global level.[13]

Of course, these strategies are based upon choosing the lesser of two evils, and are not effective for *transforming* the negative aesthetic value of a wind farm to positive. The opponents could still claim that, although it is not as bad as the aesthetics associated with oilrigs and more power plants, the aesthetics of wind farms is still negative and their approval of this form of clean energy is not sufficient to overcome the aesthetic drawback.

4.2.2 Historical precedents

At this point the proponents may resort to another strategy by invoking past examples of changed aesthetic response from negative to positive and by arguing that the opponents' negative reactions are not so much against the pure aesthetics involved in this issue but are rather based on a knee-jerk reaction to something new and unfamiliar. It is widely acknowledged among cultural geographers and landscape architects that we tend to be rather conservative about the landscape we live with and generally resist change, particularly if the change is brought about by something associated with technology. However, it is also generally recognized that, given enough time and history, what was once considered as an intruder and spoiler of a landscape will eventually be assimilated into the landscape as an integral part. For example, we now look upon windmills as a familiar, appropriate, and almost romantic ingredient of a farmscape. But there is some evidence that those windmills that we now appreciate with nostalgia were not uniformly accepted when they first started appearing in farms.[14] Even in the Netherlands, where the landscape is now inseparable from windmills, the residents' reactions to them have not always been uniformly positive.[15] We can also point to the Parisians' initial uproar against the Eiffel Tower, without which we cannot even picture Paris today. As for the Statue of Liberty, its "installation was resisted and delayed because, as newspapers declared, it 'was neither an object of art [n]or beauty'."[16] Even the Golden Gate Bridge, when new, was decried as an "eye-sore to those living and a betrayal of future generations."[17] *And* many of us old enough still vividly remember the vehement objections to the V-shape scar and wound on the earth that became the Vietnam Veterans Memorial.[18] So it is conceivable that what is today considered a state-of-the-art machine can become an object of nostalgia and affection in the future.

Indeed, despite persistent resistance to wind farms in Europe and the United States, there is some indication that there has been a gradual acceptance of the appearance of wind turbines in the landscape. If this trend continues, eventually a new aesthetic sensibility embracing the aesthetics of the wind farm may emerge, eliminating the necessity for engaging in an aesthetic debate surrounding this issue. I am, and want to be, optimistic about this possibility, but I believe that it has to be part of a more general, larger aesthetic movement, which I will take up in Chapter 7. For now, however, we have to admit that this 'test of time' argument will not quell the opponents' concern because, while they may agree with the possibility of the change in their aesthetic judgment, nobody can predict whether and how soon it will happen, and in the meantime they will be forced to live with what they consider to be a ruined seascape.

Furthermore, history does not lack examples which make us question in retrospect: "What were we/they thinking about?" One writer thus reminds us that "the test of time works both ways."[19] Consider, for example, the past history regarding renewable energy, hydropower in particular. Dams were regarded with awe because of their sheer size and spectacle, not to mention their inexhaustible supply of electricity. Supporters of damming up Hetch Hetchy in Yosemite even invoked an aesthetic argument, accompanied by a touched-up photograph, to foster their cause (although the primary reason for building Hetch Hetchy was not for hydropower but as a water reservoir for the residents of San Francisco who suffered from perennial water shortage).[20] People at the time would not have anticipated the current de-damming projects.

Another example is suppression of forest fire. Even John Muir, like most conservationists at the time, argued for suppression of any fire in the Sierra forests, contrary to the long-held practice by the resident Native Americans who, through periodic burning, maintained the health of redwood forests. Those early conservationists would have argued against the current 'let burn' policy because of their belief that care-taking of forests include putting out fires, as well as the perception that burnt forest is not aesthetically pleasing, a problem specific to the American National Parks because their primary purpose was considered to be to provide aesthetic pleasure to the American populace.[21] So, how do we know that the wind farm will not suffer the same fate as such historical precedents?

One response to this argument is that these historical precedents, such as constructing dams and suppressing fire, took place when the general environmental awareness was not raised to today's degree and the various environmental repercussions were neither considered nor anticipated. In his account of the history of Hetch Hetchy, Alfred Runte comments that "perhaps increased knowledge of its plants and animals, coupled with scientific evidence corroborating the requirements for survival, could have swayed a few proponents of development to reconsider their stance. Even so, the argument was in the future."[22] One could say that people should have predicted the decimation of salmon population, for example, when they were busily constructing dams in the Western United States. But people didn't even know the harm caused by DDT until Rachel Carson pushed the alarm button in 1962, nor did they understand for a long time the environmental harm of losing wetlands which are now recognized to play at least twenty ecological functions.[23] Today, we are much more aware of environmental ramifications of our projects and, because of these past precedents, we proceed cautiously with environmental impact studies, such as the one done for Cape Wind. When people were enthralled with dams, environmental impact was not on their radar, unfortunately. Can we then feel confident that we know once and for all the environmental impact, positive and negative, of today's projects? Of course not. There may be unforeseen consequences in the future that none of us have even dreamed of, but that is true of any 'knowledge' we hold.

One may then ask whether it is wise to decide on the environmental value/disvalue of something and adapt our aesthetic sensibility to it, when it may possibly be subject to revision. This raises an important question, particularly in everyday aesthetics, because so much of our aesthetic evaluation seems to be affected by what we perceive to be the object's social, political, and environmental value. An extreme skeptic view would render any aesthetic evaluation impossible, because we can never have omniscient knowledge regarding all possible future ramifications. However, is it the most reasonable stance to take—that we should never engage in assigning aesthetic values, positive or negative, to any objects with possible ramifications, environmental or otherwise? This would be similar to making it impossible for us to decide or act on anything because we can never have complete knowledge about all the possible consequences of the contemplated action, because, as a good Cartesian would claim, nothing is indubitable except for the *Cogito*. Utilitarianism in fact is sometimes criticized for the impossibility of completing the utility calculation. However, there has to be a middle ground between reckless disregard or complete ignorance and omniscience, and we conduct our everyday life, decision-making process, and academic pursuit on that middle ground, that is, on the basis of best available evidence.

This extreme skepticism will certainly impoverish our aesthetic life, as well as deprive us of the opportunity to tap into the power of aesthetic persuasion that I will discuss in the final chapter. But I believe we do need to heed this cautionary warning and educate ourselves with available materials and data before formulating an aesthetic judgment. The aesthetic estimation of an object is subject to modification and revision with newer findings, just like everything else. We cannot but change our perception and judgment of a painting if it turns out to be a forgery. Similarly, as I will discuss in the final chapter, once we are educated about the environmental harm resulting from maintaining the velvety-smooth, weeds-free green carpet, our attraction to the green lawn will never be the same (though I don't think it will make it all of a sudden ugly, either). In a sense, our aesthetic perception is fragile, vulnerable to be influenced by associated facts, or, to borrow David Suzuki's phrase, "we see beauty through filters shaped by our values and beliefs."[24] So, although I currently hold the wind farm project generally in the positive light and hence argue for its positive aesthetic value, I do reserve the possibility of revision and modification if new, unexpected harms inherent in the technology and structure were to occur or be discovered in the future. At the same time, it seems to me that the same reserved attitude should be advised for all parties to the debate.

4.2.3 Analogy with art

Another strategy is to draw an analogy between this project and some examples from environmental art. There are successful cases of unfamiliar and new constructions that 'intrude on' or 'invade' a landscape, yet with positive aesthetic results. A number of projects by Christo immediately come to mind, such as *Valley Curtain* (1970–72), *Running Fence* (1972–76), *Surrounded Islands* (1980–83), *The Umbrellas* (1984–91), and *The Gates* (1979–2005).[25] *The Running Fence* is perhaps the most interesting example because of the fierce opposition he received from the farmers and ranchers whose fields were going to be affected by the project. His persistence eventually convinced them not only to approve, but also to participate in the project, and the end result was a breathtaking view of the rolling hills of California, the contour of which was accentuated by the white curtain. Even the roughneck farmers and ranchers were captivated and mesmerized by what should have been the most familiar and everyday landscape of their lives made both prominent and fresh by the project.[26] This and other works by Christo illustrate that something seemingly foreign and unfamiliar added to a landscape does not necessarily 'ruin,' 'spoil,' or 'destroy' it; if anything, it *can* enhance its aesthetic values by highlighting, illuminating, or intensifying some of its features.

Another example is Walter de Maria's *Lightning Field* discussed in the previous chapter. Though the real focus of this work is the phenomenon of lightning captured by metal poles, which of course occurs only sporadically and unpredictably, we can also appreciate the flatness and wide openness of the site made more prominent by the rows of poles placed with geometric precision.

It is true that there are important differences between these art works and wind farms. For example, Christo's projects are temporary installations[27] and *Lightning Field* is located in a remote area, not affecting people's everyday landscape. In addition, the design of Christo's projects changes from place to place, reflecting and enhancing its local characteristics, but the design of wind turbines cannot respond similarly to the sense of place.[28] Finally and more importantly, these art constructions do not serve any utilitarian function and are not regarded as 'machines.' Despite these differences between art projects and wind turbines, their analogy does suggest a *possibility* that human constructs *can* enhance the aesthetic of a landscape.

The comparison made to art projects highlights the importance of attending to the purely sensuous appearance of the turbine structure. In discussing the "aesthetic guidelines for a wind power future," one commentator illustrates different ways in which the design and arrangement of wind turbines can detract from or enhance the aesthetics of the landscape. For example, the following will generally take away from the aesthetic value of the existing landscape: visual clutter resulting from inadequate spacing between individual wind towers; unsynchronized directions of the movement of the blades; mixture of two- and three-blade turbines; inconsistent height, color, and design of the turbines; neglect of broken blades; unreclaimed access paths for construction vehicles; application of colors incongruous with the surrounding; and general neglect of the surrounding space strewn with construction debris and broken parts.[29]

On the other hand, it is possible to create an aesthetically pleasing effect by choosing the color, shape, and height of the turbines appropriate and responsive to the particular landscape, making them uniform in their appearance and movement, and spacing and arranging them in proportion to the landscape. Indeed, one writer admires the windmills in Sweden as "graceful objects" because "the slender airfoils seem both delicate and powerful at the same time while their gentle motion imparts a living kinetic nature."[30] These are indeed useful guidelines and some localities have in fact created ordinances to regulate the appearance of wind farms in their communities.[31] There has also been improved design, particularly of wind turbines in urban areas, such as on roof tops or integrated into the architectural design, that sometimes feature stunning aesthetic effects in its own right. Such new designs are created specifically in response to the aesthetic concerns in urban areas, where many people's visual experience is affected.[32] Finally, some recent proposals of land-based wind farm include turning it into parks with walking paths and landscaping, rendering the projects into a proactive vehicle for providing aesthetic experience for the visitors and passersby.[33]

There is another aesthetic dimension to consider regarding wind turbines: the *site-specific* relationship between the wind turbines and surrounding environment. For example, the extreme size of the turbines proposed in the Cape Wind project will be inappropriate in certain other contexts, not only aesthetically but probably psychologically as well. I would imagine that, if a series of them are erected near a residential area, the residents, their dwellings and other buildings will be dwarfed in the turbines' shadow and people will most likely feel threatened, not to mention that their size makes the structures incongruous in such a context. In the New England town where I live, the proposal to erect one wind turbine on the high school athletic field surrounded by houses was rejected for this very reason, and I believe it was the right decision. But the Cape Wind project is 4.7 miles out in the ocean at its closest proximity to land whose view from onshore will measure half an inch or two-thirds of a thumbnail. So in *this* case, I don't think their super-size will be aesthetically inappropriate.

At the same time, this advantage of the distance from which to view the Cape Wind project also poses a disadvantage. With the inland installation, it is often possible to view the turbines from varying distances and directions. Furthermore, it is possible to live in proximity with them, as we walk or drive on the road, or literally have them in our backyards. With the offshore projects like Cape Wind, our visual experience will lack perspective, distance cues, or a sense of gradual progression enjoyed by successful inland projects. As a result, the residents' experience is confined to a bunch of small spokes sticking out of water in the distance, or a bunch of blinking lights above water at night, neither of which is likely to help enhance and highlight the wide expanse of the ocean. I have to admit that this fact does pose a particular challenge to make offshore wind farms aesthetically positive.[34] These aesthetic considerations regarding the sensuous surface of the wind turbines and their relationship to the surrounding environment indicate that the specifics of each case matter.

Furthermore, the site-specific aesthetic considerations also include the cultural and historical character of the place. The 2004 Draft Environmental Impact Statement does indeed point out the loss of historic character of several nearby places, specifically two National Historic Landmark properties, four historic districts, and ten individual historic properties, that will result from the Cape Wind project. "The visual alteration to the historic Nantucket Sound settings of these properties, caused by the addition of the W(ind) T(urbine) G(enerator)s and related structures, will constitute an alteration of the historic character, setting and viewshed of the properties and will have an adverse visual effect on them."[35]

I think the relative weight of the loss of historic character of several places affected by the wind farm depends upon the degree of significance of the oceanscape to their historic import. For example, to what degree is the ocean view integral to the historic value of Kennedy Compound, one of the historic places that the DEIS identifies as being adversely affected by the wind farm? It is true that the Kennedy family is well-known for their enthusiasm for sailing, but is the historic legacy of the site going to be completely ruined by the wind farm? Or, is it rather going to be compromised without being destroyed altogether? Can there be a cost–benefit analysis of aesthetic values?

4.3 Life Value-Based Aesthetics of Wind Farms

4.3.1 'Thick' and 'thin' aesthetic qualities

Consideration of the aesthetic loss caused by damaging the historic and cultural values takes the discussion beyond the realm of the purely sensuous, such as the color and spatial arrangement of the turbines. The historic character and cultural significance of a site requires knowledge and associative imagination. At the same time, a similar strategy of going beyond the sensuous surface can also be employed in favor of wind turbines. That is, to invoke the notion of 'thick' aesthetic qualities which are based upon, but go beyond, the purely sensuous 'thin' qualities.

Sometimes 'thick' aesthetic qualities refer to what Kant would call "dependent beauty" or, more recently, "functional beauty" proposed by Carlson and Parsons. Another aesthetician, John Hospers also points out that "the design of the streamlined automobile seems to express speed, efficiency, ease, power (all of them values from life…)" and "the graceful curve of the arrowhead is not apprehended merely as a line, but as admirably designed for its purpose."[36] Another way that 'thick' aesthetic quality is characterized concerns ethical values.

Allen Carlson, for example, advocates developing an aesthetic appreciation of human environments by incorporating "the life values that such environments express."[37] Take, for example, an exclusive, upper-middle class suburban community that looks attractive in the purely sensuous way. Carlson maintains, and I agree, that if this attractive façade results from social injustice and racism, for example, it will be difficult to aesthetically appreciate its 'thin' qualities.

It is important to note that the 'thick' qualities are constituted by the 'thin' sensuous qualities that are organized under conceptual considerations, such as the arrowhead's function and the political ideology that gave rise to a gated community. For example, an arrowhead's smooth, well-polished surface, sharp edge, and pointy tip become appreciated as their fittingness to fulfill its function of spearing. Or, the specific size and design of a wall or a fence surrounding a gated community seems to say to the passersby, "keep out," and an extremely large, though gorgeous, house with multiple car garages exudes conspicuous consumption and disregard for their carbon footprint. The aesthetically relevant expression of life values, thus, needs to be presented by the sensuous appearance of 'thin' qualities, rather than life values imposed upon the object regardless of its sensuous appearance.[38]

Generally, it is easy to argue that some human environments or artifacts are aesthetically negative when they symbolize ecological harm or express negative life values. This is not to deny the benefit of sharpening our aesthetic sensibility toward the 'thin' surface that is unencumbered by life and environmental concerns associated with littering, belching black smoke from factories, strip-mining, clear-cutting, and green lawn maintained by toxic brew.[39]

However, the case of the wind farm is challenging because it provides an opposite case: the object in question is, by all accounts, environmentally positive. But this does not seem to transform its aesthetic value accordingly, from negative to positive. What should we make of this challenge then? Does it indicate a kind of asymmetry, in that environmental values are aesthetically relevant only when they are negative but not when they are positive, so that they can uglify but not beautify, so to speak? Or is there still room for modifying and possibly transforming the opponents' aesthetic judgments? If so, what sort of argument has to be developed to educate, convince, and finally convert the naysayers? Or, does this case indicate the limit of the aesthetics discourse, so that the argument in support of the wind farm has to proceed *despite* its negative aesthetic values and exclusively on the basis of its environmental benefit, along the lines of "eat your spinach because it's good for you—never mind its taste" mode of persuasion?[40]

I do believe that there is a limit to the extent to which environmental values can positively affect aesthetic values. For example, particularly with respect to a more body-oriented sensation, smell, I think there is a threshold of what we can tolerate. Even the die-hard environmentalists among us will be hard pressed to tolerate the odor caused by composting. Does the aesthetic objection to wind farms, directed primarily toward its visual aspect, also pose the same limitation?[41]

Vision has traditionally been regarded closest to the intellect, rendering it more receptive to modification by conceptual considerations. So there seems to be a prima facie hope for converting the Cape Wind opponents' view. What, then, would be an argument for the 'thick' aesthetic value of a wind farm invoking its life value?

4.3.2 The aesthetics of sustainability

In the case of wind farms, the most prominent life value associated with it is arguably its environmental benefit. Can there be a general argument for the aesthetics of sustainability?[42] I believe that some ingredients for such aesthetics have already been proposed by those who advocate and promote sustainable design, wind turbines being one example. Robert Thayer, for example, claims that "landscapes that create an illusion of a better world while depriving us of the actual means of achieving it are not sustainable" and that "the emotional state provoked by the landscape's surfaces should be congruent with and not contradictory to the manner in which the core properties of the same landscape provide for our functional needs and well-being."[43] If a landscape is unsustainable because of the incongruity between the surface value and core value, then, I would add (and I believe Thayer would agree) that such a landscape is not aesthetically appreciable. In the same vein, David Orr, in his work on the nature of design, makes an even more radical claim by defining what he calls "a higher order of beauty" needed today as something that "causes no ugliness somewhere else or at some later time."[44]

What this kind of aesthetic sensibility requires is that we judge the aesthetic value of an object, like a wind farm in the ocean, in an even larger spatial/temporal context. It is decidedly a movement beyond simply attending to the 'thin' sensuous qualities of the landscape with this structure. A wind farm will then be experienced as 'appropriate' or 'congruent' with its surrounding, because not only does it not pollute the air or water nor harm creatures, but also because it gratefully accepts and derives maximum benefit out of the site-specific gift that nature is providing—wind and open space. And we can witness this nature's gift at work in the movement of the blades.

As I discussed earlier, this new aesthetic sensibility does not deny the relevance and importance of 'thin' surface considerations—some colors, shapes, sizes, and arrangements of wind turbines and solar panels *are* aesthetically more, or less, pleasing than others. But the aesthetic debate concerning these objects responsible for determining the qualities of the environment, the world, and our life cannot be adequately addressed by simply working out better sensuous appearances.

Is this new aesthetics of sustainability asking us too much by way of conceptual knowledge (because we have to know the environmental impact and implications of the object in question)? No, I do not think it is expecting too much of our conceptual understanding, provided that there will be more societal effort to improve our ecological literacy and associated aesthetic sensibility. Implicit in Aldo Leopold's argument for the necessity of nature study, in particular ecology and natural history, and for promoting what he calls "perception" or land aesthetic sensibility, is a hopeful optimism that the general populace can be educated to hear a "marshland elegy," "the song of a river," and "the speech of hills and rivers."[45] In addition, we engage in a conceptually based aesthetic appreciation with works of art all the time—by taking courses in music, art history, and literature, and by reading program notes, reviews, and exhibition catalogues. It is just that we have not developed an equivalent formal discipline or discourse guiding our aesthetic appreciation of nature, environment, and designed objects. I will revisit the possibility of changing the aesthetic paradigm, including developing the aesthetics of sustainability, in Chapter 7.

4.3.3 Civic environmentalism

In the last section, I have tried to make a case for the aesthetics of sustainability that includes the aesthetics of wind farms based upon their life value, in this case, the environmental value. However, the fundamental problem with the 'thick' sense of aesthetic value is that this is where the ultimate disagreement lies concerning the object's symbolic import. For the proponents, wind farms express values such as stewardship, appropriateness, progress, safety, and cleanliness, while for the opponents they represent clutter, conspicuousness, monstrosity, or even a threatening feeling of militaristic power, and they resent the way in which their landscape is marred, spoiled, ruined, scarred, and destroyed by this intrusion.[46] This kind of disagreement is not unique to wind farms; in fact, such clashes of basic values that lead to aesthetic controversies are quite common, ranging from the gentrification of urban areas to the Wal-Martization of dilapidated downtowns, from utility facilities and highway infrastructures to gated communities of gorgeous estates.[47] One's aesthetic assessment of these phenomena is largely determined by one's economic, social, political, moral, and cultural orientations, and the values associated with these are as individual-dependent as aesthetic values. Though perhaps not as a way of resolving disagreement and settling disputes, I offer two possible ways in which we as a society can and should proceed.

First, when I think of the notions such as marring, spoiling, or ruining otherwise pristine and beautiful surroundings, I wonder how much of this negative reaction is based upon an underlying feeling of resentment that the project was concocted by outsiders and 'imposed' upon those affected by them. If the residents do not feel they are a part of the process, they do not have ownership of the project; in short, they feel alienated. What if, hypothetically, they took part in designing the structure, placement, and arrangement of the turbines? Of course, this scenario is implausible because the residents would refuse to participate in a project which they are opposed to from the outset. Furthermore, unlike many other community-initiated projects, such as creating a community garden or rehabilitating an abandoned building, a wind farm by necessity has to be constructed by a utility company because of its sheer scale, technological complexity, and connection to the regional or even national utility grid system.

However, what I am exploring is whether the residents' aesthetic judgment that the ocean view is spoiled, destroyed, ruined, or marred by wind turbines remains the same if the whole project was *their* idea, *their* initiative, and *their* design. If we subscribe to the traditional, art-oriented aesthetic theory, our personal relationship to and stake in an object should be irrelevant to its aesthetic value. For example, the fact that my friend composed a particular piece of music is irrelevant to its musical merit; similarly, the fact that a particular landscape photograph depicts my hometown in Japan has nothing to do with whether or not it is a good photographic work. We certainly do not want art critics and art historians to bring in their very personal associations and investment to bear upon their professional aesthetic judgments of a work of art.

However, I don't think that what is appropriate and expected in the field of art is readily applicable to our aesthetic lives outside the realm of art. A cultural geographer, Yi-Fu Tuan, for example, explains with his notion of "topophilia" that our appreciation of a place cannot be dissociated from the personal, as well as cultural and societal, relationships we have with it.[48] Particularly when planning and designing a structure which affects and alters a landscape, this affective dimension of our landscape experience should not be ignored, but rather should be addressed, possibly with the hope of turning it into an asset.

Very often, our direct involvement in altering a landscape seems to generate our affection and attachment toward the resultant landscape, which then leads to a positive aesthetic appreciation. A well-known anecdote related by William James describes how "coves" in North Carolina, recently cleared fields left with charred tree stumps and irregularly planted corn, which to him were initially "unmitigated squalor" and "a mere ugly picture on the retina," were a landscape redolent with pride and dignity to the residents because it symbolized "a very paean of duty, struggle, and success" based on their honest sweat and labor.[49] I believe that a similar observation can be made with the way in which urban dwellers take pride and find aesthetic appeal in what otherwise may appear as a crude- and amateurish-looking community garden.

So, one effective way of promoting a positive aesthetic experience of a particular environment is for us to be participants in creating it, which would help generate our affection and attachment. Particularly regarding environment, I believe such a personal relationship and affective response is inseparable from its perceived aesthetic value. And this "topophilia" resulting from people's involvement and engagement should be fully attended to and utilized.[50]

My thinking here stems from a newly emerging environmental ethic called civic environmentalism, which recognizes and emphasizes that solutions to various challenges facing the environment need the citizens' commitment to better their environment.[51] That is, no matter how environmentally sound and well-meaning a certain goal, policy, or project may be, if it is perceived as something imposed on citizens from above or outside, such as by a government or an outside environmental organization, its success and cultural sustainability are doubtful.[52] Citizens need to be enfranchised, and this sense of empowerment will positively affect their aesthetic experience of the object and project.[53]

But, as I mentioned earlier, wind farms in general do have disadvantages compared to other community projects. We can 'engage' with them only visually, but not literally.[54] Offshore facilities have further disadvantages compared to inland facilities because there are very few possibilities for each resident to actively interact with the structures. It is not impossible, however. For example, the residents can be a part of the process of choosing colors, spacing, and arrangement. They can also act as a distant and visual caretaker by reporting damaged or malfunctioning turbines. Or, after the example of Austin, Texas, which made a tourist attraction out of a bat colony, this seascape with wind farm, the first in the United States and the biggest in the world, could be promoted as a new tourist destination.[55]

A potential pitfall of this strategy of community involvement is that it may create the unwelcome mentality that all we care about is our own community or those projects with which we are personally or communally engaged. It may encourage our civic-mindedness on a micro-scale at the expense of its application on a macro-level. In addition, it may encourage, rather than discourage, the NIMBY mentality and environmental racism. I do believe that we have to be wary of this potential danger always lurking in the background. But the following two considerations may help mitigate, if not eliminate, this possible problem.

First, if each of us cared about, and cared for, our respective community environment, the cumulative results would go a long way toward covering many parts of the habitable environment. Second, like the saying goes, in order to cultivate a civic and green sensibility with a truly global perspective, we have to "think globally, act locally."

Ultimately, however, this case of wind farms should not be addressed as a unique, isolated issue, but rather should be thought of as one example of larger aesthetic, environmental, and social concerns. That is, if we are to respond to various environmental and ecological challenges and problems with sustainable designs, and if the social acceptability and cultural sustainability of green design are partly dependent upon its perceived aesthetic values, then it is our responsibility, both as designers/creators and as users/viewers, to clarify and formulate our aesthetic vision of what our world should be like. Do we want to hang on to the long-held ideal of a picturesque landscape and keep creating velvety smooth, lush green lawns adorned with exotic plants? Do we also want to maintain a pastoral ideal by hiding or rejecting machines as much as possible? Once we become aware of various harms and losses incurred by these aesthetic ideals, it does, and should, become more difficult to maintain them.

I would like to think we are in the midst of such an aesthetic paradigm shift. Even regarding wind farms, a number of reports from the United States and Europe state that the initial aesthetic objections not only subsided but also changed into positive responses, embracing and celebrating the altered landscapes. In fact, Lefteris Pavlides, Professor of Architecture at Roger William University, who has been working to install wind turbines in various parts of the State of Rhode Island, shared with me that, to his pleasant surprise, he is encountering more and more "YIMBYism" (Yes In My Back Yard) rather than "NIMBYism." When there are enough cases of such aesthetic endorsement, landscapes with wind farms will become integrated into our aesthetic vocabulary through what Thayer calls "an accrual of positive environmental symbolism"[56] that adds to the cumulative and collective memories of our cultural landscape. There are other examples that contribute to facilitating the aesthetic paradigm shift and developing this aesthetics of sustainability, such as promotion of laundry hanging and misshapen fruits and vegetables, as well as alternatives to green lawn. In the subsequent chapters, I will revisit and explore further the development of the aesthetics of sustainability, the role that aesthetics plays, and its cumulative effect in humanity's project of world-making.

Notes

1. An earlier version of this chapter, titled "Machines in the Ocean: The Aesthetics of Wind Farms," was published in *Contemporary Aesthetics* 2 (2004) http://www.con tempaesthetics.org/newvolume/pages/article.php?articleID=247. This chapter also incorporates "Response to Jon Boone's Critique," *Contemporary Aesthetics* 3 (2005) http://www.contempaesthetics.org/newvolume/pages/article.php?articleID=321.

2. This project went through numerous twists and turns regarding obtaining permits. The primary source of the problems was many residents' objections, and as I will show in this chapter the aesthetic objection was the major reason. For the timeline of these twists and turns, go to http://www.capewind.org/when/timeline.

3. Pointed out by Elinor Burkett in "A Mighty Wind," *New York Times Sunday Magazine* (June 15, 2003). Details of this project, accompanied by a map and visual simulation of the wind farm can be found at the company website at www.capewind.org.

4. At the time of initial writing for *Contemporary Aesthetics*, the Draft Environmental Impact Statement was available from The United States Army Corps of Engineers at http://www.nae.usace.army.mil/projects/ma/ccwf/deis.htm. "Executive Summary," sec. 3 (accessed August 25, 2005), no longer available online. The final report was filed in January 2009 as *Environmental Impact Statement for the Proposed Cape Wind Energy Project* by U.S. Department of the Interior (MMS EIS-EA, OCS Publication No. 2008-040, OCS EIS/EA MMS 2010-11 and OCS EIS/EA BOEMRE 2011-024) http://energy. gov/sites/prod/files/DOE-EIS-0470-Cape_Wind_FEIS_2012.pdf. My discussion in this chapter is based upon the Draft EIS.

5. Cited from "Consumer Attitude and Choice in Local Energy Development," by Robert Thayer and Heather Hansen, Department of Environmental Design, University of California—Davis, May 1989, in Paul Gipe, "Design As If People Matter: Aesthetic Guidelines for a Wind Power Future," in *Wind Power in View: Energy Landscape in a Crowded World*, eds. Martin J. Pasqualetti, Paul Gipe, Robert W. Righter (San Diego: Academic Press, 2002), pp. 173–212; ref. on p. 178. For the sake of argument, I am assuming that the wind turbine is environmentally beneficial, particularly in comparison with other unsustainable means of generating electricity. I shall also put aside the problem of wind turbines' inability to produce a large volume of electricity.

6. In my "Response to Jon Boone's Critique," I discussed several non-aesthetic objections raised by Jon Boone, namely questions of effectiveness of wind turbine-generated electricity, harm to humans and non-humans, and financial incentive to Cape Wind (sections 1, 2, 3). Since the discussion here should focus on aesthetic issues, I will not repeat these points here.

7. That aesthetics continues to be a perennial obstacle to wind farm proposals both in the United States and United Kingdom is also pointed out by Tyson-Lord Gray in "Beauty or Bane: Advancing an Aesthetic Appreciation of Wind Turbine Farms," in *Environmental Aesthetics: Crossing Divides and Breaking Ground*, eds. Martin Drenthen and Jozef Keulartz (New York: Fordham University Press, 2014), pp. 157–73.

8. For example, Charles Komanoff characterizes the opposition as "NIMBYs Everywhere: Even Wind Power Can't be Invisible," the title of his article in *The Providence Journal* (June 6, 2003). The visibility problem is also pointed out by Robert W. Righter in

"Exoskeletal Outer-Space Creations" (p. 29) and Martin J. Pasqualetti in "Living with Wind Power in a Hostile Landscape" (p. 161), in *Wind Power in View*.

9. Quoted in Burkett, "A Mighty Wind."

10. Leo Marx, *The Machine in the Garden: Technology and the Pastoral Ideal in America* (Oxford: Oxford University Press, 2000). In the case of the Cape Wind project, there is an additional social/political dimension which complicates the aesthetic debate. That is, many of the homeowners whose ocean view will be affected by this project are wealthy people who use their beach houses only as summerhouses for vacation. Part of the appeal of the beachfront properties, of course, is the unobstructed ocean view, but, unlike other wind farm projects on the land, their everyday lives are not going to be profoundly affected by these machines in the water. After all, many of them are not even year-long residents of the area and do not live with this oceanscape year-long. I do believe that there are important qualitative differences between the residents' reactions and part-time residents' or outsiders' reactions that affect the aesthetic debate, but for the purpose of the discussion here, I will not address this issue.

11. One cartoon which appeared in *The Providence Journal* at the height of the Cape Wind controversy depicts a sinking tanker with oil spill all around and an oil-covered seagull's comment is captioned as: "Oh, yes, much better-looking than wind turbines." For a good discussion of the aesthetic harm of elsewhere, see Jonathan Maskit's "The Aesthetics of Elsewhere: An Environmentalist Everyday Aesthetics," *Aesthetic Pathways* 1/2 (2011), pp. 92–107.

12. Indeed, in his letter to the editor entitled "While Tilting at Windmills, Consider the Aesthetics," Robert Skydell asks: "Did we already forget last year's spill of nearly 100,000 gallons of light crude oil into the waters of Buzzards Bay?" *Martha's Vineyard Gazette* (Nov. 11, 2003).

13. Another layer of this issue is so-called environmental racism. That is, those places that host various utility and resource extraction facilities (which cause environmental harm) are usually located in or near impoverished communities dominated by minority residents. One critic of the opponents of the Cape Wind project thus points out: "Nor does it seem to matter to them that other precious—*albeit less prosperous*—places, from West Virginia mountaintops to Wyoming sandhills, are sacrificed daily to yield the very fuels that the wind farm would displace." Komanoff, "NIMBYs Everywhere," emphasis added.

14. Documented by Righter, "Exoskeletal," pp. 25, 27–8.

15. Pointed out by Robert W. Righter, *Wind Energy in America: A History* (Norman: University of Oklahoma Press, 1996), p. 286.

16. Lefteris Pavlides, "The Aesthetics of Wind Power," *The Providence Journal* (March 5, 2005). I thank Pavlides, professor of architecture at Roger Williams University, for sharing his view, materials, and teaching experience regarding wind turbines.

17. Cited by Virginia Postrel, *Substance of Style: How the Rise of Aesthetic Value Is Remaking Commerce, Culture, & Consciousness* (New York: HarperCollins, 2003), p. 156. Tom Leddy called my attention to an excellent discussion of the history and aesthetic issues regarding the Statue of Liberty and the Golden Gate Bridge in Philip E. Davis' *A Pragmatic Theory of Public Art and Architecture* (North Charleston: CreativeSpace Independent Publishing Platform, 2015).

18. See the documentary film *Maya Lin: A Strong Clear Vision*, dir. Freida Lee Mock (2003).
19. Postrel, *Substance of Style*, p. 157.
20. Various issues associated with Hetch Hetchy are discussed by Nancy Lee Wilkinson in her "No Holier Temple: Responses to Hodel's Hetch Hetchy Proposal," *Landscape* 31/1 (1991), pp. 1–9 and it is accompanied by a number of photographs, including the touched-up photograph used by supporters to show its presumed positive aesthetic effect. Its historical accounts can be found in Alfred Runte's *National Parks: The American Experience* (Lincoln: University of Nebraska Press, 1989), *Yosemite: The Embattled Wilderness* (Lincoln: University of Nebraska Press, 1990), as well as Roderick Nash's *Wilderness and the American Mind* (New Haven: Yale University Press, 1982).
21. Runte, *Yosemite*, p. 60.
22. Runte, *Yosemite*, p. 82.
23. The sorry history of American wetlands is chronicled by Ann Vileisis in *Discovering the Unknown Landscape: A History of America's Wetlands* (Washington, D.C.: Island Press, 1997).
24. David Suzuki, "They're Welcome in My Backyard," *New Scientist* 186/2495 (April 16, 2005), p. 20.
25. I thought of this possible analogy before researching the literature on wind power, but it was interesting to discover in my subsequent research that some people dealing with this issue also made the same analogy. See, for example, Righter, "Exoskeletal," pp. 33–4.
26. A documentary film captures the farmers' and ranchers' change of attitude quite nicely. See *Running Fence: Christo's Project for Sonoma and Marin Counties, State of California* (New York: Maysles films, 1978).
27. Wind turbines obviously are not meant to be temporary structures in the same way that Christo's works are. However, Martin J. Pasqualetti points out that, in comparison with dams, mines, and nuclear waste sites, wind turbines *can be* dismantled and removed, rendering their alteration of landscape reversible. He concludes from this fact that "wind power need not produce a lasting landscape legacy" and he takes "this positive trait" as "one of the most conspicuous environmental advantages of wind energy." Pasqualetti, "Living with Wind Power," p. 167.
28. The impossibility of designing turbines to be site-specific is pointed out by Gordon G. Brittan, Jr., "The Wind in One's Sails: a Philosophy," in *Wind Power in View*, p. 71.
29. Gipe, "Design As If People Matter." Gipe's discussion is accompanied by a number of photographs to illustrate what is/is not visually appealing in various wind turbines. The fact that these 'thin' surface aesthetic considerations do make a difference in the overall aesthetic value of an object challenges what I would call environmental determinism, which renders the aesthetic value wholly dependent upon the object's environmental value, so that anything with negative ecological significance is deemed automatically aesthetically negative and anything with positive ecological significance is deemed aesthetically positive, *regardless of* its sensuous appearance. I will explore the problem with environmental determinism in later chapters regarding laundry hanging and green lawn.

30. Skydell, "Did we already forget?"
31. Riverside County and Palm Springs, both in California, have regulations regarding "height, noise, and color" of turbines. In addition, "advertising and logos are prohibited, and electrical distribution lines must be buried underground." *Aesthetics, Community Character, and the Law*, Christopher J. Duerksen and R. Matthew Goebel (Chicago: The American Planning Association, 1999), p. 145.
32. See Tim Sharpe's "The Role of Aesthetics, Visual and Physical Integration in Building Mounted Wind Turbines—An Alternative Approach," in *Paths to Sustainable Energy*, ed. Jatin Nathwami (Rijeka, Croatia: InTech, 2010), pp. 279–300 for many visual images of newer wind turbines, some actual and some sketches.
33. I thank Arnold Berleant for pointing out these recent developments. It is encouraging that there has been an increasing effort to merge art and utility structures, such as the projects by Aero Art, NewWind, and Land Art Generator Initiative.
34. One could make an opposite argument by pointing out that inland structures pose more threat of intrusion to our everyday environment, while the offshore structures do not 'intrude' on our environment in the similar way or to a similar degree.
35. DEIS, "Executive Summary," sec.16.
36. John Hospers, *Meaning and Truth in the Arts* (Hamden: Archon books, 1964), p. 13.
37. Allen Carlson, "On Aesthetically Appreciating Human Environments," *Philosophy & Geography* 4/1 (2001), p. 19.
38. Of course the ultimate question regards how to determine the life values associated with an object. One could list positive values such as success in life, hard work, and ambition associated with the large size and opulent appearance of a gated community. I will address the issue of disagreement over life values in the final chapter.
39. For example, a series of John Pfahl's photography depicting the smoke coming out of a steel factory smokestack and David T. Hanson's aerial photographs of coal-mining landscape are eerily beautiful on the surface level. So are Edward Burtynski's photographs of queries. Also see Thomas Leddy's "The Aesthetics of Junkyards and Roadside Clutter," *Contemporary Aesthetics* 6 (2008) http://www.contempaesthetics.org/newvolume/pages/article.php?articleID=511.
40. In my past writings I have always used this "eat your spinach because it's good for you (don't mind how it tastes)" mode of persuasion in characterizing one way of encouraging us to recognize the value of environmentally sound objects, landscapes, etc. I was intrigued when I found the same reference used by Gordon G. Brittan, Jr. in the same context: "the grudging 'You must eat your spinach' directive works only slightly better with children than with adults, particularly since there seems to be a clear alternative, namely to put the turbines anywhere else but 'my' view," p. 62 of Brittan, "The Wind in One's Sails."
41. At the initial stage of wind power development, the whirling sound of the blades was another problem. However, with improved technology that problem seems to be overcome; plus, it would not be a problem with the Cape Wind project because of the distance between the turbines and the shore.

42. I will be exploring this aesthetics of sustainability more fully in Chapter 7, in the section 7.2.3 on the "Aesthetic paradigm shift."

43. Taken from "Gray World" and included in *Theory in Landscape Architecture*, ed. Simon Swaffield (Philadelphia: University of Pennsylvania Press, 2002), pp. 189–96; ref. on pp. 189, 190.

44. David Orr, *The Nature of Design: Ecology, Culture, and Human Intention* (Oxford: Oxford University Press, 2002), pp. 185, 134.

45. The importance of developing "perception" is discussed in "Conservation Esthetic," in Leopold's *A Sand County Almanac: with Essays on Conservation from Round River* (New York: Ballantine Books, 1977). "Marshland elegy" is a title of a section in "The Quality of Landscape" and he also describes a marsh chorus in pp. 65–6. "The song of a river" and "the speech of hills and rivers" are discussed on p. 158.

46. These terms are culled from a number of academic writings, as well as from newspaper and magazine articles on this issue.

47. Some of these and similar examples are explored by Carlson, "On Aesthetically Appreciating Human Environments," and Duerksen and Goebel, *Aesthetics*.

48. Yi-Fu Tuan, *Topophilia: A Study of Environmental Perception, Attitudes, and Values* (Englewood Cliffs: Prentice-Hall, 1974).

49. William James, "On a Certain Blindness in Human Beings," in *Talks to Teachers* (New York: Henry Holt and Company, 1915), pp. 231–4.

50. The importance of attending to people's attitude toward their landscape is explored by Laurence Short in "Wind Power and English Landscape Identity," included in *Wind Power in View*. For example, he claims that "the wind industry must respect our cultural connection to the land, an attachment to the landscape that has been reaffirmed in the United Kingdom as a metaphor for national identity" (p. 57).

51. The notion of "civic environmentalism" was proposed and developed by Andrew Light. See his "Urban Ecological Citizenship," *Journal of Social Philosophy* 34/1 (2003), pp. 44–63. I discuss the role of aesthetics in civic environmentalism in "The Role of Aesthetics in Civic Environmentalism," in *The Aesthetics of Human Environments*, eds. Arnold Berleant and Allen Carlson (Peterborough: Broadview Press, 2007), pp. 203–18.

52. I am here using the notion of "cultural sustainability" proposed by Joan Nassauer. An object (in her case a constructed landscape) is culturally sustainable when its features make people take notice, develop an affection, as well as a caring and protective attitude toward it. Even when an object is ecologically sound, if it does not thus appeal to people, it will not be culturally sustainable because people do not care about it and end up neglecting it. For the articulation of this view, see her "Cultural Sustainability: Aligning Aesthetics and Ecology," in *Placing Nature: Culture and Landscape Ecology*, ed. Joan Iverson Nassauer (Washington, D.C.: Island Press, 1997), pp. 67–83.

53. The importance of empowering citizens in a project like a wind farm is stressed by a number of writers in *Wind Power in View* (Short, Brittan, Pasqualetti, Gipe).

54. Brittan points out that wind turbines "preclude engagement. The primary way in which the vast majority of people can engage with them is visually. They cannot climb

over and around them. They cannot get inside them. They cannot tinker with them." Brittan, "The Wind in One's Sails," p. 71.

55. I thank Sheila Lintott for this reference. There are also precedents for marketing wind farms by using them as a backdrop for advertising or a film scene. See Brittan, "The Wind in One's Sails," p. 63, Pasqualetti, "Living with Wind Power," p. 165, and Robert L. Thayer, Jr., *Gray World, Green Heart: Technology, Nature, and the Sustainable Landscape* (New York: John Wiley & Sons, 1994), p. 131.

56. Cited by Righter, "Exoskeletal," p. 36.

5

The Aesthetics of Laundry

As a quintessential part of everyday life, 'laundry' seems like an item that does not belong to an aesthetic basket full of things like art, beauty, sublimity, scenic landscapes, and the like. Despite the gradual expansion of the boundary of aesthetics discourse, to include nature aesthetics, aesthetics of popular arts, and even everyday aesthetics, laundry has yet to be mainstreamed as a legitimate subject matter of aesthetics.[1] In this chapter I challenge this status of laundry as an aesthetic outcast and argue for enfranchizing it in the aesthetic arena. The challenge of doing so brings up a number of criticisms posed to the legitimacy of everyday aesthetics reviewed in Part I. The aesthetics of laundry thus can be regarded as a test case for legitimatizing the most ordinary and mundane activity as a worthy subject of aesthetics discourse. As such, the following discussion in this chapter makes frequent references to Part I.

5.1 Exclusion of Laundry from the Aesthetic Arena

First, why has laundry been excluded from aesthetics discourse? Perhaps what comes to one's mind immediately is its rather lowly status when compared to the lofty nature of the traditionally held quintessential subject matters of aesthetics: art and aesthetic values such as beauty and sublimity. This is the reason that has excluded most everyday aesthetic matters from aesthetics discourse, and laundry appears to be a prime example for justifying this exclusion. Even when subjects other than art, such as food, game, and sports, are included in the aesthetic arena, the discussion generally centers on the extent to which they are like art. Specifically, the discussion focuses on whether or not those non-art objects and activities can involve compositional order, power to 'move' people, originality and creativity, and the possibility to make social commentary.[2]

What would happen if we subjected laundry to the same discussion regarding the degree of its likeness to art? One could argue that the orderly way in which clothes are hung on a clothesline or the neat and meticulous manner in which items are folded and put away can be aesthetically pleasing. So are the fresh smell and soft feel of properly laundered items. However, such 'order' and nice feel do not compare to the highly sophisticated compositional features and intensity of impact characteristic of many works of art, such as the compositions of Bach or the *Mona Lisa*, discussed in Part I. Specifically, the arrangement of clothes and linen is necessarily limited by the laundry items; the norm for proper laundering leaves little room for originality or creativity; laundry does not make a profound statement or express a deep emotion; and laundry is always done out of practical necessity rather than in pursuit of providing an aesthetic experience or deriving amusement. So laundry seems to share very little in common with art, at least less so than other non-art objects and activities.

If including laundry within the aesthetic circle via its analogy to art does not work, another possibility may be to focus on some of the aesthetic qualities engendered by laundry: beauty, cleanliness, sweet smell, crisp feel, and the like. For example, one writer on laundry declares that "a closet or armoire full of freshly laundered linens is an *object of beauty*."[3] However, we encounter more obstacles here. First, the 'beauty' of freshly laundered items, one could argue, is not an inherent quality in itself but a relative quality in comparison to the item's pre-washed state. Essentially the 'beauty' of laundered item is the cleanliness, such as white fabric being bright white without any stain or soil. Furthermore, one could argue that cleanliness, if it is an aesthetic quality at all, is not in the same league as other, more typical examples of aesthetic quality such as bona fide beauty, elegance, expressive intensity, and the like.[4] Recognition and appreciation of something being 'clean' does not require any special sensibility, training, sophistication, or connoisseurship, and presumably this fact disqualifies laundry from being a legitimate subject matter for aesthetics.[5]

Another challenge is that the sweet smell of freshly laundered linen and the nice feel of fabric against one's skin are pure bodily sensations, and I examined in Chapter 2 the reasons why some aestheticians still exclude them from the aesthetic arena proper. Namely, bodily sensations are regarded akin to knee-jerk reactions with no room for contemplation or reflection; nor do they have any objectivity or intersubjective validity because they are purely private sensations.

Finally, one may also point out that laundry includes not only the clean beauty of washed items but also disgusting pre-laundered items, such as smelly socks and soiled diapers. There are at least two possible responses to this point. The first response seems too contrived, though a typical move that can be made by those who advocate aesthetic distancing and disinterestedness. If the classical aesthetic attitude theory is correct that there is virtually nothing that cannot be aesthetically appreciable, then dirty laundry should be no exception. If "anything that can be viewed is a fit object for aesthetic attention," including "a gator basking on the mound of dried dung," as Paul Ziff claims, it seems at least theoretically possible to appreciate soiled diapers.[6] Furthermore, one can adopt an artistic eye and look at dirty laundry as if it were the subject matter of a painting or a photograph, such as a soiled table cloth depicted in Catherine Murphy's painting.[7]

While such an aesthetic experience may be possible, it seems too contrived to argue for the aesthetic dimension of laundry in this manner. Furthermore, since the aesthetic attitude theory is predominantly concerned with the visual experience, as indicated by Ziff's discussion of anything that can be "viewed," it will have a harder time accounting for how bad odor of dirty socks and diaper can induce an aesthetic experience.

A much less contrived response is to go along with our most common reactions to dirty laundry—it is unpleasant, disgusting, and sometimes downright repulsive. Such negative reactions also belong to the aesthetics discourse, understood in the classificatory sense, as I argued previously in Chapter 1. Membership in the aesthetics discourse does not require the qualities or experiences to be positive. So, it may appear that by virtue of the aesthetically negative qualities of dirty clothes and the aesthetically positive qualities of clean laundry, laundry should be considered legitimately belonging to the aesthetic basket.

However, this quality-oriented model, whether yielding positive or negative experience, does not capture the full aesthetic dimensions involved in laundry. This approach typifies what I termed 'spectator-oriented' aesthetics rooted in the conventional model in which a person perceives the aesthetic object and experiences a certain quality that affects her. As I argued in Chapter 2, when food or sports is considered for its aesthetics, discussion is primarily conducted from the point of view of tasting food or watching a sporting event, instead of the actual, physical experience of cooking or participating in a sport. While we could be a spectator of laundry by watching somebody else do laundry and having aesthetic reactions to dirty or clean laundry, our experience with laundry is most often gained by actually engaging in the laundering activity. In fact, quite a few activities are involved in laundering, beginning with gathering and sorting items, washing them, drying them either in a dryer or hanging them on a clothesline, ironing them, and folding them or hanging them.

At this point, one may pursue Dewey's line of thinking by pointing out that what characterizes the aesthetic is the feature of any experience rather than a particular object or a quality. If "any practical activity will, provided that it is integrated and moves by its own urge to fulfillment, have esthetic quality," nothing prevents washing linens, hanging them on the clothesline, and ironing them from becoming "*an* experience."[8] I don't deny the possibility of having *an* experience while doing laundry. A sudden intense experience is possible, similar to the way in which many Zen practitioners reach enlightenment by engaging in the most mundane activity such as sweeping a floor.

However, I believe that enfranchising laundry into the arena of aesthetics this way again restricts its aesthetic dimensions. It is because Dewey's account of *an* experience is quite stringent that he himself admits such experiences are rare. He characterizes the prevalent mode of experience to consist of either "loose succession that does not begin at any particular place and that ends...at no particular place" or "arrest, constriction, proceeding from parts having only a mechanical connection with one another" and observes that "there exists *so much* of one and the other of these two kinds of experience." Against this background, "when the esthetic appears, it...sharply contrasts with the picture that has been formed of experience."[9] I do believe that when we engage in the regular chore of doing laundry, we sense the aesthetic involved in laundry rather frequently, though our experience is so prevalent and mundane that it generally does not form "*an*" experience that is "complete in itself, standing out because marked out from what went before and what came after."[10] As I argued in Chapter 1, if we do the laundry chore on autopilot with no attention to what we are doing, there is no experience to speak of, although we are not unconscious, either. However, I believe that we can experience the ordinary activity in its ordinariness and familiarity without lifting it out of the mundane as a standout, extraordinary moment.

Thus, an attempt to account for the aesthetics involved in laundry by applying the established models of art, aesthetic quality, and aesthetic experience is not adequate. This is not to deny that there can be an art-like quality in laundered items: there are aesthetic qualities, both positive and negative, experienced from a spectator's point of view. Neither is it to deny the possibility of having *an* experience while doing laundry. However, doing so compromises the mundane humdrum nature of the experience integrated into the flow of everyday life. Furthermore, it does not adequately capture how our *decisions* and *actions* regarding laundry are motivated by aesthetic concerns. These concerns are so entrenched in our daily lives and taken for granted that we seldom reflect upon, let alone scrutinize, them from the aesthetic point of view. Just as there are pragmatic or moral reasons for our actions, there are aesthetic reasons for our actions, and such aesthetic reasons that guide our decisions and actions in our daily lives should be included as legitimate subject matters for aesthetics discourse, along with aesthetic objects, qualities, and experiences.

5.2 Aesthetics Specific to Laundry

Then what are those aesthetic considerations that guide our decisions and actions regarding laundry? Why do we wash our clothes and linen in the first place? The obvious answer is to 'clean' them. Now the notion of cleanliness may appear to be a hygienic concern, which it often is. We don't even want to imagine what it would be like if we never clean our underwear and socks. As such, somebody may dismiss considering laundry as a legitimate aesthetic subject by pointing out that it is a purely pragmatic activity exclusively concerned with practical concerns, namely hygiene. The relationship between the practical and the aesthetic has been a contentious issue particularly since the eighteenth-century aesthetics discourse. Until recently, the tendency has been to emphasize their separation and secure the independence of the aesthetic for fear that it may be subsumed under the practical. However, a strict separation between them has been challenged in recent years in a number of ways, many pointing out their inseparability in functional objects, the most notable example of which is architecture.[11] So, even if laundering is done primarily for practical reasons, that itself does not disqualify it from the realm of the aesthetic.

However, more importantly, as well as interestingly, hygiene alone cannot account for many decisions we make and actions we undertake when laundering. Consider the following list of do's and don't's of laundry that are motivated purely by aesthetic considerations to produce the best-*looking*, best-*feeling*, and best-*smelling* results.[12] The list is quite lengthy. It starts with sorting the laundry items by the color and fabric type to avoid light-colored items from getting darker from dark-colored items as well as making sure that the delicate fabric does not get mixed with others, as delicate fabric has to be washed with milder detergent, lukewarm water, and the gentle wash cycle to retain its quality. Dark-colored items should be washed in cold water to minimize fading, unless that's the desired effect, as in the faded look of denim jeans. Pre-treatment to remove stains needs to be done carefully, as sometimes it will discolor the treated area; hence, when in doubt we are supposed to test the pre-treatment detergent on an inconspicuous area such as the back side of the hem. When loading the washer, some items, such as made of corduroy, should be turned inside out in order to prevent lint from sticking. The use of bleach also is determined by whether or not the fabric color will become brighter or rather faded.

As for drying the laundered items, the heat and time settings of the dryer are crucial not only to avoid shrinkage (which is a practical consideration because we cannot fit into pants and shirts that have shrunk) but also to minimize wrinkles. Some items, such as shirts, should be removed and hung on hangers as soon as the drying cycle is complete in order to minimize wrinkles and maintain their shape. If drying on the clothesline, the same concern regarding wrinkles and maintenance of shape dictates certain measures, such as stretching or hitting the fabric before hanging and draping the item over the line rather than hanging so that the item does not get overly stretched by the weight of wet fabric. The use of clothes pins also needs some thought in order not have a pinch mark in the middle of a shirt, for example. While today's fabric softeners are scented so that the washed items have a nice smell, those who advocate outdoor drying insist that nothing can beat the fresh fragrance of sun-soaked and wind-blown laundry. On the other hand, line-drying hardens the texture of the wash, creating a stiff feel of jeans and coarse texture of towels. Then there are proper temperature and ways of ironing the laundered items, followed by 'how-to' regarding folding the items so that the crease will appear in the appropriate place.[13]

Adherence to these extensive do's and don't's is motivated by aesthetic considerations alone. For example, most of the time, stains do not compromise the functionality or hygiene of the items, whether clothes, linen, or towels. A white shirt made dingy and grayish because it was washed with dark-colored items is no less clean than a bright white shirt. Fabric softener, starch, or ironing does not increase the cleanliness of the laundered items. Neither does proper hanging on the clothesline to retain the shape of the clothing item, nor is proper folding of laundered items. In short, a shirt can function as a clothing item (to cover a naked human body as well as protecting it from the cold or the sun) with a stain, wrinkle, coarse texture, and dingy color. Similarly, functionality and hygiene of my corduroy pants are not compromised by a stain that has not been removed, lint that accumulated on their surface, and the coarse texture because they were line-dried. One may argue that a shirt and pants with such an appearance do compromise their practicality because they will most likely give a bad impression of the wearer to others; that is, the clothes' practical function of giving a favorable presentation of the wearer is not fulfilled. I will take up this issue later in more detail, but here I will simply point out that such 'function' of the clothes is derived from their appearance and feel, thereby invoking their aesthetic dimension.

It is thus somewhat surprising that what we do on a daily basis as a 'chore' without any thought to aesthetics actually is full of aesthetic considerations enumerated above. It is true that very rarely do any of these concerns lead one to a lofty thought or a profound aesthetic experience. However, there is no denying that these are all aesthetic considerations insofar as they are concerned with the sensuous appearance of the objects: the look, feel, and smell of the laundered items.

Now that I have established the number of specific ways in which aesthetic considerations determine our decisions and actions regarding laundry, I want to explore three more ways in which aesthetics is integrated into this daily chore: (1) the kind of aesthetic experience derived from engaging in *doing* laundry that is different from a standout experience; (2) the way in which one's character is assessed through the condition of one's clothes; and (3) the environmental ramifications of aesthetics involved in laundering activity.

5.3 Aesthetics of Doing Laundry

Housework usually conjures up an image of drudgery, particularly those having to do with cleaning. Nobody envies what Cinderella had to do on a daily basis or what Snow White found herself doing after discovering the mess in the seven dwarves' house.

Cleaning, whether of the house or clothes, has traditionally been regarded with disdain because nothing creative or sophisticated is thought to be required of the task; hence the task has been typically relegated to women or servants. Indeed, before the advent of washing machine and dryer, laundry *was* a time-consuming and back-breaking chore. Imagine washing diapers on a washboard or wringing bath towels to get rid of excess water, as my mother's generation had to do. Although many contemporary writings on laundry reminisce on their mothers' and grandmothers' routine with a sense of nostalgia and celebration, as I do when recalling my childhood, it is not clear whether our mothers and grandmothers found any joy and delight in this routine, unavoidable household chore. Cheryl Mendelson recalls her childhood in rural Appalachia where her grandmother and great-grandmother had to do the wash in the old fashioned way—everything by hand. She dispels any romantic notion of "good old days" by pointing out the "dreary" experience of slithering "between cold, wet sheets hanging in a dark, dark, moldy cellar" and the "cheerless and exhausting" physical labor.[14] As I have argued in Chapter 1, work both inside and outside of home is sometimes characterized as dreadful drudgery while other times providing stability and comfort. If it is experienced as sheer drudgery, one could still make a case that it belongs to the realm of aesthetics as a negative aesthetic experience.

Today, however, with labor-saving devices such as washing machines, all-purpose stain removers, electric irons with temperature setting, and so forth, this otherwise boring and labor-intensive daily chore does not exclude the possibility of a more positive aesthetic experience, though typically not in the form of having "an" experience. Not only from my own experience, but also from various people's (not surprisingly all women) writings regarding laundry, it is clear that there can be a quiet pleasure felt when the task is well done. Such delight is subtle and felt quite frequently as we engage in the chore on a daily basis, but it is hidden in plain sight because it is all-too-familiar and all-too-common. However, as I argued in Chapter 1, the almost exclusive focus on extraordinary experiences in traditional aesthetics discourse severely limits the scope of our aesthetic lives. If those standout experiences dominate the aesthetics discourse because of their intensity and profundity, more mundane aesthetic experiences should equally garner our attention because of their prevalence.

Let me compile some examples that recount such quiet and subtle aesthetic delights as engaging in the daily chore of cleaning. Pauliina Rautio's research on the place of beauty in everyday life provides a wealth of materials in this regard.[15] Her research consists of her monthly letter correspondence with a mother of three in a rural area of northern Finland. It is noteworthy that this woman, Laura, chose the act of laundry hanging as the focal point of reflecting on the place of beauty in her daily life. Laura's narrative covers a wide-ranging reflection on season, nature, family, and life, the purely sensuous experience of colors, scents, and sounds gained during this chore, constantly changing according to the season, weather, and time of the day. Rautio summarizes the nature of such an aesthetic experience that is folded into daily life as follows:

Everyday life is a contextual process but one that nevertheless defies definitions bound in time and space. This is because as subjectively experienced it entails simultaneously the past, the present, and the future as necessary for managing it. By managing everyday life I mean a practice that consists of constant reflection, evaluation and steering, but one that we are mostly unaware of engaging. In a way we are making our everyday lives. This makes the everyday a subjective construct instead of an objectively definable unit.[16]

For the author of a book titled *Laundry*, Cheryl Mendelson, laundry is "sensually pleasing, with its snowy, sweet-smelling suds, warm water, and lovely look and feel of fabric folded or ironed, smooth and gleaming."[17] She feels similarly about ironing by declaring that it

gratifies the senses. The transformation of wrinkled, shapeless cloth into the smooth and gleaming folds of a familiar garment pleases the eye. The good scent of ironing is the most comfortable smell in the world. And the fingertips enjoy the changes in the fabrics from cold to warm, wet to dry, and rough to silky.[18]

She characterizes such experience as "modest, quiet, private pleasures" and "valuable even though they are nothing that there ever could—or should—be a buzz about."[19] The additional reward of such a humble delight is further "physical pleasures—the look of favorite clothes restored to freshness and beauty, the tactile satisfaction of crisp linens in beautifully folded stacks"; "crisp, smooth sheets (that) dramatically change the aesthetic appeal of your bed and heighten your sense of repose"; and "the anticipation of feeling good or looking good in garments and linens restored to freshness and attractiveness through one's own competence and diligence."[20] Other writers join this observation: "there's something so satisfying about the fresh, steamy scent of just-ironed linens."[21] Note that there are two layers of aesthetic pleasure described here. One is the physical delight in the process of washing and ironing, and the other regards the end result of such physical labor. The former tends to be neglected in the usual spectator-based aesthetics discourse. The latter is also generally excluded from the aesthetic domain because the pleasure gained by freshly laundered and ironed items is predominantly derived from proximal senses of touch and smell.

Furthermore, writings on laundry indicate that there is a satisfaction in participating in the same task that women over the centuries and across the globe have undertaken: "the lifting, hauling, pinning and folding connects me to the generations of women who came before me, those who had fewer choices in their chores."[22] This theme of sharing the camaraderie with women throughout ages and across geographical borders is recurrent in most writings on laundry, as indicated by another writer: "over the years I have come to realize that, throughout shocking political and cultural upheavals, one thing that connects women over the generations is the making and tending of cloth."[23]

The sense of satisfaction and quiet delight thus experienced are woven into the fabric of daily life and as such rarely stands out from the rest of our lives. However, I characterize such sense of satisfaction as aesthetic insofar as it is rooted in the sensuous feelings gained from the bodily engagement with the activity as well as the condition of the objects resulting from our accomplishing the task. This feeling is akin to the sense of satisfaction related by Yi-Fu Tuan in his account of vacuuming and other mundane activities:

When I vacuum the carpet and create neat swathes of flattened fibers, when I look at a cleanly typed page, ... there is necessarily an aesthetic tinge to the satisfaction. All these activities are attempts to maintain or create small fields of order and meaning, temporary stays against fuzziness and chaos, which can be viewed, however fleetingly, with the pleasure of an artist.[24]

Tuan follows by observing "how rarely we attend to the world aesthetically," though "alert individuals do, glancingly, during the pauses and among the interstices of practical life." I agree with his observation that there is "an aesthetic tinge" to the satisfaction one gains from engaging in these chores, but I do not agree with his characterization that the experience can be "viewed ... with the pleasure of an artist" and that we "rarely" do so. This characterization is still based upon a commonly accepted assumption that the aesthetic experience needs to somehow dislodge everyday experience as if one were experiencing a work of art, thereby implying that it happens infrequently.

While I include the ordinary experienced as extraordinary as part of everyday aesthetics, I locate the core of everyday aesthetics in the ordinary experienced as ordinary: the quiet, unarticulated aesthetic satisfaction interwoven with the flow of daily life. Yanagita Kunio, a Japanese ethnologist, describes a similar aesthetic experience felt by farmers as they engage in their agricultural work: "Though the farmers clearly experience the beauty of the soybean field, they do not have a need to describe this experience in detail because their whole community shares this feeling in the first place."[25] Domestic cleaning is usually a private, rather than communal, affair, but it also rarely involves articulation. In fact, Tuan's account of farmers' experience describes better the kind of aesthetic experience typical of daily chores: "aesthetic appreciation is present but seldom articulated...the working farmer does not frame nature into pretty pictures, but he can be profoundly aware of its beauty."[26]

In all of these examples, what is noteworthy is that the aesthetic satisfaction is felt as one engages in an activity: laundering, vacuuming, farming. This mode of aesthetic experience does not fit the spectator-oriented mode of aesthetics, even if we were to liken our activity to performing.[27] Nor does it quite fit the Deweyan model, as such experiences are usually integrated into, rather than standing out from, the mundane humdrum. This suggests the need for another model for aesthetic experience: the kind that is experienced through one's engagement with everyday tasks and that is thoroughly integrated into the mundane. I argued for such a need, as well as a possibility, in Chapter 1 by discussing the possibility of experiencing the familiar as familiar, and in Chapter 2 by proposing activity- rather than spectator-oriented aesthetics.

5.4 Judgments of a Person's Appearance

Another aesthetic issue involved in laundry is the way in which we are concerned about the impression we give to others according to the degree of cleanliness of our clothes and other household objects. Now, as Mary Douglas points out, the notion of "dirt" is not an independent sensuous quality, but rather necessarily depends upon some kind of ordered system: "dirt" is something that is "out of place."[28] So, the coffee stain on my shirt is dirty, though there is nothing dirty about coffee; it just does not happen to belong on a shirt. Similarly, our (meaning contemporary American and I suspect many other Westernized) society has constructed an implicit ordered system which dictates how clothes should look and feel like: stain-free, white remaining white, wrinkle-free (unless the fabric is supposed to be wrinkled from the outset like seersucker), and a crease appearing only at the right places (such as the center of front and back of trouser legs). It is possible to imagine a different culture where the norm for clothes includes patterns created by various stains, grayish dinginess preferred over bright white, and random wrinkles and creases created by crumpling the washed clothes without stretching or ironing. But given the system we (again meaning referring to the Western and Westernized societies) do have, such a condition of clothes leads us to assume that the person who did the laundry or the person who wears those clothes (if they are two different people) does not care about the societal norm or one's appearance.

If I wear a shirt that has not been washed or laundered and ironed properly, hence sporting stains, bad smell, dingy color, and wrinkles, I don't normally suffer in the functional sense (except perhaps hygienically); the shirt will still cover my body, keep me warm, and shield my body from the sun's rays. However, most likely I will suffer from other people's judgment of me, particularly on public occasions requiring some degree of respectability and decorum, such as when I teach, go for a job interview, or attend a meeting. I may be judged to be disrespectful, improper, and inconsiderate. Whether we like it or not, Mendelson points out that cloth "is an astonishingly fertile means of expression for our aspirations to beauty, *sociability*, and *individuality* in our lives."[29] Furthermore, the moral assessment of one's character can extend to the person assumed to be responsible for laundry in a household. Given that my society still adheres to a gender-specific role, if my husband and children wear clothes that have not been properly laundered and ironed, others will most likely form a negative judgment not only of my laundry skills but also my character—that I am lazy, slovenly, irresponsible, or uncaring as a wife and a mother (unless they have a good reason to suspect that I or my family members are intentionally wearing poorly laundered clothes to make an extreme fashion statement of some sort). One writer characterizes old diaries that compile the correct way of laundering passed down from mother to daughter as "an encyclopedia of *correct behavior*."[30]

Now, we are often taught not to judge the book by its cover, but in daily life we do, in particular regarding personal appearance, to which the choice of our clothes and their condition make a major contribution. One may worry that such a judgment is too superficial and hasty. Those of us who try to get to know the person inside before passing any judgment based upon her appearance, in particular, may be inclined to refrain from forming such a judgment. However, there is also a pull toward assessing to what extent the person respects propriety and decorum. Despite the fact that what counts as 'clean' may be culturally and socially constructed, there is a sense in which we are justified in regarding a person with suspicion if she does not seem to care at all about social norms and propriety.[31] By adhering to the social norm by putting our best foot forward, so to speak, we are not simply conforming to the social norm but more importantly we are showing respect for others by giving a pleasant impression, or at least by not giving an unpleasant impression through poorly maintained clothes.

The moral assessment based upon the external appearance also happens with regard to the care for the outside of our house—such as the exterior paint and the yard. This constitutes our face to the outside world, and if it is shabby, neglected, and unkempt, not only is it considered aesthetically displeasing but also it disrupts the ambience of the neighborhood. It is like greeting people with a frown or scowl, instead of a smile. There is a sense in which the homeowner is justifiably judged as irresponsible and not sufficiently neighborly, civic-minded, and community-oriented by being totally indifferent to the appearance of her house and yard.[32] Just as most of us are put off by peeling paint, broken windows, a haphazardly leaning porch, weed-infested and garbage-strewn yard in our neighborhood, we are also put off by a wrinkled shirt, lint-laden pants, stained jacket, and discolored white dress. Provided that the wearer has a means and wherewithal to launder them correctly, we do make a moral assessment of her character through aesthetic means. Aesthetics involved in laundry, therefore, has this important dimension—the way in which its results can affect a judgment on a person's moral character.[33]

5.5 Environmental Impact of Laundry Aesthetics

Debates regarding the environmental impact of laundry normally do not involve aesthetic considerations. Environmental considerations involved in laundry typically address issues such as: whether cloth diapers are environmentally preferable to disposable diapers; the harmful effect of phosphate in detergents; toxic chemicals used in dry cleaning; improving washing machine performance to minimize the use of water, recommendations to wash most items in cold water, and the like. Although, as I argued before, much of laundering is motivated by aesthetic considerations, these environmental concerns do not seem to have a direct relationship with aesthetics.

There are, however, at least two ways in which our aesthetic concerns regarding laundry lead to environmentally harmful consequences. First is the poor performance of green detergents compared to regular detergents. Green detergents do not contain optical brightener, an environmentally harmful fluorescent blue dye contained in popular detergents, which helps make whites appear bright white. Without optical brightener, laundered whites appear dingy, even though clean. According to a 2014 *Consumer Report* testing, "no green detergents made our winners' list, in part because they often do without optical brighteners and grime-fighting polymer compounds. Many from our latest tests were downright dismal."[34] As a result, according to an observation from UK, the environmentally conscientious consumers have resigned themselves to "the reduction in standards from the 'whiter-than-white' effect we have come to expect from conventional washing powders to the noticeably less-than-white we get from bleach-free, environmentally friendly ones."[35]

Another way in which aesthetic considerations regarding laundry have a negative environmental ramification is outdoor laundry hanging, and this is the subject that occupies the rest of this chapter. This is an issue specific to the United States (and possibly Canada); at least I am not aware of the same issue outside of the United States.

Once a ubiquitous sight, after the introduction of the electric dryer, most households in the United States stopped drying laundry on the clothesline, except in rural areas, such as farming communities, where it is still relatively common, as well as recreational areas with no access to dryers, such as camping grounds and beach cottages. As one writer observes, "until about 50 years ago the clothesline was a part of the American backyard, but as the electric dryer spread to the masses, it quickly became viewed as a mandatory appliance." She quotes the 2006 Pew survey that found "83% consider them a necessity, as opposed to 62% a decade ago."[36] The electric dryer's popularity is understandable, as it does away with the time-consuming task of hanging each item of laundry secured with clothes pins, not to mention the problem of carrying a heavy basket full of wet items, soiling a freshly laundered item by accidentally dropping it on the ground, and the disaster of not taking the laundry in before rain. As more women began to participate in the workforce outside their home, the convenience of the electric dryer became all the more attractive.

Now with the heightened awareness regarding the environmental cost of running home appliances, among which a dryer ranks second after a refrigerator,[37] clotheslines are making a comeback in many American households, except for one problem. Many communities *prohibit* clotheslines for 'aesthetic' reasons. According to one estimate, "clotheslines are banned or restricted by many of the roughly 300,000 homeowners' associations that set rules for some 60 million people."[38] Laundry hanging is considered an "eyesore," an "'unsightly condition' up there with 'litter, trash, junk,'" comparable to "storing junk cars in driveways," and is believed to lower property value.[39] A *New York Times* article reports that "most private home associations which govern perhaps half of all subdivisions in Connecticut...forbid hanging laundry outside," as typified by one association's ban on "any apparatus designed for the purpose of drying clothing outside."[40] The clotheslines and wash hanging on them are treated in the same way as other items, such as lawn ornaments, flags, picket fences, porches, and the like, which are also regulated in many homeowners' associations (e.g., no plastic pink flamingo on the front yard). The major difference is that nobody disputes the environmental benefit of clotheslines, while the other ornamental items do not contribute to reducing carbon footprint.

Part of the negative perception regarding laundry hanging appears to come from the historical association with poverty. A number of writers comment on the association of laundry hanging with "scenes depicting dire poverty," "a flag of poverty," "low class," and "tenement living."[41] Even today those who still hang laundry on clothesline in the United States are not associated with affluence, such as farmers and immigrants who live in impoverished inner city areas.

While one can question the overall positive environmental value of wind turbines (because of the possible harm to birds, marine creatures, among others), the environmental benefit of drying clothes outdoors is indisputable. Compared to the energy consumption of using electric or gas dryers, a solar dryer is cost-free, both literally and carbon footprint-wise. It is therefore all the more ironic that even those communities priding themselves on being green by creating a park and a bike path in their midst and encouraging solar panels on each house prohibit clothesline in their yard.[42]

Considering this aesthetic regulation, along with various community ordin-ances regarding the front lawn, it is striking that, in the so-called "land of freedom" for which the First Amendment right to free speech and expression is regarded almost sacrosanct, when it comes to the aesthetics of everyday envir-onments, the tyranny of the majority still seems to prevail in favor of "homoge-neous exteriors."[43] This underscores one of my theses of this book that aesthetic matters in everyday life are never trivial; instead, they are surprisingly powerful in determining the quality of life and the state of the world, for better or worse.

In response to this prohibition of what otherwise is an environmental win–win activity, nineteen states in the United States to date have laws that in effect protect clotheslines[44] by "encourage(ing) the use of solar power" and overriding existing community ban on outdoor laundry hanging.[45] An organization like Project Laundry List based in New Hampshire advocates "right to dry" and is active in trying to have similar legislations passed in other states. For them it is a matter of "live free or dry."[46]

In addition to the environmental benefit, there are several aesthetic reasons given in support of outdoor laundry hanging. One argument attends to the sheer sensuous appeal. In addition to the sensuous satisfaction of laundry described by Mendelson and the fresh smell of air and sun that is pointed out by almost every writer writing about clothesline, there are visual attractions as well, according to their account. For example, Cindy Etter-Trunbull states: "You can still find linen lines and they are very pretty to look at; the colour of the different sized rectangles blowing in the wind or simply hanging still is very picturesque."[47] Some liken them to a work of art: "done properly, it can put a Calder to shame. It takes on a life of its own. Shirts shudder. Pants dance. Towels flap and snap."[48] Indeed, some photographers focus on laundry hanging the world over, particularly with the colorful combination among hung items as well as the clothesline against building facades, balconies, or streets.[49] Some writers also point out the interesting interplay of the view up close (hanging items themselves) and the glimpse of distant landscape, such as a mountain or a field, peeking through the gaps between hung items.

Other appreciators of clothesline go further by incorporating associated values. For the family themselves, their laundry hanging outside is "banners of familial pride just as sure as a coat of arms hanging from a castle wall in Olde England!"[50] One writer recalls that "when I had three babies, I *loved* hanging out the cloth diapers on the line...The significance was: it was like an announcement that this house had a baby."[51] For those doing the chore, washed clothes can symbolize the care and tenderness toward the family. In addition, laundered items ground the family with a feeling of at-home-ness, as described by Mendelson: "it...helps reawaken us to the part of the physical world that we experience most intimately—on our skin—and reacquaints us with it in a way that makes us more at home in our homes."[52]

For the outsiders, they offer glimpse into the family life: "Amazing what you can deduce from viewing a line. Your clothesline instantly reflects any household news" and "one glance at a clothesline told everything about the new family down the block," such as: "workshirts and overalls said there was a laborer in the house. White shirts and dozens of handkerchiefs meant an office worker."[53] As one writers recalls, "To us, clotheslines offered clues to the mystery of each house we passed. One old lady lived alone, and her bloomers often puffed out in the breeze in a sad, solitary sort of way."[54] One could argue that such information-gathering about a family's private life amounts to voyeurism. Perhaps. However, it can also conjure up "a homey, close neighborhood feeling" or a feeling that people are "connected to one another—by extended family, by neighborhood, by communities, and by the simple tasks that sustained life and gave it continuity."[55]

Even if the onlooker does not attend to the hung laundry items of the individual household, the sight of drying laundry signals 'life.' This is particularly true when laundry hanging graces what otherwise is an inhuman, inhospitable environment, such as a battle-scarred city or an area of dire poverty. As mentioned in Chapter 1 regarding the minimalist architectural aesthetics in Gaza Strip, such sign of life, no matter how small and modest, signals that the residents are managing everyday life with dignity and resilience, though with unimaginable difficulties.

How do we reconcile these positive responses toward clotheslines and the negative view that considers them to be an unsightly eyesore? As in the case of wind turbines, we can't simply dismiss the conflict as a matter of taste, because there is a real life consequence of how we adjudicate the conflicting taste. In the case of homeowners' associations' ban of clotheslines, there is an issue of aesthetic tyranny imposing its will on others,[56] as well as the substantial environmental ramifications of forcing everyone to use energy-guzzling dryers instead of nature's harm- and cost-free dryer. Because of its clear-cut environmental benefits as well as the fact that advocates of clotheslines are not forcing others not to use the electric dryer, it seems that the direction of changing the aesthetics of the issue seems to be in emphasizing the positive aesthetic aspect of the clothesline, or at least to mitigate its presumed 'eyesore' status. However, is it possible?

Several possibilities exist. First, we can learn from streetscapes from countries such as Italy and Japan that are enlivened by ubiquitous laundry hanging in windows and balconies without apparently suffering from the 'eyesore' phenomenon. Learning here is made easy because we tend to be more objective about foreign cultural practices (it is not my neighbor's backyard).[57] Here, many paintings and photographic works that depict such scenes may help, because of their artistic treatment that encourages us to attend to the possibility of picturesque composition and colorful palette, such as "the play of light and shadow, with the motion created by the wind, with the shimmer of damp garments in the sunlight, with the classical drape of towels and sheets," summarized as "a simple, honest beauty."[58] Exposure to them may make us more sensitive to the way in which properly, thoughtfully, and artistically hung laundry can simply enliven the atmosphere with colorful display.

Another strategy is to encourage active engagement. As I pointed out in Chapter 2 and earlier in this chapter, everyday aesthetics is not limited to deriving aesthetic pleasure from a spectator's point of view. An important aspect of everyday aesthetics resides in experiences gained while *doing* something. Laundry hanging as an activity that we literally engage in lends itself to this aspect of everyday aesthetics. It is instructive that many writings in praise of this activity point out that it is a delightful experience both for aesthetic creativity and contemplation. Because of its time-consuming nature of hanging clothes on line, some appreciate the way in which they are forced to slow down, comparable to the slow food movement: "The simple act of picking clean, wet clothes out of a wicker basket, shaking them out, and hanging them up makes me slow down, giving me time to compose the rest of my day." The same writer even calls this chore "one of life's luxuries."[59] It should also be pointed out that outdoor laundry hanging not only engages the body in movement but also in interacting with the environment, often nature and always consisting of air, sun, and wind. As with visual arts being helpful in facilitating the appreciation of visual images of hung laundry, poetic accounts of doing laundry help inspire aesthetic experience of engaging in laundry activities.[60]

Many also talk about the 'art' of laundry hanging, such as creating an order by hanging similar kind of things or items of the same color together or by hanging objects in order of size. It also means that, when hanging socks, they should all face the same direction.[61] Some go so far as to color-coordinate laundry with clothes pins, as well as their precise arrangement so that they "stand up in perfect rows like little soldiers."[62]

Furthermore, the reward of skillful laundry hanging is also aesthetic: the properly hung clothes retain their shape and carefully stretching clothes before hanging minimizes wrinkles. Finally, the fresh smell of sun-soaked clothes and linens cannot be duplicated by scented laundry detergent or softener, as described by one writer:

I wondered how anything as invisible and intangible as sunlight could have an odor. Nothing else I could ever think of smelled like the sun. But I loved getting into bed at night with those clean sheets and the scent of summer.[63]

In addition to these purely sensuous appeals of laundry hanging, we can encourage activation of imagination and association. Emily Brady provides several ways in which imaginative power enhances, or sometimes constitutes, the aesthetic appreciation of nature.[64] Her discussion can be applied to the act of laundry hanging here. For example, an acute sense of season dominates literature on laundry hanging. One writer suggests that line drying makes one sensitive to seasons, as "clotheslines are a sign of spring" just like "the return of dandelions and the first tender sprouts of creeping thyme between the flagstones of the walk," while clothes hung in the autumn air "carry with them the nostalgic smell of distant woodsmoke that lightly perfumes the clothesline."[65] Another writer remarks that "when conditions are right and the laundry is on the line, you feel harmonious with nature."[66] The imaginative power can also extend to a sense of participating in the age-old domestic practice done the world over.

Another imaginative association that enhances the aesthetic appreciation of laundry hanging is the satisfaction of environmental benefit that accompanies these sensuous experiences. In nature aesthetics, one of the most contentious issues has been regarding the scientific cognitivism advocated by Allen Carlson. Controversy surrounds whether basic scientific knowledge is necessary for an 'appropriate' appreciation of nature. Common criticism of scientific cognitivism is that it unduly excludes other forms of appreciation, often accompanied by imagination engaged with non-scientific associations, such as cultural and historical.[67] My current view is that the notion of 'appropriateness' is context-dependent, and appreciation informed by scientific cognitivism is necessary if the context of making an aesthetic judgment is concerned with environmental issues, such as preservation. However, if we accept the context-dependent nature of 'appropriateness,' holding scientific cognitivism is compatible with acknowledging other associated imaginations informing the aesthetic experience of nature. It would be odd to ignore the historical and cultural associations when viewing the Gettysburg battlefield and to focus exclusively on its geological and botanical aspects. Similarly, I don't think there is a good reason to reject imagined participation in the communal activity of laundry hanging with other women across cultures and histories. At the same time, there is no reason to deny the relevance and importance of experiencing laundry hanging with the associated environmental (based upon scientific) benefits. That is, the laundry hung outside can be appreciated not only for its orderly and colorful arrangement but also for the nature's gifts that are perceptible: the wind that makes the items flutter and the sun that imparts fresh scent that cannot be duplicated by any artificial fragrance.

In cultivating this aesthetic sensibility toward laundry hung outside, however, we must avoid what I call environmental determinism, whereby environmental value of an activity automatically determines its aesthetic value, making its sensuous appearance irrelevant. As I discussed in Chapter 4, no matter how environmentally valuable wind turbines may be, there *are* some cases of eyesore due to uneven arrangement, size and color not congruous with the surrounding landscape, and the like. The same applies to laundry hanging. Some instances of laundry hanging *are* disorderly, giving an impression that sufficient care was not given in making its appearance pleasant or at least less offensive to the passersby. As one writer comments,

If you compare a line where time was taken to insure things were consistently hung evenly and straight to one more randomly hung, with no established pattern or unity, it becomes clear where the harmony rests ... You wouldn't want Mrs. Jones up the road or Mrs. Smith down the road to drive by, see the clothes on the line and not hanging right. They would know, for sure, that your house must look the same, messy and untidy.[68]

Just as one judges the other person by the condition of her clothes, one often judges her also by the way her laundry is hung on the line, as it is reported that "our mothers were also making up their minds about the new folks in town, based on the way they hung their clothesline."[69] There has to be some detectable order, whether by size, color, or the kind of items, a sign of paying respect and being thoughtful to whoever is subjected to the sight.

Furthermore, most of us would not object to seeing shirts, towels, and linen on the line, but we react differently toward a parade of underwear bluntly exposed to us in an 'in your face' fashion. But such offensive appearance can be mitigated by a 'discreet' hanging method that hides those 'unsightly' items behind innocuous items. As one writer recalls:

It wouldn't do to put one's bloomers and other dainties out there to wave in the breeze where they might be seen by the fellow delivering ice or hauling coal. No, undergarments were hung under the sheets, where they could dry in the morning breeze—without being seen.[70]

Today in the developed nations, some of the older practices in daily life are making a comeback due to the increasing concern about the environment. For example, more shoppers are bringing attractive cloth bags to grocery shopping to alleviate the need for plastic or paper bags supplied by the market. Such was the practice before the ubiquity of plastic bags, and it still is the practice in many parts of the world. The same phenomenon exists with carrying a stylish canteen instead of a disposable plastic water bottle. Rather than being regarded as 'old' fashioned or a practice of the poor, bringing one's own cloth bags or canteen is now regarded as 'chic' and 'fashionable.' The same applies to cloth diapers. There is hope, then, that a similar change in taste can occur with respect to clothesline. One writer calls for renaming it as "solar dryer," because anything "solar" nowadays has good currency in the green market.[71] In short, the director of Project Laundry List suggests that "what the American clothesline needs is a new image...We want Martha [Stewart] and Oprah [Winfrey] to make the clothesline into a pennant of eco-chic."[72]

I have to confess I do not feel totally comfortable with making older, sustainable practices 'fashionable' and 'chic,' as it implies that it is simply a fad and can be overridden any time by a different mode of fashionableness. Furthermore, such retro-fashionableness is often associated with morally questionable 'shabby chic' or 'grunge,' a kind of aestheticization of poverty whereby the wealthy plays at looking poor by sporting torn and faded jeans that cost a lot of money. However, we need to be pragmatic about what works, and at the moment, the eco-chic of cloth grocery bags and canteens seem to be working, so there is no reason not to embrace it if it can be done with clothesline. In addition, unlike the case of $200 tattered jeans, clotheslines are quite affordable by most people.

I started this chapter with a common perception that there is nothing aesthetically worthy in the lowly, mundane activity of laundry and objects associated with it. I tried to show that this assumption couldn't be further from the truth. Laundry has so many aesthetically related dimensions that it is like a treasure trove for aesthetic inquiry. Actually, most of our domestic activities are laden with aesthetic considerations: house cleaning; cooking; maintenance and care of the house, yard, clothing, and furnishing. Just as laundry goes beyond simply maintaining hygiene, as I tried to show in this chapter, many activities involved in these chores also go beyond fulfilling needs and functions such as hygiene, safety, nutrition, and health. This underscores my claim that everyday aesthetics surrounds us all the time.

Philosophy is often characterized as the art of wondering at the obvious. Putting laundry under aesthetic scrutiny reveals a number of interesting issues. It is particularly fascinating because we take it for granted that soiled clothes and linen need to be laundered and seldom give even a passing glance at their potential aesthetic import. The experience is a slice of our everyday life shared the world over, and it is teeming with aesthetic gems. Although I limited my discussion here to laundry, I have no doubt that the same rich reservoir of aesthetic issues can be found in other domestic chores.

Notes

1. In this regard, I found it interesting and fitting that the cover of Ben Highmore's *Ordinary Lives: Studies in the Everyday* (London: Routledge, 2011) is a photograph of indoor laundry hanging. I also want to highlight the following two articles published in *Contemporary Aesthetics* as an exception to the neglect of laundry as an aesthetic issue: Pauliina Rautio, "On Hanging Laundry: The Place of Beauty in Managing Everyday Life," 7 (2009) http://www.contempaesthetics.org/newvolume/pages/article.php?articleID=535, and Jessica J. Lee, "Home Life: Cultivating a Domestic Aesthetic," 8 (2010) http://www.contempaesthetics.org/newvolume/pages/article.php?articleID=587.
2. I discuss these dimensions of the aesthetics of food and sports in *Everyday Aesthetics* (Oxford: Oxford University Press, 2007), pp. 15–16.
3. Irene Rawlings and Andrea Vansteenhouse, *The Clothesline* (Layton: Gibbs Smith, Publisher, 2002), p. 62.
4. While allowing different power and intensity of various aesthetic qualities, Thomas Leddy argues in support of qualities such as clean and messy. See his "Everyday Surface Aesthetic Qualities: 'Neat,' 'Messy,' 'Clean,' 'Dirty,'" *The Journal of Aesthetics and Art Criticism* 53/3 (1995), pp. 259–68. D. W. Prall also points out that neatness and cleanliness have both practical and aesthetic values in our daily life: "What does

move in the direction of improving the surface of this world for our contemplation, is evidenced in the fulfillment of such aesthetic demands as those of neatness, cleanliness, polished surfaces, finished and efficient apparatus of all sorts, such apparatus as happen to be useful or to be thought useful for our practical everyday purposes." *Aesthetic Judgment*, first published in 1929 (New York: Thomas Y. Crowell Company, 1967), p. 42.

5. This reason for exclusion and a response to it was discussed in Chapter 2, particularly by reference to Thomas Leddy's view developed in "Defending Everyday Aesthetics and the Concept of 'Pretty,'" *Contemporary Aesthetics* 10 (2012) http://www.con tempaesthetics.org/newvolume/pages/article.php?articleID=654.

6. Paul Ziff, "Anything Viewed," in *Oxford Readers: Aesthetics*, eds. Susan L. Feagin and Patrick Maynard (Oxford: Oxford University Press, 1997), pp. 29 and 23.

7. See the discussion of Murphy's work in Francine Prose, "A Dirty Tablecloth, Deconstructed," *ARTnews* 98/9 (October 1999), pp. 126–7.

8. John Dewey, *Art as Experience* (New York: Capricorn Press, 1958), p. 39.

9. Dewey, *Art as Experience*, p. 40, emphasis added.

10. Dewey, *Art as Experience*, p. 36.

11. A thorough discussion of the relationship between aesthetic values and function can be found in Glenn Parsons and Allen Carlson's *Functional Beauty* (Oxford: Oxford University Press, 2008).

12. I am sure that this list of instructions is limited to the Western and Westernized societies and will need adjustment depending upon other cultural norms.

13. The list here is compiled from Cheryl Mendelson's *Laundry: The Home Comforts: Book of Caring for Clothes and Linens* (New York: Scribner, 2005).

14. Mendelson, *Laundry*, p. xii.

15. Pauliina Rautio, "On Hanging Laundry."

16. Rautio, "On Hanging Laundry," Sec. 4.

17. Mendelson, *Laundry*, p. xiv.

18. Mendelson, *Laundry*, p. 99.

19. Mendelson, *Laundry*, p. xv.

20. Rick Marin, "A Scholar Tackles the Wash," *New York Times* (Sept. 29, 2005), Mendelson, *Laundry*, pp. 99 and xiv–xv.

21. Rawlings and Vansteenhouse, *The Clothesline*, p. 59.

22. Marcia Worth-Baker, "HOME WORK: The Quiet Pleasures of a Line in the Sun," *The New York Times* (July 23, 2006).

23. Rawlings and Vansteenhouse, *The Clothesline*, p. 8.

24. Yi-Fu Tuan, *Passing Strange and Wonderful: Aesthetics, Nature, and Culture* (Washington, D.C.: Island Press, 1993), pp. 101 and 100.

25. Yanagita Kunio, *Mame no Ha to Taiyō* (*Leaves of Beans and the Sun*) (Tokyo: Sōgensha, 1942), p. 5, my translation. Lucy Lippard makes a similar observation: "the feeling of farmers and farm workers, who directly experience the land, are rarely articulated from the inside," *The Lure of the Local: Senses of Place in a Multicultural Society* (New York: The New Press, 1997), p. 141.

26. Yi-Fu Tuan, *Topophilia: A Study of Environmental Perception, Attitudes, and Values* (Englewood Cliffs: Prentice-Hall, 1974), p. 97.

27. A good critique of interpreting the aesthetics of body actions involved in daily chores as a performance can be found in Jessica Lee's "Home Life."

28. Mary Douglas, *Purity and Danger: An Analysis of Concept of Pollution and Taboo* (London: Routledge, 2002), p. 44. She further states that in our society "dirt avoidance is a matter of hygiene or aesthetics" (p. 44) and repeats that "with us pollution is a matter of aesthetics, hygiene or etiquette" (p. 92). I have more extensive discussion on the notion of dirt, cleanliness, orderliness, and the like in *Everyday Aesthetics*, pp. 154–8.

29. Mendelson, *Laundry*, p. xi, emphasis added.

30. Rawlings and Vansteenhouse, *The Clothesline*, p. 9, emphasis added.

31. Here and in subsequent discussion, I am assuming that a person knows the cultural norm, has a means of affording clean clothes and a tidy house and yard, and is not trying to make an extreme fashion statement by challenging the cultural norm.

32. As I discuss in Chapter 7, one of the objections to front yards consisting of wild flowers, vegetables, and/or fruits is their unkempt appearance that is regarded as the homeowners' indifference to the neighborhood.

33. David Novitz has an extended discussion on the judgment of a person based upon his/her appearance. See Chapter 6 of *The Boundaries of Art: A Philosophical Inquiry into the Place of Art in Everyday Life* (Philadelphia: Temple University Press, 1992).

34. *Consumer Report*, Aug. 2014, p. 41.

35. Nigel Whiteley, *Design for Society* (London: Reaktion Books, 1993), p. 92.

36. Kirsten Dirksen, "Clothesline Wars: The Solar Dryer," *Faircompanies Sustainable News* (March 11, 2008).

37. According to Christine Woodside, the dryer is second to the fridge in energy consumption among household appliances. "Drawing a Line on Outdoor Clothes Drying," *New York Times* (Dec. 2, 2007).

38. Kathleen A. Hughes, "To Fight Global Warming, Some Hang a Clothesline," *New York Times* (April 4, 2007).

39. Reference to "eyesore" is by Amy Quinton, "Clothesline: Solar Device or Eyesore?" *New Hampshire Public Radio* (Nov. 1, 2007) http://nhpr.org/post/clothesline-solar-device-or-eyesore, "unsightly condition" by Nancy Bartley, "Clothesline Crusaders Calling Laundry Flap Overblown," *Seattle Times* (August 13, 2013) citing the home-owners' covenants in Sammamish's Heritage Hill near Seattle, and "junk cars" by Jenna Russell, "Clothesline Rule Creates Flap," *The Boston Globe* (March 13, 2008). It is interesting to note that in the past, laundry hanging was prohibited on Sundays in New Jersey, according to the "1796 Act to Suppress Vice and Immorality." Marcia Worth-Baker speculates that "perhaps the peek-a-boo factor helped give rise to the rule; maybe fluttering frilly underpants inspired thoughts unsuitable for Sunday." Worth-Baker, "HOME WORK." Most likely for the same reason derived from morality, Minnesota once prohibited hanging men and women's underwear on the same clothesline, according to Deborah Sharp in "Neighborhood Rules on the Line; Want to Hang Clothes Outside? Better Check City, Local Bylaws," *USA Today* (Dec. 10, 2004).

40. Woodside, "Drawing a Line."

41. Hughes, "To Fight Global Warming;" Alexander Lee interviewed by Orli Cotel, "The Answer, My Friend," *Sierra* 92/5 (Sept./Oct. 2007), p. 8; Quinton, "Clothesline;" Sharp, "Neighborhood Rules."

42. Jon Howland cites an example from The Forest Heights neighborhood, Oregon's largest ever new-home community, located in Portland's posh West Hills, in "Clothesline Bans Void in 19 States," *Sightline Daily* (Feb. 21, 2012) http://daily. sightline.org/2012/02/21/clothesline-bans-void-in-19-states.

43. Elisabeth Salemme, "The Right to Dry," *Time* (Dec. 2, 2007), p. 100.

44. Salemme, "The Right to Dry."

45. Sharp, "Neighborhood Rules."

46. http://laundrylist.org.

47. Cindy Etter-Turnbull, *Fine Lines: A Celebration of Clothesline Culture* (East Lawrencetown, Nova Scotia: Pottersfield Press, 2006), p. 54.

48. Craig Wilson, "Three Sheets to the Wind: The Only Way to Dry," *USA Today* (April 8, 1999).

49. Annalisa Parent is cited by "To Fight Global Warming," and others mentioned by Rawlings and Vansteenhouse.

50. Roger Welsch, "Musings from the Mud Porch," *Successful Farming* 99/7 (May–June 2001), p. 62.

51. Etter-Turnbull, *Fine Lines*, p. 102.

52. Mendelson, *Laundry*, p. xvi.

53. Mendelson, *Laundry*, p. 101 and Rawlings and Vansteenhouse, *The Clothesline*, pp. 7 and 17.

54. Edie Clark, "Summer's Scent," *Yankee* 65/6 (July/Aug. 2001), p. 144.

55. Hughes, "To Fight Global Warming," and Rawlings and Vansteenhouse, *The Clothesline*, p. 7.

56. To be fair, homeowners' associations are constituted by those residents who all chose to come and live there, implicitly agreeing to abide by their rules.

57. It can be a disadvantage because of the possibility of exoticizing the foreign cultural practice. Pauliina Rautio also cautions against looking at laundry hanging in rural Finland from a wholly outsider's viewpoint, whether "through the mythical rhetoric of tourism or is reflected in the depressing results of national statistical welfare research," and points out that "between these poles there seems to be gap in need of filling with accounts of everyday life from the viewpoint of the villagers themselves." Rautio, "On Hanging Laundry," Sec. 2.

58. Rawlings and Vansteenhouse, *The Clothesline*, pp. 81 and 83.

59. Rawlings and Vansteenhouse, *The Clothesline*, pp. 8 and 13. It is true that this activity can be considered a luxury because many of us in the workforce simply cannot afford the time to engage in laundry hanging; even when we are home there is no guarantee that the weather will cooperate.

60. One example of a collection of poems regarding laundry hanging with illustrations is *Washing Lines: A Collection of Poems*, selected by Janie Hextall and Barbara McNaught (Lechlade: Lautus Press, 2011). I thank Reiko Goto for this gift.

61. Etter-Turnbull, *Fine Lines*, pp. 84–6.

62. Etter-Turnbull, *Fine Lines*, pp. 41 and 42.
63. Clark, "Summer's Scent," p. 144.
64. Emily Brady, "Imagination and the Aesthetic Appreciation of Nature," in *The Aesthetics of Natural Environments*, eds. Allen Carlson and Arnold Berleant (Peterborough: Broadview Press, 2004), pp. 156–69.
65. Rawlings and Vansteenhouse, *The Clothesline*, pp. 47 and 52.
66. Etter-Turnbull, *Fine Lines*, p. 16.
67. I will not present a thorough overview of this issue in environmental aesthetics. For those who are not familiar with this discourse, the following resources provide a good overview: Entries on "Environmental Aesthetics" by Arnold Berleant and Emily S. Brady and an entry on "Nature: Contemporary Thought" by Allen A. Carlson in *Encyclopedia of Aesthetics*, 2nd edn, ed. Michael Kelly (Oxford: Oxford University Press, 2014), Vol. 2, pp. 493–503, and Vol. 4, pp. 474–8; Allen Carlson's entry on "Environmental Aesthetics" in *Stanford Encyclopedia of Philosophy* http://plato.stanford.edu/entries/environmental-aesthetics/; and *The Aesthetics of Natural Environments*, eds. Allen Carlson and Arnold Berleant (Peterborough: Broadview Press, 2004).
68. Etter-Turnbull, *Fine Lines*, p. 62.
69. Rawlings and Vansteenhouse, *The Clothesline*, p. 7.
70. Welsch, "Musings from the Mud Porch," p. 62.
71. Worth-Baker, "HOME WORK."
72. Russell, "Clothesline Rule Creates Flap."

PART III

Consequences

Everyday Aesthetics and World-Making

In Chapter 1, I argued for the value of cultivating everyday aesthetic sensibility to enrich one's life and encourage a mindful way of living. The example of sky art in Chapter 3 explored one way in which art can help facilitate a sharpened aesthetic sensibility toward an aspect of our daily lives. The cases of wind turbines and laundry in Chapters 4 and 5, on the other hand, suggested that everyday aesthetics has consequences that affect the state of the world in a significant way. I am particularly concerned with this aspect of everyday aesthetics: its contribution to the world-making project.

6

Consequences of Everyday Aesthetics

Since my discussion concerns mostly the aesthetic lives of people who are not professional world-makers like artists, designers, architects, and other creators, it may sound counterintuitive, as well as a bit grandiose, to refer to everyday aesthetics' contribution to the world-making project. Despite my claim that everyday aesthetics should attend to the daily activities we undertake, such as laundering and cooking, we generally regard ourselves as recipients, dwellers, and consumers of the world fashioned by professionals. However, in addition to the aesthetic objection to wind turbines and outdoor laundry hanging, there are many other ways in which our seemingly trivial and inconsequential aesthetic preference and taste have unexpected serious implications that determine the state of the world and the quality of life. This chapter compiles more examples to illustrate this point.

I maintain that, despite the lack of our awareness, we all contribute to this world-making enterprise, and aesthetics plays a surprisingly important, indeed crucial, role. I call this 'the power of the aesthetic.' The considerable power of the aesthetic to guide people's behavior, decisions, and actions has been recognized and utilized by psychologists, advertisers, and propagandists, but curiously not sufficiently by aestheticians. I believe we need to address this lacuna in the aesthetics discourse.

6.1 Environmental, Political, and Social Consequences

6.1.1 Environmental consequences

In my earlier work, I compiled many examples to illustrate how our seemingly trivial aesthetic tastes, preferences, and judgments lead to decisions, actions, and policies that have serious environmental or political consequences.[1] Let me give a brief summary of these examples here, with additional examples.

First, until recently and even sometimes today, many of us, particularly in the United States, are commonly attracted to scenic landscapes typified by the early National Parks with wondrous, gorgeous, and exquisite beauty. Aldo Leopold characterizes this scenic aesthetics "an under-aged brand of esthetics which limits the definition of 'scenery' to lakes and pine trees" and "proper mountains with waterfalls, cliffs, and lakes."[2] In comparison, we tend to judge that "the Kansas plain is tedious" because of its monotonous appearance. The pragmatic consequence of this scenic landscape aesthetics is that, while we loudly protest the destruction of scenic beauty, we tend to neglect protecting unscenic lands, with devastating consequences, such as the decimation of wetlands in the United States by rendering them more 'productive' through filling and paving.[3]

The reverse situation occurs when the public resists the destruction of beautiful-looking plants that are invasive and damaging the health of an ecosystem. Marcia Eaton points out, "a patch of purple loosestrife, with its brilliant color, may cause a lot of pleasure."[4] In the area I live (on the northeast coast of the United States), phragmites poses a threat to salt marshes because of its invasive character with a network of sturdy root systems, destroying the delicate ecological balance of the area that negotiates between the different saline content of the water. Before becoming aware of their ecological threat, I used to be rather upset to see a patch of phragmites that are cut at the roots or sometime burned, the most effective way of eradicating this species, because I thought the uniform stalk with fluffy tops swaying in the wind was an attractive sight.[5]

The same scenic aesthetics plagues nondescript-looking or unattractive creatures, such as fish, invertebrates, and insects. They do not garner the same kind of publicity and support when endangered, compared to creatures that are cute, cuddly, graceful, or awesome, such as a seal pup, crane, whale, polar bear, or bald eagle. Stephen Jay Gould points out the consequences of this aesthetic preference: "environmentalists continually face the political reality that support and funding can be won for soft, cuddly, and 'attractive' animals, but not for slimy, grubby, and ugly creatures (of potentially greater evolutionary interest and practical significance) or for habitats."[6] Marcia Eaton points out that the aesthetic attractiveness of deer, coupled with the literary, and subsequent Disney film's, portrayal of Bambi, creates a challenge to forest managers who sometimes need to reduce its population rather than allowing massive starvation and other ecological problems.[7] This challenge would most likely not occur if deer were not attractive creatures.

Our environmental awareness is also influenced by the power of the aesthetic. We often refer to belching smoke stacks from factories and massive oil spills, such as the Exxon Valdez and BP disasters, as the quintessential examples of air and water pollution. Their aesthetic impact consists of dramatic images and an effective narrative structure of 'an event' with a beginning, middle, and end, accompanied by an identifiable villain and hapless victims such as oil-covered seagulls. Such aesthetically powerful events tend to eclipse our daily individual actions which are equally, if not more, serious as a source of pollution, because they lack the comparable aesthetic effects.[8]

A green lawn is considered a symbol of American domesticity. Constant vigilance and work, described by one critic as "a perpetual torture" and "constant amputation," are required to achieve the aesthetic ideal of weed-free, velvety smooth, and (ideally perpetually) green, not brown, lawn sporting a uniform crew-cut.[9] The aesthetic norms governing this ideal lawn are order, uniformity, neatness, and cleanliness, although the contemporary critics of this aesthetic ideal point out that the green lawn instead expresses monotony, conformity, lifelessness, and sterility.[10] Its cultivation and maintenance is thought to reflect the homeowner's industriousness, work ethic, orderliness, propriety, neighborliness, and civic-mindedness. The prototype of this aesthetic ideal goes back to Thomas Jefferson's Monticello, but it came to be promoted most heavily during the post-war period, thanks in no small measure to the chemical industry that created the market for lawn maintenance products.

Americans spend an inordinate amount of time, energy, resources, and money to continue this practice, sometimes even risking their own health and safety.[11] In addition, what one observer calls this American "lawnoholic" obsession exacts a considerable environmental cost: heavy use of water, fertilizer, herbicide, insecticide, and gas-guzzling lawn-mower.[12] For example, it is estimated that 30 percent of urban water is used for lawn care on the East Coast and 60 percent in the West.[13] The toxicity of chemicals used in maintaining the green lawn is indicated by the fact that companies like Chemlawn warn residents not to let their children play on the lawn for a few days after the application of their chemicals. The workers must protect themselves by wearing protective gear so as not to breathe in the toxins they are spraying.

It is no accident that the color, shape, and size of fresh produce we find at the supermarket are uniform. One commentator on America's food points out that "the apparent perfection" of "strangely uniform and incredibly shiny red tomatoes and picture-perfect peaches" reflects "the fact that perhaps one-third of the farm's fruits and vegetables have been discarded by the farmer or the supermarket for *aesthetic* reasons."[14] This wasteful practice motivated primarily by aesthetic considerations is not limited to the United States. The 1988 European Economic Community law stipulates the shape and size of fruits and vegetables that are fit to be sold directly to consumers. It includes, for example, "a mathematical definition for the acceptable curvature in the highest class of cucumber," although the law was superseded in 2009 by legislation that "allows for many nonstandard fruits and vegetables to be sold directly to consumers as long as they are labeled 'intended for processing'."[15] Another regulation stipulates that "a spear of asparagus could not be sold unless at least 80% of its length was green."[16] In addition, without the use of chemical insecticides and pesticides, organic fruits may have holes created by worms, which may turn off the consumers not only because of the possible contamination by worms but also by the blemished surface.

The problematic consequences of discarding ugly, deformed, misshapen, inglorious fruits and vegetables are not limited to food waste which, according to several estimates, amounts to one third of the global food supply. It also includes environmental impact, as "the energy used to produce and then dispose of food is a huge greenhouse gas emitter" and, according to a UN report, "the carbon footprint of waste food is equivalent to 3.3 billion tonnes of CO_2 per year worldwide."[17] Furthermore, rotting fruits and vegetables that end up in landfill produce methane gas, a major contributor to climate change.

6.1.2 Landscape aesthetics and nationalism

Art's contribution to promoting political agendas is well-known. The most notorious example is Nazi Germany's utilization of film and music. Even without the same kind of negative consequences, today's political campaigning, particularly in the United States, is unimaginable without posters, music, buttons, and spectacle-like events, not to mention the aesthetic considerations regarding the political candidates' attire, hairdo, gesture, posture, and way of speaking.[18]

Historically, however, people's attitudes toward the aesthetics of the everyday environment also has played a significant role in promoting nationalism and political agendas, although this is not as well-known as art's contribution. For example, Nazi Germany's promotion of native plants and its effort to eradicate alien species had a political purpose. According to their agenda, "the area must be given a structure which corresponds to our type of being ... so that the Teutonic German person will feel himself to be at home so that he settles there and is ready to love and defend his new home"; hence, it is necessary "to cleanse the German landscape of unharmonious foreign substance."[19]

Even less known is an example from pre-World War II Japan. After two and half centuries of isolation from the rest of the world, Japan finally opened its doors in 1868, initiating a sudden and rapid process of Westernization. In its own estimation, Japan could not compete against Western civilization, except through its aesthetic tradition.[20] This construction of the national aesthetic heritage included the so-called 'uniquely' Japanese art forms and aesthetic sensibilities. Equally important was the aesthetic value of their everyday environment and its ingredients.[21] For example, Japanese bridges were praised for their design to blend in with the surrounding nature, and considered superior to Western, particularly Roman, structures, which were interpreted as being designed to dominate nature.[22]

By far the most prominent example, however, is cherry blossoms. Their ephemerality, signaled by graceful parting after a short-lived life, was celebrated for embodying the moral virtue of not clinging to life unnecessarily. The most poignant reference to this aesthetics of cherry blossoms can be found in the praise for Kamikaze pilots for their readiness to depart life, as well as the planting of cherry trees on the invaded soils of Korea and Manchuria.[23] The aesthetics of these natural and everyday objects promoted by various intellectuals of the time was not intended as political propaganda. However, it was appropriated by the military for uniting Japanese citizens in their war-time effort. One commentator thus emphasizes the potency of "policies and rhetoric [that are] ostensibly meant to beautify work, the workplace, and everyday life."[24]

Perhaps with less dire consequences, the American wilderness aesthetics that developed during the nineteenth century was also motivated by the relatively young nation's attempt to formulate and promote national identity and pride. At first plagued by an inferiority complex with regard to America's uncultivated, crude, and uncouth land in comparison to civilized European lands, nineteenth-century American intellectuals sought to put a positive spin on their land by turning the initial disadvantage into an asset. Landscape painter Thomas Cole, for example, declared that "the most distinctive, and perhaps the most impressive, characteristic of American scenery is its wildness."[25] The implications of this wilderness aesthetics are far-reaching, both positive and negative, ranging from the formation of the national park system to the displacement of indigenous Native American population and suppression of forest fires.[26]

The aesthetic appreciation of one's native landscape is critical in the formation of national identity and pride. Indeed this is one of the legacies of landscape aesthetics. Simon Schama observes that "national identity...would lose much of its ferocious enchantment without the mystique of a particular landscape tradition."[27] Arnold Berleant also points out that "national groups commonly possess a mystique about their land" and "part of that mystique is an affection for their landscape and its beauty."[28] However, when such cultural nationalism becomes political nationalism, particularly with a militaristic agenda, it often leads to problematic consequences. While the creation of desired landscapes in these historical examples was primarily carried out by the government and the military, many citizens of these respective societies participated in these world-making projects, even if unwittingly, by supporting such landscape aesthetics. With or without problematic consequences, there is no denying that such an aesthetic tradition exerts a powerful influence on the course of a nation's history.

6.1.3 Consumer aesthetics

Aesthetics also plays a significant role in consumers' purchasing decisions and the subsequent handling of their possessions today in many industrialized nations. Virginia Postrel declares that "aesthetics, whether people admit it or not, is why you buy something."[29] Thomas Leddy also observes that "we increasingly choose things (e.g., products) based on aesthetic, rather than more appropriate criteria—religious, political or economic."[30] Contemporary aesthetic persuaders consist of qualities such as new, fashionable, cool, cutting-edge, novel, state-of-the-art, and stylish. This aesthetic obsession is orchestrated by the strategy of 'perceived' obsolescence, a version of planned obsolescence, employed by the manufacturing industry to encourage consumers to throw away perfectly functional products that are no longer considered fashionable. We as consumers are constantly 'updating' our appearance by buying new clothes, household items, automobiles, and other gadgets that are 'in style,' although their functional value may not differ from the older models. This creates the 'keeping up with the Joneses' mentality whereby people "ripped out perfectly good appliances just to replace them for *aesthetic reasons*, in part because they saw their neighbors doing the same thing."[31] Sometimes referred to as 'fast fashion,' this frenzy of today's consumer culture creates a number of environmental problems. As the 2007 animated film *Story of Stuff* illustrates, the staggering volume of 'stuff' created to satisfy the consumer appetite, fueled primarily by aesthetic desire rather than genuine need, is responsible for resource extraction, a high carbon footprint, pollution associated with manufacturing and transportation, and ever bulging landfills and incinerators.[32]

There are also increasingly devastating incidents of human rights violation in developing nations related to manufacturing processes and waste dumping: sweatshop-like factories, inhumane working conditions, child labor, and toxic e-waste materials that are dismantled for recycling and reuse by villagers with no protective gear, while children play in their midst. Today's mechanism of global capitalism is such that, often, developing nations are caught in the inescapable cycle of exploitation in which they have to ignore environmental devastation and human rights violation in order to meet the developed nations' demand for more and more goods to be manufactured. One of the most dramatic results is the infamous garment factory collapse in Rana Plaza, Bangladesh, in 2013 with the death toll of 1,127 people and roughly 2,515 injured. This is after 112 workers were killed in 2012 in a factory fire in Bangladesh that sewed US Marines logo onto clothing. Poor working conditions also persist in Chinese computer factories that led to an increased suicide rate among workers to the point that the buildings now have a built-in net to capture those suicides who throw themselves from the rooftop. All of these problems result from satisfying the industrialized nations' consumer appetite for aesthetically attractive products.

The concern over factory workers' well-being goes back to Karl Marx. He was particularly concerned about the 'surplus value' whereby the workers do not receive the full fruits of their labor, as well as the nature of mechanical, repetitive work of industrial capitalism which alienates them from the products they are helping to create. He was also critical of injury to the workers' sense experience caused by "artificial elevation of temperature," "the dust-laden atmosphere," and "the deafening noise"[33] of the workplace. William Morris shared similar concerns. He points out "there is a great deal of sham work in the world, hurtful to the buyer, more hurtful to the seller, if he only knew it, most hurtful to the maker."[34] One of the results is the degradation of townscape caused by "squalor and hideousness" and "thoughtlessness and recklessness." Factories also "blacken rivers, hide the sun and poison the air with smoke and worse." He particularly calls attention to "the *everyday squalors* that the most of men move in" which are often ignored by highly cultivated men engaged in affairs of arts. Leddy summarizes and updates their concern: "Such thinkers as Marx, Morris, Ruskin, and Dewey all were concerned about the moral implications of everyday aesthetics, and so should we be. This would imply recognition of *aesthetic pain* in everyday life, for example..., the alienating *lack of aesthetic satisfactions* experienced by workers in Mexican maquiladoras and on Chinese factory floors."[35]

The place of aesthetics in today's consumer culture does not stop with the products themselves. Today's economy is referred to as "experience economy," premised on the belief that it is no longer sufficient for today's business to sell goods and services.[36] The experiences associated with the sale of their goods and services are necessary. The branding of Apple distinguishes not only the Apple products but also the whole atmosphere of the Apple Store. The same applies to phenomena such as Niketown, Hard Rock Café, and Starbucks. Sometimes referred to as "shoppertainment" or "entertailing," everything in the store is scripted and designed to promote "customer participation," an "environmental relationship," and "a well-defined theme" through "engage(ing) all five senses."[37] For example, "the mist at the Rainforest Café appeals serially to all five senses. It is first apparent as a sound: Sss-sss-zzz. Then you see the mist rising from the rocks and feel it soft and cool against your skin. Finally, you smell its tropical essence, and you taste (or imagine that you do) its freshness."[38] Or, the recent proliferation of a bookstore combined with café is based upon the discovery that "the aroma and taste of coffee go well with a freshly cracked book," while one chain of laundromats went bust after installing a bar inside because it was found that "the smells of phosphates and hops, apparently, aren't mutually complementary."[39]

Aesthetics concerns not only the creation of a certain physical environment for the shopping experience. Many stores have strict policies regarding the employees' appearance, ranging from attire and hairdo to prohibition of tattoos and body piercing. There are also piped in music and fragrant air-fresheners. In short, there is a concerted effort to provide an aesthetically pleasing multi-sensory ambience surrounding consumers' shopping experience.

Finally, various aesthetic strategies employed in advertising are well-known. Whether employing sexual images, or images of cute and cuddly puppies and kittens, or presenting an idealized life-style, the aesthetic bombardment on TV, internet, billboards, and magazines permeates the everyday environment in many parts of the world. One advertising phenomenon that is receiving attention today is 'food styling.' It can be considered almost as an art. A fast food hamburger is carefully dressed up for an advertising photo shoot through the application of shoe polish to make the meat patty appear moist and appetizing, placement of the tomato, lettuce, and a pickle slice to protrude toward the viewer to indicate their crispness, and the arrangement of individual sesame seeds with tweezers for the most attractive appearance of the bun. Such advertising strategies must be effective; otherwise, companies would not invest considerable amount of their profit to creating ever-changing ad campaigns.

The central role played by aesthetics in today's consumer culture is noted by many thinkers. Terry Eagleton, for example, observes that "the wholesale aestheticization of society had found its grotesque apotheosis for a brief moment in fascism, with its panoply of myths, symbols, and orgiastic spectacles. . . . But in the post-war years a different form of aestheticization was also to saturate the entire culture of late capitalism, with its fetishism of style and surface, its culture of hedonism and technique, its reifying of the signifier and displacement of discursive meaning with random intensities."[40] Similarly, Paul Duncum points out that "aesthetics have been used to support any number of political regimes, social causes and economic systems. It is the particular characteristic of our own time that aesthetics is used to support the consumerist aesthetics of designer capitalism."[41] Specifically, "with the packing and styling of products, along with a host of cross-media promotional images all intended to stimulate desire, aesthetics has become indispensable to the capitalist cycle. If in an earlier period of capitalism, aesthetics was a last thought, the icing on the cake, the decorative but non-essential cheery [sic] on top, it is now central to the entire capitalist enterprise."

There is a growing concern with the role of aesthetics in today's consumer culture. First, it is highly probable that this prevalent aesthetics stunts the development of people's aesthetic sensibility. There is a worry that people are seduced by easy and instant gratification that does not require much discrimination, effort, or reflection. For example, Leddy points out that "commercialization is...thought bad because it encourages consumers to revel in shallow pleasures at the expense of ones that are deeper and more fulfilling," emphasizing "relatively superficial aesthetic properties in a way that is detrimental to human flourishing."[42] Promotion of this kind of easy aesthetics, according to Duncum, "encourages self-indulgence, not self-discipline; desire, not denial; hedonism, not abstinence—aesthetics, not ascetics."[43]

Furthermore, within the capitalist framework, positive aesthetic values that may be beneficial to the consumers (such as being able to enjoy a nice environment in which to shop) are exploited ultimately for the sake of increasing the company's bottom line. They are strategies to manipulate the consumer purchasing decisions and, as such, need to be regarded with a dose of skepticism. Berleant complains that "the ubiquity of canned music in public spaces is a particularly flagrant aesthetic-moral intrusion, the former by attempting seduction by perceptual techniques and the latter by psychologically manipulating moods to promote vulnerability."[44] And the reason that "makes these practices morally culpable is the fact that they are perpetrated intentionally, their motive being to impinge on passersby for the purposes of influence and profit."[45]

However, the most problematic aspect of consumer aesthetics is that, at least according to the way in which manufacturing processes operate today, there are too many moral, political, and environmental problems that result from the industry's effort to satisfy consumers' aesthetic demands (although these demands are often artificially created by the industries themselves).[46]

6.2 Moral Consequences

The last section compiled examples of everyday aesthetics' consequences on a macro-level, that is, the ways in which the state of the world becomes affected, and sometimes determined, whether environmentally, politically, or socially. This section will focus on everyday aesthetics' consequences on a micro-level. This regards our interactions with others.

In contemporary Western ethical discourse, virtue ethics, such as its classical Aristotelian formulation, has been receiving increasing attention. At the same time, ethics of care has developed as one of the consequences of growing feminist concerns. They both complement, or sometimes compete with, ethical theories that emphasize justice, rights, and utilitarian considerations. While I welcome and support this development, I also note a lacuna that needs to be addressed, and that is the contribution aesthetics makes to ethics. This section explores how moral virtues such as respect, care, consideration, and thoughtfulness are often expressed, appreciated, and cultivated through *aesthetic* means.

Ethical discourse is primarily concerned with what gets accomplished by an action: carrying out one's duty; helping a person in distress; telling the truth even if it hurts; making a difficult decision in a no-win situation; sharing a gift with others, and so on. Typical debates ensue regarding the nature and content of one's duty, what should be the criteria for deciding in the case of an ethical dilemma, and whether or not fulfilling negative duty is sufficient. What is generally not addressed is that *the way in which* an action, whatever its goal, is carried out affects its moral value. Furthermore, the sensuous appearance of artifacts often expresses moral virtues or lack thereof. I maintain that both are aesthetic, as well as moral, concerns insofar as our experiences and judgments of moral values are derived from the sensuous appearance of the actions and objects.

Examples in this section are predominantly from Japan. I find in Japanese aesthetics a long tradition of regarding moral virtues and aesthetics as insepar-able. I do not imply, however, that Japan is unique in this respect, and some of the examples I give should substantiate this point. Nor do I claim that this moral-aesthetic ideal is always adhered to by everyone in Japan or in every situation. My interest here is that the principle behind the ideal of this inseparability demon-strated in many aspects of Japanese art and culture can be applicable in different cultural and geographical contexts, as some of the non-Japanese examples below will show. Thus, I hope that this section will not be read as a presentation of a cultural and artistic practice of 'the other' or 'the exotic' experienced from the Western viewpoint; my aim is rather to tease out the general principle which I believe can transcend a particular cultural context.

6.2.1 Respect for humans expressed aesthetically through objects

The substantial part of our moral life regards how we interact with other humans. The focus is usually on the nature of our direct dealing with other humans through actions or conversations. What does not receive sufficient attention is our moral life mediated by the aesthetics of objects we create or handle. The Japanese artistic tradition offers a rich array of examples.

The best aesthetic expression of a caring attitude toward others is found in the art of tea ceremony, established in the sixteenth century and usually credited for providing the model for civilized behavior and rules of etiquette that are still alive and well in Japan today. The almost excessive fussiness of the host's preparation for the ceremony is guided by the host's desire and obligation to please the guests. This includes not only the obvious, like preparing tea and snacks and choosing the tea bowl, but also such considerations as (1) when to refill water in the stone basin and sprinkle water on plants in the garden through which the guests arrive at the tea hut; (2) what implements and decorations to choose for providing a cool feeling in the summer and warmth in winter; (3) whether or not to brush off the snow accumulated on trees, rocks, and basins; and (4) how to leave water droplets on the kettle's surface to allow for appreciation of the way they gradually dry over the hearth.[47]

Decisions regarding these minute details are guided by imagining what would make the guests feel most comfortable and entertained. Interpreting *Nambōroku* (南方録), the compilation of teachings of Master Sen no Rikyū (千利休) (1521–1591) by his disciple Nambō Sōkei (南方宗啓), contemporary commentator Kumakura Isao notes Nambō's frequent use of the term "*hataraki*," literally meaning "function." Kumakura explains that it refers to the way in which the host's heart and intention are expressed in his body movements, his manner of tea making, and various objects' appearance.[48] Another Japanese philosopher, Hisamatsu Shin'ichi, comments on the moral dimension of tea etiquette: "Inherent in the way of tea is the morality that goes beyond everyday life. Thoughtfulness toward the guest is the foundation of tea manners, which realize this attitude in the formal manner. This heartfelt consideration is both profound and elevated in its moral dimension."[49] What is relevant for my purpose here is not the specifics of the host's aesthetic decisions, but rather the fact that the host's concern for the feelings of guests is expressed through aesthetic means.

Japanese garden design also responds to the visitor's experience, in addition to respecting the innate characteristics of the materials. Stepping stones and stone pavements, both ubiquitous features of Japanese gardens, illustrate this attitude most effectively. For example, the selection and arrangement of stepping stones are guided not only by practical considerations, but more importantly, by the desire to provide an optimal aesthetic experience to the visitors.[50] Normally, we seldom take note of the ground under our feet when walking, but in the case of stepping stones in Japanese gardens, the juxtaposition of rocks with differing sizes, shapes, textures, and colors (both when dry and wet) forces us to look down and pay attention (Figures 6.1).[51] Their variety delights our senses and heightens aesthetic experience. So does the stark contrast sometimes created by the placement of natural stones with their irregular shape and rough texture alongside geometrically shaped and smooth-surfaced hewn stones or temple foundation stones and millstones that are re-used (Figures 6.2).

Figure 6.1a Katsura Detached Villa (Kyoto)

6.1b Portland Japanese Garden (Portland, USA)

Figure 6.2a Garden (Kyoto)

Figure 6.2b Garden (Kyoto)

Care is also taken to avoid an *impression* of instability, regardless of the actual stability of the stones. This means, among other things, that the *appearance* that the pavement may fall apart must be avoided by making the line-like space between stones to be about 1.5–1.7cm in width. Furthermore, such line-like space that runs uninterrupted for more than four stones, called 'potato vine,' should also be avoided because of its impression of looseness.[52] Similarly, in the case of stepping stones, the space between stones should not run repeatedly in the same direction. Moreover, the side of the stones facing each other should be complementary and 'attuned to' each other, such as a convex side responding to a concave side of the next stone, in order to provide a more stable impression. If facing sides are both convex, they appear as if they are repelling each other.

While the choice and arrangement of stepping stones and pavements explained above concern their spatial dimension, their composition also responds to the temporal aspect of our sensual experience by affecting, or sometimes dictating, the sequential order in which our experience unfolds. Some sequences, such as those accentuated by anticipation, surprise, or fulfillment of expectation, are more likely to satisfy us by holding our attention and interest than other sequences characterized, for example, by repetition and monotony.

One frequently employed strategy for making the walking experience enriching and stimulating is to make the path marked by stepping stones and pavements meandering rather than straight (Figures 6.3).[53] Stepping stones that use the same kind of stones repeatedly are placed in an almost random-looking manner, encouraging the walker to slow down and savor the constantly and subtly changing view of the garden. Another method of avoiding a straight line is to place long rectangular pavements, planks, or slates in a staggered manner to create a path or a bridge (Figures 6.4). This avoidance of a strictly straight line is an application of the principle of *suji kaete* (すじかへて), changing the axis, one of the principles of design articulated in the eleventh-century treatise on garden-making, *Sakuteiki* (作庭記). It originally referred to how a bridge over a pond in the middle of a courtyard garden in an aristocrat's residence must avoid lining up with the axis extending from the center of the building. This design strategy was subsequently generalized for any garden pathways, including bridges and stone pavements. The effect of such an arrangement is that the walker is encouraged to pause and slightly alter the direction in the middle of the otherwise straight path or bridge, which provides a different view of the garden.

Sometimes stepping stones are followed by pavement or vice versa. While stepping stones generally force us to look down, pavement facilitates easier passage, thus enabling us to look up. This way, the experience of a garden shifts, sometimes focusing downward while other times freeing us to look up and around. This constantly shifting sequential experience facilitated by the arrangement of stepping stones and pavement stones is described by one practitioner as "accumulated layers in the garden" and "sensory experience or scenic views layered in space."[54] Our experience becomes a gradually unfolding panorama, a synthesis of multi-perspective views, rather than a one-directional view. The same practitioner states: "through careful design of the paths, the gardener

Figure 6.3a Garden (Kyoto)

Figure 6.3b Garden (Kyoto)

Figure 6.4a Garden (Kyoto)

Figure 6.4b Garden (Kyoto)

controls not only the cadence of motion through a garden but what is seen as well. Paths are not simply an element of the overall plan, but a technique the garden designer utilizes to control how the garden will be revealed."[55]

It is true that stepping stones made with variety of stones, meandering paths, and staggered placement in pavements and bridges compromise easy walkability, *if* we are solely interested in getting from point A to point B in the most efficient manner. However, paths in Japanese gardens are primarily geared for encouraging multisensory and multidimensional aesthetic experience of the objects and environment surrounding the walker, after certain practical requirements such as safety are met. These design strategies are calculated to slow down our walk and encourage us to pause and attend to the stone underneath our feet and the subtly changing view of the garden.

I should note, however, that sometimes strict geometry and the straight line of pavements *are* favored, when the primary purpose of the walker is not aesthetic enjoyment. Paved paths leading to temple buildings are often straight, composed of geometrically shaped stones arranged in a stiff and formal manner. Here the purpose of the stone pavement is to help the religious practitioners concentrate on preparing for a spiritual practice, rather than taking in the rich aesthetic tapestry of the surrounding environment. The formally arranged stone pavement helps them assume the composure and fortitude required for a rigorous religious discipline.

Another design strategy often employed in Japanese gardens in order to maximize the aesthetic experience is *miegakure* (見え隠れ), literally meaning "now you see it, now you don't," sometimes also referred to as "Zen view" by Western designers.[56] This is achieved by intentionally blocking or partially obscuring a scenic view of a tea hut with dense planting, giving us only hints and glimpses. For example, the garden path in Figure 6.5 is located behind the tall hedge-like planting on the upper left side that blocks the view of the garden offered by this photo until one goes around the hedge. In Figure 6.6, the wide vista with the foreground of an artificial lake and the background of the borrowed scenery of distant mountains opens up only after the visitor walks on an uphill path surrounded by dense planting higher than human height (indicated by the diagonal line in the middle of the bush in this photo) and turns around when reaching a tea hut in the middle of the mountain. Anticipating a full view excites us and invites us to proceed, and the final, usually sudden, opening of the full vista is quite dramatic. A series of gates found in tea gardens as well as in temple or shrine compounds also accentuates the sequentially ordered spatial experience. Gates make us conscious of the unfolding layer of spaces along the passageway into *oku* (奥), translated as the innermost, the remote depth, or

Figure 6.5 Taizōin (Kyoto)

Figure 6.6 Shūgakuin (Kyoto)

deep recess, invoking a sense of "unwrapping."[57] The choreography of these devices that enhance the temporal dimension of our experience in Japanese gardens can result in stunning effects.

These examples indicate that Japanese garden design takes into consideration the desired experience for the garden visitor or religious practitioner. That is, the garden designers empty their own ego and imaginatively experience the space from the visitor's point of view, in addition to paying respect to the materials by honoring their native characteristics. The respectful attitude is directed both to the materials themselves and the people who experience them. Praising the stepping stones in a contemporary garden, one gardener remarks:

When walking on the stepping stones, I did not feel "I was walking on the stepping stones," but instead I felt that "the stepping stones are gently inviting my legs and directing them forward quite naturally." As I followed the stepping stones, I felt heartened and touched by the maker's warm heart. The maker's thoughtfulness and care were beautifully expressed . . . (and) the resulting design bears his considerateness.[58]

Although my discussion so far regards a spatial environment specifically designed for aesthetic enjoyment, that is, a garden, the same sensitivity and caring attitude informing these garden design features are found in everyday environments in Japan today. For example, a winding path is often found leading to the entrance of a condominium (Figure 6.7). Most noteworthy is the design of what we step on, which is often very much like the stepping stones and pavement in the garden. We normally do not pay attention to what we step on, such as a floor or a patch of ground, except for pragmatic concerns for not tripping or avoiding a puddle. However, things underfoot can provide a rich aesthetic experience, reflecting the caring and thoughtful attitude of the designer. For example, in my hometown of Sapporo, the subway station near a zoo features a corridor floor with tiles depicting zoo animals in a cartoon-like style, enhancing the anticipation and excitement particularly for children whose low stature makes this visual experience of the floor effective (Figure 6.8). Some underground corridors also sport tiles with drawings depicting built structures and native fauna and flora associated with the city. Finally, even a manhole cover, usually an exclusively utilitarian object, displays an embossed image such as a well-known clock tower building, TV tower, and salmon in a river, all historically associated with the city's sense of place (Figures 6.9).[59]

So that my discussion is not taken as simply an explanation of Japanese aesthetic sensibility, let me give two examples from the United States. The Seattle-Tacoma airport's corridor floor has inlaid salmon shapes, sometimes swimming upstream while other times gathering near the image of a pool of

Figure 6.7 Condominium entrance (Sapporo, Japan)

Figure 6.8 Maruyama Park subway station (Sapporo, Japan)

Figure 6.9a Manhole cover (Sapporo, Japan)

Figure 6.9b Manhole cover (Sapporo, Japan)

water (Figures 6.10). What could otherwise be an uninteresting and monotonous walk becomes a fun experience trying to follow where salmon are headed. Closer to my (American) home, an outdoor plaza floor in downtown Providence has a metal inlaid depiction of several well-known sights from Rhode Island, enhancing the sense of place. These things underfoot are heartwarming because one senses that whoever designed them took time imagining the experience of whoever walks on them and thinking about how to enrich their experience by providing a greeting and sense of place of the city.

Some of today's cutting-edge design practices in Japan continue the time-honored tradition of other-regarding consideration. For example, Kenya Hara, a contemporary designer well-known as the art director of MUJI (no mark) design group, relates his thoughts on emptiness:

"Emptiness" (*utsu*) and "completely hollow" (*karappo*) are among the terms I pondered while trying to grasp the nature of communication. When people share their thoughts, they commonly listen to each other's opinions rather than throwing information at each other. In other words, successful communication depends on how well we listen, rather than how well we push our opinions on the person seated before us. People have therefore conceptualized communication techniques using terms like "empty vessel" to try to understand each other better.[60]

A similar point is made by his designer colleague at MUJI, Naoto Fukasawa, who also claims that "if a designer believes that people and time have created a form,

Figure 6.10a Seattle Tacoma Airport

Figure 6.10b Seattle Tacoma Airport

then they want to *get rid of the ego* that says, 'I designed this object.'"[61] The resultant products are characterized by minimalism, simplicity, understatement, and the absence of showy self-assertion, while maintaining meticulous and thoughtful attention to details. However, these qualities are not a mode of styling or branding. They are rather generated as a response to the body's movement when using the products and integrate the cumulative wisdom of user experience. As such, MUJI does not identify the designer behind the product and often emphasizes 'anonymous' design.[62]

Of course, this other-regarding attitude toward materials and people is hardly unique to the Japanese tradition. Particularly in the field of design today, there is an increasing attention to and call for 'care' and 'thoughtfulness.' It is noteworthy that such a plea is a reaction against the prevailing design process in the West, which the designers themselves admit has not paid enough attention or respect to the experiences of users and inhabitants. They take recent designs to task for exuding the qualities of "ego trips," such as "arrogance," "narcissism," "impudence," "formal authority," and "showiness."[63] Himself an architect, Juhani Pallasmaa criticizes the contemporary architectural profession as encouraging the super-stardom of individual "geniuses" whose creations exist for the sake of self-aggrandizement, alienating the users and inhabitants.[64] Similarly, Victor Papanek writes that designers and architects tend to think of themselves as artists whose mission is to make artistic "statements." As a result, he observes that "a good deal of design and architecture seems to be created for the personal glory of its creator."[65] Sim Van der Ryn and Stuart Cowan express a similar sentiment by criticizing the architect in Ayn Rand's *The Fountainhead*, depicted as a hero committed to the "'pure' process" that is not "'contaminated' by any real-world constraints or needs: social, environmental, or economic."[66]

These critics offer an alternative model of the design process that reflects other-regarding attitudes, such as "courtesy," "responsiveness," "humility," "patience," and "care." These qualities are embodied in an appropriate size for humans, with a spatial arrangement sensitive to the bodily-oriented experience as well as its temporal sequence, and design features that are simply delightful to the senses. The resulting design not only provides a positive aesthetic experience, but also leads to serious pragmatic consequences, such as a healthy environment instead of a 'sick' building. The degree of healthfulness is commensurate with the way in which our sensory experience is affected. For example, consider the recently emerging 'green' buildings that utilize the benefits of such sustainable materials as sunlight, fresh air, breeze, rain water, and vegetation. Such a building "honors" the senses, one critic points out, and it is "comfortable, humanizing and supportive," "healthy and healing," "caring for the environment," "nourishing to the human being;" in short, it is where we feel "at home."[67]

Perhaps the area where the absence or presence of due care in design becomes most manifest regards environments and objects surrounding vulnerable populations, such as senior citizens and those suffering from illness. Because they often live in an institutional setting such as a nursing home or a hospital, it becomes all the more crucial that the utmost care goes into designing it with consideration. For example, Susann Vihma presents her fieldwork in various senior citizens' institutional living environments and stresses the importance of empowering the residents to create a 'homey' atmosphere for themselves.[68] Usually in institutional settings, choice and placement of decorative objects in public or shared spaces are decided not by the residents, thus compromising the feeling of at-home-ness and the dignity and integrity of the inhabitants.

Another important design factor to consider for senior citizens is their relative unfamiliarity and unease regarding technology. Speaking from my personal experience, when my parents in Japan moved into a senior citizens' facility there, we were dismayed by the high-tech mechanisms such as light switch, temperature control, and even water faucet. Probably designed by designers and architects of the younger generation who grew up with and feel at home with high-tech gadgetry, what may be considered to be a convenient device became an obstacle to my parents' daily life for a long time until they got used to how things worked. Although it was not the designer's and architect's intention, the residents were set up for failure, exacerbating their already insecure feelings. This is an example of how the design features do not reflect care and consideration for this specific group of users.[69]

Regarding medical facilities, Hilary Moss and Desmond O'Neill argue for the importance of addressing the "aesthetic deprivation" that often plagues both patients and medical professionals in a hospital setting.[70] In addition to the benefits gained by art therapy, live music, and the like, they also call attention to "everyday aesthetics, such as food, the texture of bed sheets, crockery, and interior design" which contribute to the quality of life of the patients. They also point out that healthcare settings are often "poorly designed, aesthetically barren, and polluted by noise" in a way that has a negative impact on the healthcare workers' well-being, as well as their work performance.

The aesthetic value of designed objects and built environments that respond to our experiences is not only in the enhancement of pleasure. It also communicates a moral attitude, affirming the importance of others' experiences. "Good design," Donald Norman writes, "takes *care*, planning, thought" and "*concern* for others."[71] Similarly, in discussing the importance of "care" in architecture,

Nigel Taylor points out that a building that appears to be put together thoughtlessly and carelessly, without regard to our experience as users or its relationship to the surrounding,

> would offend us aesthetically, but, more than that, part of our offense might be ethical. Thus we might reasonably be angered or outraged, not just by the look of the thing, but also by the visible evidence that the person who designed it didn't show sufficient *care* about the aesthetic impact of his building.[72]

He cites Roger Scruton's discussion of "appropriateness" as a criterion of architectural criticism, which Scruton calls "an embodiment of moral thought." Commenting on Scruton's praise of a railway wall in London, Taylor points out that "the anonymous designers of this wall *cared* about the wall they designed" and asserts that "'caring' is a moral concept." He concludes by stating that "to care like this for how something looks, and thereby for the people who will look at it, is to exhibit not just an aesthetic but also a moral concern. Or rather, it is to exhibit an aesthetic attentiveness which is itself moral."

One example close to my (American) home illustrative of a lack of care and thoughtfulness is the Providence train station. It is an embarrassing disgrace, with its bare concrete walls and platform with no welcoming gesture, not even the signage to indicate where it is and which way is New York or Boston. A skeptic could claim that it is my personal judgment that this structure exudes thoughtlessness and indifference.[73] A person seeking adventure exploring unknown places without any help or someone who welcomes the challenge of finding his own way without any guidance may prefer this train station to other stations with clear signage and signs of greeting. I don't deny such a possibility, nor the fact that the number of signage and announcements to guide passengers in some Japanese train stations can at times become excessive and annoying. However, given that the train station's *primary* function is to facilitate easy travelling experience for passengers and greeting visitors, I believe that I am justified in considering the Providence train station to be an example of thoughtlessness and unconcern, particularly when this function is relatively easy to satisfy and many other stations indeed succeed in doing so.

Those objects and structures that are created for glorifying the designer, and those that are put together thoughtlessly and carelessly, such as the Providence train station, exemplify negative aesthetics, which unfortunately characterizes some of our everyday environments. I agree with Taylor that what amounts to a lack of consideration and graciousness, particularly to visitors, is both an aesthetic *and* a moral offense. Or to put it another way, the attitude of inattentiveness and indifference is expressed aesthetically (in the classificatory sense).

All the examples in this section are designed by professionals, such as architects, tea masters, and garden designers. As such, it may appear that many of us who use or visit those places as dwellers, visitors, and guests, have no role to play in the project of world-making. However, I maintain that we still do participate in this project insofar as we recognize and respond to the aesthetic expression of care and respect (or their opposites). If we detect and appreciate that we are surrounded by objects and environments expressive of care and thoughtfulness, we tend to pass on kindness and consideration to those around us, while if our experience is dominated by negative aesthetics, either we become indifferent and demoralized and tend to give up making an effort for better world-making or we will be spurred to correct those instances of negative aesthetics. I shall return to the issue of negative aesthetics in the final chapter, because I maintain that the detection of negative aesthetics with an eye toward correcting and improving it is one of the important contributions that everyday aesthetics can make to the project of world-making.

6.2.2 Aesthetic expression of respect for inanimate objects

In the prevailing Western ethical discourse, inanimate objects have traditionally been excluded from the moral domain. They become relevant only if their treatment affects the bona fide moral agents' rights or well-being. For example, destroying someone's car is not doing anything wrong to the car itself but rather violating its owner's property right. Handling a package roughly has no moral significance until or unless its content gets broken, thus depriving the gift receiver of her right. A car and a package cannot have a membership to the moral domain because they don't have a good of their own, unlike humans and non-human creatures (and possibly plants). Environmental ethics widened the scope of the moral sphere by following Aldo Leopold's land ethic, but artifacts are usually regarded as remaining outside the moral domain.[74]

However, the following examples demonstrate that there can be a moral significance to the way in which we handle and interact with inanimate objects beyond possible consequences to other humans and non-human creatures. First, consider Robert Carter's description of how a master potter, Hamada Shōji, designated in 1955 as a Living National Treasure of Japan by the Japanese government, handled a pottery piece:

He would sit down on the floor ... carefully unwrap a piece ... We would talk about each piece, touch each piece in order to get the feel of it, and then he would slowly and carefully rewrap it, for this, too, was part of the journey of appreciation that he had taken me on ... for Hamada, the rewrapping, the care of each piece, was part of being drenched in the beauty of each object. It was done as a sign of respect and appreciation.[75]

Carter also observes how "landscape gardening brings about a *gentleness* in the designer, the builders, and the caretakers."[76] The gentle attitude is reflected in the treatment of materials through certain bodily movements. He reports on the making of a garden for the Canadian Museum of Civilization in Ottawa by a contemporary master gardener, Masuno Shunmyo:

The work began on a cold, rainy day, and as the sand and rocks were being positioned by the Japanese crew under Masuno's detailed instructions, the Canadian workers were surprised by the way in which the Japanese crew entered and left the actual site by walking in the footsteps of a single pathway, which had already been established in the mud on the site, rather than tracking mud all over the newly placed sand, or on or around the rocks, keeping tracking and foreign markings to a minimum. It was a degree of *caring and concern* for the state and cleanliness of the site that was itself quite foreign to the Canadians on hand.[77]

A similarly respectful attitude informs the art of flower arrangement. "The *tender* way in which the materials for flower arrangements are handled"[78] includes carefully unwrapping the bundle of flowers to be used, gently bending and twisting when shaping the branches and stems, and neatly arranging unused remnants of flowers for disposal. Ultimately, the aim of flower arrangement is "not just to teach techniques and basic skills, but to convey attitudes which would apply both to flower arranging and to living one's life generally."[79]

The gentle and caring attitude toward plant materials can be seen outside the art of flower arrangement. In Japan, trees and shrubs in public spaces like a street and an entrance for a building or in a residential garden receive protection from cold and snow before every winter. Termed yukitsuri (雪吊り), tall trees are protected by a bamboo pole support with ropes attached to tree limbs, displaying a cone-shape structure (Figure 6.11). Short trees are clothed by straw mats that have been meticulously woven and fastened (Figures 6.12). Low shrubs are enclosed by woven bamboos tied with straws, exhibiting a geometrical pattern (Figures 6.13). These sights are ubiquitous in snowy areas of Japan, in particular northwestern part of the main island, Honshū, facing the Japan Sea and the northern island of Hokkaidō. Unlike rather unsightly wrapping by tarp often seen in the United States for the same purpose, these examples of protective gear are aesthetically pleasing in their own right for their grace and elegance. Beyond pure aesthetic attractiveness, however, they express a caring attitude toward the protected trees and shrubs, as well as providing a seasonal reminder and an aesthetic enjoyment to the passersby.

Finally, consider the thirteenth-century Zen priest Dōgen's instructions regarding food. Whether cooking or eating, one must be respectful not only of the other humans involved in the process but also of the ingredients.

Figure 6.11 Streetscape (Sapporo, Japan)

One's attitude should not change whether one is dealing with an expensive luxury item or an ordinary, inexpensive material:

When you prepare food, do not see with ordinary eyes and do not think with ordinary mind...do not arouse disdainful mind when you prepare a broth of wild grasses; do not arouse joyful mind when you prepare a fine cream soup. Where there is no discrimination, how can there be distaste? Thus, do not be careless even when you work with poor

Figure 6.12a Streetscape (Sapporo, Japan)

materials, and sustain your efforts even when you have excellent materials. Never change your attitude according to the materials.[80]

These expressions of respect, care, and gentleness shown toward inanimate objects, such as rocks, flowers, trees, and cooking ingredients, may strike one versed in the mainstream Western ethical tradition as falling outside of moral discourse because these objects don't have a 'good of their own' which gets

Figure 6.12b Streetscape (Sapporo, Japan)

damaged by soiling or rough handling. According to this view, if they deserve to be treated with care, it is because of the indirect effects of our actions to other humans, such as the object's owner or prospective appreciators. However, I agree with Simon James, who argues that such an attitude toward inanimate objects *is* morally relevant in the sense that "part of what makes someone morally good or virtuous is the fact that she will tend to exhibit...a 'delicacy' towards her surroundings, taking care not to damage the things with which she deals, even when those things are neither sentient nor alive."[81] There is something odd about a person, if s/he exists, who may act morally and caringly toward sentient beings while treating non-sentient objects callously or even violently with no good reason even when such an action does not indirectly harm other sentient beings.[82]

6.2.3 Body aesthetics and the expression of respect for humans

So far I discussed the ways in which the respectful and caring attitude toward objects and humans are expressed by how we make, handle, and appreciate objects. I now want to turn to body aesthetics, such as body movements, facial

Figure 6.13a Condominium entrance (Sapporo, Japan)

Figure 6.13b Streetscape (Sapporo, Japan)

Figure 6.13c Condominium entrance (Sapporo, Japan)

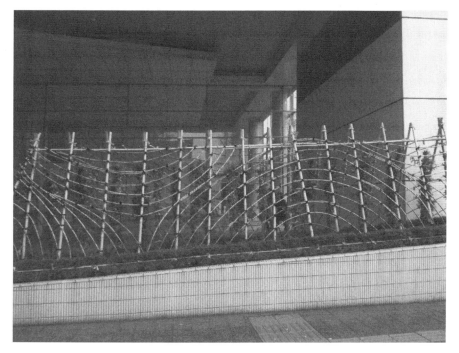

Figure 6.13d Streetscape (Sapporo, Japan)

expressions, and tone of voice, and argue that they, too, also act as a vehicle for expressing moral virtues or lack thereof.

Let us start with considering how we act respectfully toward other humans. At the very minimum, we should not violate their rights by injuring them and their property, restricting their freedom, or slandering their reputation. Carrying out these negative duties toward others is necessary, but not sufficient in respecting them. Sometimes we should fulfill positive duties toward them, such as helping them when they are in dire need. Ignoring their plea for help may not violate their negative right, but it will be a sign of our disrespect, particularly when helping them does not place an unreasonably heavy burden on us.

Ethics of care places emphasis on this latter kind of action. The virtues of care and consideration for others are manifested in things we do for others, rather than or in addition to refraining from certain actions. In fact, for many of us, our everyday moral concerns seem to be directed more toward caring for a sick neighbor and bailing out a friend from a troubling situation than refraining from such acts as murder, rape, assault, and theft. A person who never goes beyond not violating others' rights is certainly better than a murderer or a rapist, but seems morally deficient. Similarly, a society where no egregiously immoral acts occur but neither do human interactions expressive of care and respect is certainly preferable to the Hobbesian state of nature, but I doubt our lives there would be satisfying or fulfilling.[83]

What does not receive sufficient attention, however, is that the moral character of an action motivated by care and respect is determined not only by what gets accomplished but, sometimes even more importantly, by the *manner* or the *way* in which it is carried out. For example, Nel Noddings observes that "I cannot claim to care for my relative if my caretaking is perfunctory or grudging."[84] Similarly, citing Seneca, Nancy Sherman remarks that "we spoil kindness...if our reluctance is betrayed in inappropriate 'furrowed brows' and 'grudging words'" and concludes that "playing the role of the good person...has to do with socially sensitive behaviour—how we convey to others interest, empathy, respect, and thanks through the emotional expressions we wear on our faces (or exhibit through our body language and voices)."[85] Even if I accomplish the goal of kindness and caring, say by taking a relative to the doctor, the way in which I carry out the action changes the nature of the act: I can do so kindly and gently or spitefully and grudgingly.

The manner in which one carries out an action is often considered to be a matter of etiquette, civility, and courtesy. Compared to the issues of justice and rights that have grave social consequences, they are considered superficial and trivial, not worthy of the same kind of attention. When writing *Why Manners Matter*, Lucinda Holdforth admits "it's hard not to wonder if, among the grand and awe-inspiring issues of our day, manners must come a long way down the list," when considering that "the planet is hotting up, the Middle East is imploding, terrorists plot our demise and much of Africa is starving."[86] Furthermore, manners and etiquette often raise "questions of social hierarchy and identity politics," and they have historically been used as a gender- or class-specific means of discrimination and exclusion, as well as constructing a gender stereotype.[87]

However, these seemingly trivial aspects of our daily lives go a long way toward determining the quality of life and society. As Karen Stohr observes, "rules of polite behavior play a far more important role in helping us live out our moral commitments than most people realize" and "morality is incomplete unless we attend to its manifestation in ordinary human interaction."[88] It is because, as Sherman observes, courteous interactions in our everyday life are "the ways in which we acknowledge others as worthy of respect" and "the communication of those appearances is a part of the glue of human fellowship."[89] Holdforth also reminds us that "manners are a civil mode of human interaction" and "they matter because they represent an optimal means to preserve our own dignity and the dignity of others."[90] D. W. Prall points out that if we "neglect the discriminating of appearances, not the cut of clothes and color of skin, but the thousand and one marks left by life upon the surface of men's bodies, their motions, their features, their manner of speech, their whole bearing," we will have no clear criteria for judging a person except, for example, pertaining to "the distinction between foreigner and compatriot."[91] Referring to Iris Murdoch's notions of people's "total vision of life" and the "texture of man's being" consisting, among other things, of "their mode of speech or silence, their choice of words, . . . what they think attractive or funny," Marcia Eaton points out that "we have to pay attention to the tone with which something is said, as well as to the content, and the relations between the speakers, or to meanings of other words spoken earlier or later."[92]

What do these considerations regarding the moral character of an action have to do with aesthetics? It is simply this: we interact with others through handling of objects, tone of voice, facial expressions, and bodily movements, all of which are *aesthetic* factors insofar as they are perceived through senses and subject to *aesthetic* sensibility. As I explained in the first chapter, I am using the term 'aesthetic' in the classificatory sense of sensory perception rather than in the usual honorific sense associated with beauty or artistic excellence. The list of what constitutes the "*aesthetic* of character" or the "aesthetic of morals," according to Sherman, includes "how we appear to others as conveyed through formal manners and decorum, as well as manner in the wider sense of personal bearing and outward attitude," specifically "voices, faces, and gestures."[93] Sarah Buss also asks us to "think of the significance we attribute to the subtlest gestures (the curl of the lip, the raised eyebrows), the slightest differences in vocal tone."[94] Referring to Confucianism, Nicholas F. Gier points out that "bad manners are wrong not because they are immoral but because they lack *aesthetic* order: they are inelegant, coarse, or worse" and "Confucian *li* [the good] makes no distinction between manners and morality, so an *aesthetic* standard rules for all of its actions."[95] The specifics of what bodily gestures express courtesy or rudeness of course vary from situation to situation and, more importantly, from culture to culture, giving rise to all-too-familiar cases of cultural faux pas. However, the most important point for my purpose here is that the *aesthetic* dimension of the way in which we carry out an action can determine its *moral* character.

One may claim that performing an outward aesthetic expression of care and respect is simply putting on an act, not necessarily indicative of the person's virtuous character or the moral value of an action. Particularly when there is a set of socially prescribed rules of proper behavior, one could simply go through the motion to appear as if one is a caring, thoughtful person. Or worse, such an appearance may disguise a moral deficiency. It is possible that "as a 'pretense, or semblance' of respect and good will, civility makes despicable individuals appear likable, and it conceals uninterested, unflattering, and even contemptuous appraisals of others."[96] A cruel person can act with graceful manners.[97] Even within the Japanese tradition known for its emphasis on the outward display of moral virtues, "it may well be true in some instances that this caring for others is less heartfelt and more an uneasiness about being seen not to care."[98]

It is true that outward appearance of respect and care does not guarantee a virtuous character. However, admitting this does not refute the relevance of such an appearance as a way of embodying moral virtues. Respect and care for my neighbor cannot be conveyed by merely accomplishing a certain task such as taking her to a doctor, although it is better than refusing to do so. The kindness of my action is compromised or even nullified if I act in a grudging and spiteful way, even if I insist that I did show my care by driving her. As Cheshire Calhoun states, "the function of civility . . . is to *communicate* basic moral attitudes of respect, tolerance, and considerateness" and "civility always involves a *display* of respect, tolerance, or considerateness."[99]

Friedrich Schiller's discussion of grace is instructive here. He identifies grace with willful movements expressive of "moral sentiments" and distinguishes it from beauty derived from natural endowments or what he calls "beauty of frame" or "architectonic beauty."[100] He also distinguishes it from a purposeful action which is executed to accomplish a certain task, such as receiving an object.

When I extend the arm to seize an object, I execute, in truth, an intention, and the movement I make is determined in general by the end that I have in view; but in what way does my arm approach the object? how far do the other parts of my body follow this impulsion? What will be the degree of slowness or of the rapidity of the movement? What amount of force shall I employ? This is a calculation of which my will, at the instant, takes no account, and in consequence there is a something left to the discretion of nature.[101]

Grabbing an object from a friend in an indifferent, nonchalant manner is very different from receiving it gratefully and appreciatively. The specific body movements such as how far I extend my arm and how speedily I grasp the object determine the character of the attitude and action, and Schiller's point is that they are located somewhere in between intentional action and natural movement.

Lucinda Holdforth characterizes those who have not only manners but "beautiful manners" as "the ones who . . . *gently* draw out the shy stranger, or *quietly* close the window against the cold draft, or *tactfully* change the dangerous topic, or *subtly* reorganize the seating so that the slightly deaf person is able to hear better."[102] Although the emphasis in this passage is mine, she makes it clear that the manner of carrying out each action determines the beauty of the action.

If these actions are done roughly, loudly, tactlessly, and blatantly, the beauty of the action diminishes considerably or disappears altogether. Eaton also points out that "both aesthetic and moral sensitivity are demanded in making judgments such as 'This situation calls for bold action' or 'This situation calls for subtlety.'"[103] Such discernment and judgment requires aesthetic skills often nurtured by works of art, literary arts in particular.

Let me first take one of Holdforth's examples: the mundane act of closing a window. Consider the behavior of a man who leaves a lady's chamber after a night of love-making described by Sei Shōnagon (清少納言), a court lady of eleventh-century Japan. Though separated from our life in time and cultural context, her assessment of the man's act and ultimately his character should ring a bell. Here are some examples of "hateful," "charmless," "improper," "distasteful," and "distressing" behavior:

He is so flurried, in fact, that upon leaving he bangs into something with his hat. Most hateful! It is annoying too when he lifts up the Iyo blind that hangs at the entrance of the room, then lets it fall with a great rattle. If it is a head-blind, things are still worse, for being more solid it makes a terrible noise when it is dropped. There is no excuse for such carelessness...When he jumps out of bed, scurries about the room, tightly fastens his trouser-sash, rolls up the sleeves of his Court cloak, over-robe, or hunting costume, stuffs his belongings into the breast of his robe and then briskly secures the outer sash—one really begins to hate him.[104]

It is noteworthy that her attention is focused not only on the man's hurried and careless movements but also the various noises created by his actions. His behavior at the time of leave-taking, according to her, is such an important indicator of his worthiness as a lover that she declares that "one's attachment to a man depends largely on the elegance of his leave-taking."[105] This commotion-filled leave-taking is contrasted with an elegant one:

A good lover will behave as elegantly at dawn as at any other time. He drags himself out of bed with a look of dismay on his face...Once up, he does not instantly pull on his trousers. Instead he comes close to the lady and whispers whatever was left unsaid during the night. Even when he is dressed, he still lingers, vaguely pretending to be fastening his sash. Presently he raises the lattice, and the two lovers stand together by the side door while he tells her how he dreads the coming day, which will keep them apart; then he slips away.[106]

Although her assessment of each man concerns his worthiness as a lover, the ultimate criterion is a moral one. That is, what is "hateful" about banging and rustling noises is the fact that such annoying sounds were created by a man who is preoccupied by what he must/wants to do, regardless of their effects on the lady. In short, he is not being considerate. His bumbling and commotion-causing actions indicate his neglect, thus disrespect, for the lady who must put up with the flurry of movements and untoward noise. That is, even if unwittingly, he is forcing a negative aesthetic experience on her through his body movements and the sounds he makes. If he is considerate, he would behave more gently, carefully, and mindfully, which would result in less or no noise, as in carefully lifting up a head blind and opening a sliding door.

Even a head-blind does not make any noise if one lifts it up *gently* on entering and leaving the room; the same applies to sliding-door. If one's movements are *rough*, even a paper door will bend and resonate when opened; but, if one lifts the door a little while pushing it, there need be no sound.[107]

One's bodily movement accompanied by a loud noise and a hurried and fidgety motion communicates thoughtlessness or indifference, while a gentle and elegant bodily movement implies a caring and respectful attitude. How many of us are annoyed, and sometimes angered, by the sound of a door being slammed by somebody? Every parent (myself included!) who dealt with a disgruntled teenage child, I am sure, is familiar with the feeling. Even if my request of closing the door was honored and the task was accomplished, such a way of closing the door can hardly be characterized as being respectful in satisfying my request. The virtues of care and thoughtfulness or lack thereof are expressed aesthetically through bodily actions and the sensory impressions they create.[108]

Another mundane everyday act regards serving and eating food. One can serve food mindlessly and carelessly by heaping a mound of food on a plate and thrusting it in front of the person eating, typical of a cafeteria-type of place. Such serving style, though understandably necessitated by various constraints and requirements like serving many people as speedily as possible, cannot help but give an impression of an uncaring and impersonal attitude. Compare it with another way of serving in which each food item is carefully arranged for the most pleasing impression and put in front of the eating guest slowly and gently. Even if it is the same food, the latter way of serving makes it appear more inviting and appetizing, partly because we appreciate the server's care taken in honoring our experience of being served.[109]

At the same time, our manner of eating can embody various moral attitudes. Particularly if the food is presented with care, unlike the previously mentioned institutionalized food wantonly served, it will be considered both inelegant and disrespectful if we gobble up the food without taking time and care to savor its taste and texture. A Japanese author commenting on eating etiquette first establishes the cardinal principle of etiquette: "the most important rule is to be grateful for the cook's thoughtfulness and consideration . . . and to humbly acknowledge the cook's sincere heart while savoring the food . . . Failure to do so would not only diminish the taste but also ignore the thoughtfulness of the host."[110] Specifically, she discourages guests from digging some items from the bottom of an arrangement out of respect for the cook who took care in preparing a beautiful presentation.[111] It is also expected that the unappetizing remnants left on the plate, such as fish tail, head, and bones, should be collected neatly together. The care taken in preparing food requires reciprocal care in eating. That food preparation and eating is a particularly apt venue for embodying a human relationship seems to transcend cultural borders. A contemporary French writer, Luce Giard cited in Chapter 2, for example, points out that "the relationship that one maintains with one's body and with other is read, translated into visible acts, across the interest and care given to meals."[112]

Similar other-regarding considerations expressed by certain bodily movements underlie Zen priests' training in serving and eating food. Zen Buddhism denies any hierarchy among various activities for their worthiness as a vehicle for enlightenment. To underline this egalitarian view on various activities, Zen puts a particular emphasis on the importance of mundane activities, such as washing one's face, cleaning the space, cooking, serving food, and eating. Whatever activity one undertakes, one has to do it mindfully and respectfully. Part of the mindfulness and respect must be directed toward other people, whether they be cooks, servers, or eating companions. I cited in section 6.2.2 Dōgen's instructions regarding how one should handle both humble and expensive food ingredients with equal respect. He also left extensive rules regarding the manner of serving food and eating required of Zen trainees. For example, when serving, "the rice must be served carefully and never in a hurry for, if the serving is hurried, they who receive the food will be flustered; it must not be served slowly, however, for then the recipients will become tired."[113] When eating, one must assume the correct posture, hold the bowl and use chopsticks properly, and begin eating at the right time. In addition, "when the food has been received, it must not be consumed greedily."[114] One has to take time and carefully pick up each morsel to savor its taste and texture rather than devouring the food. These painstakingly detailed rules are all guided by being mindful and showing respect for the cooks, servers, and fellow eating companions. The other-regarding considerations are explicitly indicated by the following rules with which I believe we can identify even today: "fruit seeds and other similar waste must be put in a place *where it will give no offence to others*—a good place being on the lacquered table top in front of the bowl, slightly hidden by the bowl's rim—*others must never be allowed to become disgusted by such a sight.*"[115]

The Japanese tea ceremony established in the sixteenth century crystallizes the attention to other-regarding aesthetics. As discussed in section 6.2.1, some aesthetic decisions are directed toward the choice and placement of the various objects used in the ceremony. Other aesthetic considerations guide bodily movements of both the host and the guest, with almost excruciating specificities. For example, the host opens the sliding door to the tea room slowly and carefully to allow enough time to indicate his entrance without causing alarm or commotion. The host also handles implements for making tea in a gentle and elegant manner, such as by "tak(ing) care not to jar the observer by tapping the tea scoop too sharply on the bowl's rim."[116] The guest cradles the tea bowl with both hands to honor the bowl and tea inside. Through beautifully and economically choreographed actions, both the host and the guest practice conveying a respectful, considerate, gentle, caring, and pleasant impression to each other. This mutual respect should linger even after the tea ceremony is over as the guest leaves the tea hut through the garden path. The guest should not converse loudly with other guests but rather turn around to see the host, who in turn sees them off until they are out of sight before returning to the tea hut for clean-up.[117]

All of these rules are motivated by cultivating a morally sensitive way of carrying out an action. One nineteenth-century tea practitioner, also a noted statesman, remarks: "the host should attend to every detail to express his consideration and kindness so that there will not be any mishaps, and the guest in turn should recognize that the occasion is one time only and show sincere appreciation for the thorough hospitality given by the host."[118] A contemporary Japanese sociologist also states: "the host's care and consideration is expressed through *artistry of motion and gesture*" and "the guests were expected to reciprocate through their unspoken appreciation of the host's hospitality and concern for their comfort."[119] Ultimately, "the deepest human communication took place through silent *aesthetic* communion."[120] Although her interest lies in how the aesthetics of tea ceremony contributed to the formation of cultural nationalism in Japan, Kristin Surak also points out that the formalism involved in prescribed body movements in the tea ceremony is "one softened by the stylistics of action, marked by a restrained grace in movement, attention to rhythmic intervals, and *vigilant consideration of others*."[121]

Finally, consider the act of opening a gift, which is part of daily life in a gift-giving culture like Japan. Particularly if the gift is thoughtfully packaged, consider what different attitude would be expressed if the receiver were to rip apart the package in order to get to the item fast, compared to opening it carefully to minimize the unsightly remnant of torn pieces of paper and string as well as the sound of tearing paper. Even if unintended, the former act cannot help but convey a failure to recognize and appreciate the thoughtful and considerate preparation by the giver, particularly because Japanese packaging is known for embodying a "deep respect for material and process, and *respect* too for the intended user" as well as "care for the object inside, and therefore *care* for the recipient of the object."[122] Indeed, a manual for people doing business in Japan correctly advises that "if the situation makes it desirable for the receiver to unwrap the gift, he or she will do so carefully, keeping the wrapping paper in a hypothetically reusable condition before admiring the gift. This derives from a concern for appearance as well as *an expression of gratitude to the giver*."[123] The action and resultant unpleasant noise and unsightly aftermath of the ripped-up packaging material inevitably indicate a deficiency in both aesthetic and moral sensibilities.[124]

In all these examples, different moral attitudes are expressed aesthetically (in the classificatory sense) through certain bodily movements, even if the same task is accomplished: closing the door, serving food and tea, drinking tea, eating food, and receiving the gift item. The specifics of what constitute those bodily actions expressive of respect or the opposite vary, as they are context- and culture-dependent. For example, all my examples of communicating care and respect through a particular body movement are based upon what I take to be an ordinary context in which taking time and acting gently in opening a door, bidding farewell, eating food, or opening a package do not cause a problem. However, in certain contexts, extenuating circumstances may require accomplishing these tasks as swiftly as possible, and in such cases the most thoughtful way of acting will have to be adjusted and modified. The important point is that, despite variable specifics, bodily movements often reflect whether the agent is considering his action's effect on other people, thereby indicating both his moral and aesthetic sensibility. We can even go further and claim that acting with aesthetic sensitivity is a moral, as well as an aesthetic, obligation.[125]

*   *   *

This chapter was devoted to revealing moral, social, political, and environmental consequences of everyday aesthetics. I conclude from the examples compiled in this chapter that, whether we like it or not and whether we are aware of it or not, aesthetics does play a crucial role in humanity's world-making project.[126] Although many of us are not professional world-makers like architects, designers, manufacturers, or policymakers, we all participate in humanity's collective and cumulative project of world-making, and one major determinant for its direction is our aesthetic preferences, tastes, and judgments which result in various actions, such as purchasing, interacting with others, and supporting a certain cause.

I propose that one mission of everyday aesthetics is to raise our awareness of this power of the aesthetic and develop what may be called aesthetic literacy. Regarding consumer aesthetics manipulated by advertising, Leddy points out that "perhaps paying attention to these properties (of commercialized aesthetics) would help us to *understand better* the power of advertising. Although understanding the power of advertising could be used to enhance that power, it could also be used to diminish it."[127] We need to recognize and become vigilant toward the way in which our seemingly innocuous and inconsequential aesthetic tastes, judgments, and decisions significantly affect the state of the world and the quality of life, for better or worse.

However, is cultivating aesthetic literacy sufficient for everyday aesthetics? I will explore in the final chapter what everyday aesthetics discourse should do with its consequences regarding the world-making projects.

Notes

1. I discuss some of the examples below in *Everyday Aesthetics* (Oxford: Oxford University Press, 2007); "Everyday Aesthetics and World-Making," included in *Estética e interculturalidad: relaciones entre el arte y la vida*, Rosa Fernández, Luis Puelles, and Eva Fernández del Campo, eds. Supplement 17 (2012), *Contrastes. Revista de Filosofía* (publication of the University of Malaga), pp. 255–74; "The Power of the Aesthetic," *Aesthetic Pathways* 1/2 (2011), pp. 11–25.

2. Aldo Leopold, *A Sand County Almanac* (New York: Ballantine Books, 1966), pp. 268, 179–80. The following reference is from p. 268. I explored the notion of unscenic landscape in "The Aesthetics of Unscenic Nature," *The Journal of Aesthetics and Art Criticism* 56/2 (1998), pp. 101–11.

3. See Ann Vileisis, *Discovering the Unknown Landscape: A History of America's Wetlands* (Washington, D.C.: Island Press, 1997). I explore these consequences of scenic aesthetics in "The Aesthetics of Unscenic Nature," pp. 101–11. The designation of wetlands as unscenic may be dated today, as Tom Leddy has pointed out, and we are much more sensitive to their quiet and subtle beauty compared to, for example, when Leopold was writing. If so, it underscores the point I will develop later that an aesthetic paradigm shift is not only possible but actually has been taking place.

4. Marcia Eaton, *Merit, Aesthetic and Ethical* (Oxford: Oxford University Press, 2001), p. 184.

5. As pointed out by Tom Leddy, the status of phragmites in terms of its nativity is in dispute. Furthermore, as Stephen Jay Gould points out, something being native does not ensure that it does not damage its native ecosystem, nor does its alien origin automatically imply harm to its new habitat. See his "An Evolutionary Perspective on Strengths, Fallacies, and Confusions in the Concept of Native Plants," in *Nature and Ideology: Natural Garden Design in the Twentieth Century,* ed. Joachim Wolschke-Bulmahn (Washington, D.C.: Dumbarton Oaks Research Library and Collection, 1997).

6. Stephen Jay Gould, "The Golden Rule—A Proper Scale for Our Environmental Crisis," in *Environmental Ethics: Divergence and Convergence*, eds. Susan J. Armstrong and Richard G. Botzler (New York: McGraw Hill, 1993), p. 312.

7. Eaton, *Merit*, p. 182.

8. Edward Tenner, *Why Things Bite Back: Technology and the Revenge of Unintended Consequences* (New York: Alfred A. Knopf, 1996), pp. 88–94.

9. The reference to torture and amputation is by Sarah Stein, cited by Georges Teysott, "The American Lawn: Surface of Everyday Life," in *The American Lawn*, ed. Georges Teysott (New York: Princeton Architectural Press, 1999), p. 3. In addition to Teysott, other good sources on the history and aesthetics of American green lawn are Ted Steinberg, *American Green: The Obsessive Quest for the Perfect Lawn* (New York: W.W. Norton, 2006) and Virginia Scott Jenkins, *The Lawn: A History of an American Obsession* (Washington, D.C.: Smithsonian Institution Press, 1994). Jenkins discusses the perceived desirability of perpetual green on p. 141.

10. I will address such disagreement of the life values expressed by objects in the final chapter.

11. Steinberg, *American Green*.

12. Teysott, *The American Lawn*, p. 30.

13. F. Herbert Bormann, et al., *Redesigning the American Lawn: A Search for Environmental Harmony* (New Haven: Yale University Press, 1993), p. 75. At the time of writing (summer of 2015), California is suffering from severe draught and there is a ban on watering the lawn in many communities.

14. Harvey Blatt, *America's Food: What You Don't Know About What You Eat* (Cambridge: MIT Press, 2008), p. vii, emphasis added.

15. Giovanna Borasi, *Journeys: How Travelling Fruit, Ideas and Buildings Rearrange Our Environment* (Montreal: Canadian Centre for Architecture, 2010), pp. 10, 12.

16. Dan Mitchell, "Why People Are Falling in Love with 'Ugly Food'," *Times.com*, March 27, 2015 http://time.com/3761942/why-people-are-falling-in-love-with-ugly-food/.

17. Conor McGlone, "Asda's Ugly Veg Drive Divides Supermarkets," *ENDS Report* 480 (Feb. 2015), p. 40.

18. For a good analysis of the various aesthetic effects involved in "Yes, We Can" presidential campaign for Barack Obama, see Katya Mandoki's "The Third Tear in Everyday Aesthetics," *Contemporary Aesthetics* 8 (2010) http://www.con tempaesthetics.org/newvolume/pages/article.php?articleID=606. For earlier examples of presidential campaigns, see Virginia Postrel's *The Substance of Style: How the Rise of Aesthetic Value is Remaking Commerce, Culture, and Consciousness* (New York: HarperCollins Publishers, 2003).

19. Gert Groening and Joachim Wolschke-Bulmahn, "Some Notes on the Mania for Native Plants in Germany," *Landscape Journal* 11/2 (Fall 1992), pp. 122 and 123.

20. See Kōjin Karatani's "Japan as Museum: Okakura Tenshin and Ernest Fenollosa," in *Japanese Art After 1945: Scream Against the Sky*, ed. Alexandra Munroe (New York: Harry N. Abrams, 1994) and "Uses of Aesthetics: After Orientalism," in *Edward Said and the Work of the Critic: Speaking Truth to Power*, ed. Paul A. Bove (Duke University Press, 2000).

21. The most influential writing was Shiga Shigetaka's *Nihon Fūkei Ron* (*Theory of Japanese Landscape*), published in 1894, during Sino-Japanese war. Trained as a geologist, Shiga was also a member of an ultra-nationalist party.

22. Alan Tansman discusses Yasuda Yojūrō's "Japanese Bridges" (originally published in 1936, revised and lengthened in 1939) in *The Aesthetics of Japanese Fascism* (Berkeley: University of California Press, 2009).

23. Emiko Ohnuki-Tierney's *Kamikaze, Cherry Blossoms, and Nationalisms: The Militarization of Aesthetics in Japanese History* (Chicago: The University of Chicago Press, 2002) gives a thorough account of this military utilization of aesthetics regarding cherry blossoms, accompanied by a number of letters and diaries, as well as photographs, of Kamikaze pilots.

24. Tansman, *Aesthetics of Japanese Fascism*, p. 4. I don't mean to imply that the potency of the aesthetics of cherry blossoms is always problematic. It can offer a powerful remedy and comfort as seen in the people's appreciation of cherry blossoms right after the March 11, 2011 tsunami disaster in Japan. As a counterpoint to their ephemerality, cherry blossoms also offer a sense of longevity by blooming year after year despite natural calamities. See poignant interviews with a number of victims in *Tsunami and the Cherry Blossom* (Lucy Walker Film, 2011).

25. Thomas Cole, "Essay on American Scenery," first appeared in *The American Monthly Magazine*, I (January 1836), included in *The American Landscape: A Critical Anthology of Prose and Poetry*, ed. John Conron (New York: Oxford University Press, 1974), p. 571.

26. For a historical account of the development of wilderness aesthetics and the formation of American national parks, see Roderick Nash, *Wilderness and the American Mind* (New Haven: Yale University Press, 1982) and Alfred Runte, *National Parks: The American Experience* (Lincoln: University of Nebraska Press, 1987). I also give a more detailed account than presented here in *Everyday Aesthetics* (Oxford: Oxford University Press, 2008), pp. 72–7, and "Cultural Construction of National Landscapes and its Consequences: Cases of Japan and the United States," in *Humans in the Land: The Ethics and Aesthetics of the Cultural Landscape*, eds. Sven Arntzen and Emily Brady (Oslo: Unipub, 2008), pp. 219–47.

27. Simon Schama, *Landscape and Memory* (London: HarperCollins, 1995), p. 15.

28. Arnold Berleant, *Living in the Landscape: Toward an Aesthetics of Environment* (Lawrence: The University Press of Kansas, 1997), p. 15.

29. Postrel, *The Substance of Style*, p. 8.

30. Thomas Leddy, *The Extraordinary in the Ordinary: The Aesthetics of Everyday Life* (Peterborough: Broadview Press, 2012), p. 208.

31. Josh Sanburn, "The Joy of Less," *Time* (March 23, 2015), p. 50, emphasis added.

32. *Story of Stuff* is available at http://storyofstuff.org/movies/story-of-stuff/. Jonathan Maskit characterizes "capitalistic subjectivity" as follows: "that form of subjectivity that makes one not a cog in a productive machine...but rather a willing participant in a form of life that is more and more structured to produce desires and pleasures that are concordant with the products and services that can be provided through the marketplace." "Subjectivity, Desire, and the Problem of Consumption," in *Deleuze/*

Guattari & Ecology, ed. Bernd Herzogenrath (New York: Palgrave Macmillian, 2008), p. 138.

33. Cited by David Howes in "HYPERESTHESIA, or, the Sensual Logic of Late Capitalism," in *Empire of the Senses: The Sensual Culture Reader*, ed. David Howes (Oxford: Berg, 2005), p. 282.

34. William Morris, "The Lesser Arts," first published in1877, in *William Morris on Art & Design*, ed. Christine Poulson (Sheffield: Academic Press, 1996), pp. 172, 173, and the next passages are pp. 175, 175, and 176, emphasis added.

35. Leddy, *Extraordinary*, p. 216, emphases added.

36. Joseph Pine II and James H. Gilmore, "Welcome to the Experience Economy," *Harvard Business Review* (1998): 97–105.

37. Pine and Gilmore, "Experience Economy," the first two terms are from p. 99 and the other four terms are from pp. 102–4.

38. Pine and Gilmore, "Experience Economy," p. 104.

39. Pine and Gilmore, "Experience Economy," p. 105.

40. Terry Eagleton, *The Ideology of the Aesthetic* (Oxford: Basil Blackwell, 1990), p. 373.

41. Paul Duncum, "Aesthetics, Popular Visual Culture, and Designer Capitalism," *Journal of Art and Design Education* 26/3 (2007), p. 289. The next passage is from p. 291.

42. Leddy, *Extraordinary*, pp. 210, 211.

43. Duncum, "Aesthetics," p. 291.

44. Arnold Berleant, *Sensibility and Sense: The Aesthetic Transformation of the Human World* (Exeter: Imprint Academic, 2010), p. 165.

45. Berleant, *Sensibility and Sense*. I think we need to be careful in our criticism here. One could claim that the cases where we derive satisfying experience, such as at an Apple Store or Starbucks, are more subject to a negative aesthetic critique because the manipulation is more effective, hence more problematic. Or one could make a contrary case that, insofar as we have a genuine need to buy a computer or a cup of coffee, we might as well have a satisfying aesthetic experience while doing so. One could further claim that, when the commercial design succeeds in orchestrating a positive experience, we should take it with a grain of salt. That is, the profit motive does not necessarily *nullify* the success of design, although it changes the nature of the overall experience, distinguishing it from a satisfying aesthetic experience of a public space, for example. Either way, I think we need to be clear to what extent the problematic nature of a particular commercial agenda affects the *aesthetic* experience negatively. What if the aesthetic strategies are utilized to promote world peace or environmental stewardship?

46. See my "Consumer Aesthetics and Environmental Ethics: Problems and Possibilities," *The Journal of Aesthetics and Art Criticism* 76/4 (2018), pp. 429–39.

47. These items were culled from remarks scattered throughout *Nanbōroku* in *Nanbōroku wo Yomu* (*Reading Nanbōroku*), ed. Kumakura Isao (Kyoto: Tankōsha, 1989).

48. *Nanbōroku wo Yomu*, p. 242.

49. Hisamatsu Shin'ichi, *Sadō no Tetsugaku* (*The Philosophy of the Way of Tea*) (Tokyo: Kōdansha, 1991), my translation, pp. 53–4, emphasis added. By "formal," he means sensuous, rather than the contrary of "informal" or "casual." Eiko Ikegami makes a sociological interpretation of the social and political role served by the aesthetic expression of hospitality, sociability, and civility in the tea ceremony and other

traditional Japanese arts in *Bonds of Civility: Aesthetic Networks and the Political Origins of Japanese Culture* (Cambridge: Cambridge University Press, 2005).

50. Some of the practical considerations are as follows. For obvious reasons, relatively flat-surfaced stones must be chosen. In particular, concave surfaces should be avoided, as they retain water and can be messy or dangerous when frozen. To provide easy movement, a stride should be calculated a little shorter than the usual ergonomic measurement, because walking on stepping stones is by necessity slower and more measured. The space between stones should not be too wide, because it will force the walker to stretch too much or jump, hence making the pathway dangerous, particularly when the stone surface is slippery from rain or snow. By the same token, the stone should be set with roughly 3–4 cm above ground, high enough to provide protection from muddy soil while low enough to prevent tripping. Because traditional Japanese footwear includes *geta*, wooden sandals, stones should not be too hard, in order to soften the sound of footsteps, while at the same time they cannot be soft like sandstone and tuff, either, because they have to withstand being constantly stepped on. For these reasons, andesite is generally regarded as the best material. Finally, for the so-called pivotal stone which indicates the juncture of two separate paths, a large stone is chosen so the walker can pause, look around, and decide on which path to pursue.

51. This strategy to force one to pay attention to something beneath us is similar to the way in which sky art forces us to attend to the sky above us, as discussed in Chapter 3.

52. Katsuo Saito and Sadaji Wada, *Magic of Trees & Stones: Secrets of Japanese Gardening* (New York: Japan Publication Trading Company, 1970), p. 49.

53. It is interesting to note that William Hogarth's explanation of designating a serpentine line as the line of beauty refers to the fact that it "leads the eye a wanton kind of chace." *The Analysis of Beauty* (1753), in *A Documentary History of Art*, ed. Elizabeth G. Holt (Garden City: Doubleday, 1958), Vol. II, p. 271.

54. Marc Peter Keane, *Japanese Garden Design* (Rutland: Charles E. Tuttle, 1996), p. 172.

55. Keane, *Japanese Garden Design*, p. 143.

56. Donald A. Norman, *Emotional Design: Why We Love (or Hate) Everyday Things* (New York: Basic Books, 2004), pp. 109–10. He derives his discussion of "Zen view" from Christopher Alexander et al.'s *A Pattern Language: Towns, Buildings, Construction* (New York: Oxford University Press, 1977), pp. 642–3.

57. See Fumihiko Maki's "Japanese City Spaces and the Concept of *Oku*," *The Japan Architect* 264 (1979), pp. 50–62 on the discussion of the concept of *oku*. A good general discussion and various examples of *oku* can be found in Joy Hendry's *Wrapping Culture: Politeness, Presentation and Power in Japan and Other Societies* (Oxford: Clarendon Press, 1993).

58. Ryūkyo Teien Kenkyūsho, *Arukukoto ga Tanoshikunaru Tobiishi Shikiishi Sahō* (*How to Make Stepping Stones and Pavement for Enjoyable Walking*) (Tokyo: Kenchiku Shiryō Kenkyūsha, 2002), p. 71 (my translation).

59. An interesting discussion of the history and aesthetics of manhole covers, with ample photographs and diagrams, can be found in Kakishita Yoshinori's *Rojō no Geijutsu* [*Fukkoku ban*] (*Art on the Street* [*Reprint Edition*]) (Tokyo: Hobby Japan, 2015).

60. Kenya Hara, *White*, trans. Jooyeon Rhee (Baden: Lars Müller Publishers, 2010), Prologue. Hara's discussion of emptiness is also found in *Mujirushi Ryōhin no Dezain* (*Mujirushi Ryōhin's Design*), Nikkei Design (Tokyo: Nikkei BP sha, 2015), pp. 50, 67–9, and the chapter on "Simple and Empty—Genealogy of Aesthetic Sensibility," in *Nihon no Dezain—Biishiki ga Tsukuru Mirai* (*Japanese Design—Future Created by Aesthetic Sensibility*) (Tokyo: Iwanami Shoten, 2012). I find it interesting that the notion of 'emptiness' comes up in different contexts, as I have discussed in relation to sky art in Chapter 3. I believe that a work on the aesthetics of emptiness is worth exploring in the future.

61. Naoto Fukasawa and Jasper Morrison, *Super Normal*, trans. Mardi Miyake (Baden: Lars Müller Publishers 2008), p. 116, emphasis added.

62. For examples of their products and designers' own comments, see *Muji*, Masaaki Kanai et al. (New York: Rizzoli, 2013) and *Mujirushi Ryōhin no Dezain* (*Mujirushi Ryōhin's Design*).

63. These terms are culled from Juhani Pallasmaa, "Toward an Architecture of Humility," *Harvard Design Magazine* (Winter/Spring 1999), Sim Van der Ryn and Stuart Cowan, *Ecological Design* (Washington, D.C.: Island Press, 1996), and Victor Papanek, *The Green Imperative: Natural Design for the Real World* (New York: Thames and Hudson, 1995).

64. Pallasmaa, "Architecture of Humility."

65. Papanek, *The Green Imperative*, p. 203.

66. Van der Ryn and Cowan, *Ecological Design*, p. 147.

67. David Pearson, "Making Sense of Architecture," *Architectural Review* 1136 (1991), p. 70.

68. Susann Vihma, "Artification for Well-Being: Institutional Living as a Special Case," *Contemporary Aesthetics*, special volume 4 on Artification (2012), sec. 1, http://www.contempaesthetics.org/newvolume/pages/article.php?articleID=645.

69. Tom Leddy points out, and I agree, that there is a lack of other items like TV that are easy and simple to use, particularly by senior citizens with dementia.

70. Hilary Moss and Desmond O'Neill, "The Art of Medicine: Aesthetic Deprivation in Clinical Settings," *Lancet* 383 (March 22, 2014), pp. 1032–3, http://www.thelancet.com/journals/lancet/article/PIIS0140-6736(14)60507-9/fulltext?rss=yes. The following passages are from pp. 1032 and 1033.

71. Donald A. Norman, *The Design of Everyday Things* (New York: Doubleday, 1990), pp. 25 and 27, emphasis added.

72. Nigel Taylor, "Ethical Arguments about the Aesthetics of Architecture," in *Ethics and the Built Environment*, ed. Warwick Fox (London: Routledge, 2000), pp. 201–2. Citations in the next three sentences are from pp. 203, 205, and 205.

73. I thank Jane Forsey for reporting this challenge to my presentation on "Negative Aesthetics" read by the session chair in my absence at the annual meeting of the American Society for Aesthetics, 2015.

74. Possible exceptions here may include works of art and objects of extreme historical, cultural, or religious significance. That is, a case could be made that defacing a painting and destroying an ancient temple is doing something wrong to the objects

themselves, regardless of or in addition to doing something wrong to other humans who are prospective viewers, visitors, and users.

75. Robert E. Carter, *The Japanese Arts and Self-Discipline* (Albany: SUNY Press, 2008), p. 124.
76. Carter, *The Japanese Arts*, p. 70, emphasis added.
77. Carter, *The Japanese Arts*, p. 61, emphasis added.
78. Carter, *The Japanese Arts*, p. 102, emphasis added.
79. Carter, *The Japanese Arts*, pp. 108–9.
80. Dōgen, *Tenzo Kyōkun* (典座教訓 *Instruction for the Tenzo*) in *Cooking, Eating, Thinking: Transformative Philosophies of Food*, ed. Deane W. Curtin and Lisa M. Heldke (Bloomington: Indiana University Press, 1992), p. 282.
81. Simon James, "For the Sake of a Stone? Inanimate Things and the Demands of Morality," *Inquiry* 54/4 (August 2011), p. 392.
82. As discussed in Chapter 3, Stan Godlovitch discusses the moral wrongness of destroying inanimate natural objects, such as ice, even when there is no possible and future harm to sentient beings. His reason for its wrongness is different from James' reason in that he believes the proper human attitude toward nature, sentient or non-sentient, has to be acentric. It is unclear whether his view extends to artifacts. "Ice Breakers: Environmentalism and Natural Aesthetics," *Journal of Applied Philosophy* 11/1 (1994), pp. 15–30. The issue here also calls into question whether "delicacy" or "gentleness" must be expressed toward artifacts which are created specifically for evil purposes, such as a weapon of mass destruction or a torture device.
83. Sarah Buss urges us to imagine what it is like to live in such a society in "Appearing Respectful: The Moral Significance of Manners," *Ethics* 109 (July 1999), pp. 799, 804.
84. Nel Noddings, "An Ethics of Care," in *Introduction to Ethics: Personal and Social Responsibility in a Diverse World*, ed. Gary Percesepe (Englewood Cliffs: Prentice Hall, 1995), p. 176.
85. Nancy Sherman, "Of Manners and Morals," *British Journal of Educational Studies* 53/3 (Sept. 2005), p. 285.
86. Lucinda Holdforth, *Why Manners Matter: What Confucius, Jefferson, and Jackie O Knew and You Should Too* (New York: Plume, 2009), p. 3.
87. Megan Laverty, "Civility, Tact, and the Joy of Communication," *Philosophy of Education* (2009), p. 229. Gender stereotyping based upon manners seems well-entrenched in the Western philosophical tradition. David Hume, for example, declares that "an effeminate behaviour in a man, a rough manner in a woman ... are ugly because unsuitable to each character, and different from the qualities which we expect in the sexes ... The disproportions hurt the eye, and convey a disagreeable sentiment to the spectators, the source of blame and disapprobation." "Of Qualities Immediately Agreeable to Others," in *An Inquiry Concerning the Principles of Morals*, ed. Charles W. Hendel (New York: The Liberal Arts Press, 1957), p. 88. Friedrich Schiller claims that grace is found more in women and dignity more in men. "On Grace and Beauty," in *Essays Aesthetical and Philosophical* (London: George Bell & Sons, 1882), p. 204.
88. Karen Stohr, *On Manners* (New York: Routledge, 2012), pp. 166, 167.

89. Sherman, "Of Manners and Morals," pp. 273, 282. In addition to what has already been cited, see Cheshire Calhoun's "The Virtue of Civility," *Philosophy & Public Affairs* 29/3 (2000), pp. 251–75.

90. Holdforth, *Why Manners Matter*, pp. 4–5.

91. D. W. Prall, *Aesthetic Judgment*, first published in 1929 (New York: Thomas Y. Crowell Company, 1967), p. 38.

92. Eaton, *Merit*, pp. 89, 92.

93. Sherman, "Of Manners and Morals," pp. 272, 281.

94. Buss, "Appearing Respectful," p. 814.

95. Nicholas F. Gier, "The Dancing *Ru*: A Confucian Aesthetics of Virtue," *Philosophy East & West* 51/2 (2001), p. 288, emphasis added.

96. Laverty, "Civility," p. 228.

97. Indeed there is a Japanese term for this: 慇懃無礼(ingin burei).

98. Carter, *The Japanese Arts*, p. 138.

99. Calhoun, "The Virtue of Civility," pp. 259, 255.

100. Schiller, "On Grace and Beauty," pp. 171, 187, 193 for Grace expressive of moral sentiments and p. 173 for Grace distinguished from nature.

101. Schiller, "On Grace and Beauty," p. 184.

102. Holdforth, *Why Manners Matter*, p. 149, all the emphases added. For a sustained discussion on the notion of 'tact,' see Ossi Naukkarinen's "Everyday Aesthetic Practices, Ethics and Tact," *Aisthesis* 7/1 (Jan. 2014), pp. 23–44.

103. Eaton, *Merit*, p. 92.

104. Sei Shōnagon, *The Pillow Book* (枕草子) *of Sei Shōnagon*, trans. Ivan Morris (Harmondsworth: Penguin Books, 1982), pp. 49–50.

105. Sei Shōnagon, *The Pillow Book*, p. 49.

106. Sei Shōnagon, *The Pillow Book*, p. 49.

107. Sei Shōnagon, *The Pillow Book*, p. 46, emphasis added.

108. Of course the dictum of "ought implies can" applies here. If the design of the door is such that it automatically closes shut with a loud noise with even a little push, our assessment of the act of closing the door will be different. If I am the one who closed the door with a bang, I would feel horrible for making such a racket as if to express disrespect.

109. A possible complication here is that sometimes rough serving of food adds to the ambience of the restaurant, as it is typically the case in a Chinese restaurant serving dim sum.

110. Shiotsuki Yaeko, *Washoku no Itadaki kata: Oishiku, Tanoshiku, Utsukushiku* (*How to Eat Japanese Meals: Deliciously, Enjoyably, and Beautifully*) (Tokyo: Shinchōsha, 1983), p. 12. The awkward, but literal, translation of the title is mine.

111. These specifics are culled from Shiotsuki, *Washoku no Itadaki kata*.

112. Luce Giard, "Doing Cooking" in the *Practice of Everyday Life*, trans. Timothy J. Tomasik (Minneapolis: University of Minnesota Press, 1998), p. 191.

113. Dōgen, *Fushuku-Hampō* (赴粥飯法 *Meal-Time Regulations*) in *Cooking, Eating, Thinking: Transformative Philosophies of Food*, ed. Deane W. Curtin and Lisa M. Heldke (Bloomington: Indiana University Press, 1992), p. 158.

114. Dōgen, *Fushuku-Hampō*,p. 158. The same rule appears in the tea ceremony discussed below. Kristin Surak explains:

    Not to appear greedy when the drink is set out, the guest waits until the moment the host removes her hand from the tea bowl—but not so long as to appear inattentive—before moving to retrieve the tea. And when the bowl is returned, the host, careful not to convey a sense of rushing things, waits until the guest is again seated before she collects the bowl.

    Making Tea, Making Japan: Cultural Nationalism in Practice (Stanford: Stanford University Press, 2013), p. 51.

115. Dōgen, *Fushuku-Hampō*, p. 161, emphasis added.
116. Surak, *Making Tea*, p. 52.
117. Ii Naosuke, *Sayu Ikkaishū (Collection of Tea Meetings)*, finished in 1858 cited by Murai Yasuhiko, *Cha no Bunkashi (Cultural History of Tea)* (Tokyo: Iwanami Shinsho, 1979), p. 169. Details of required bodily movement can also be found in *Shoho no Sadō (Introductory Way of Tea)* by Sen Sōshitsu (Kyoto: Tankōsha, 1965) as well as in Surak, *Making Tea*, Ch. 1.
118. Ii's *Sayu Ikkaishū* cited by Murai, *Cha no Bunkashi*, my translation.
119. Ikegami, *Bonds of Civility*, p. 226, emphasis added.
120. Ikegami, *Bonds of Civility*, p. 227, emphasis added. It is instructive that meals and snacks prepared and served by the host are sometimes referred to as *furumai* (振舞), which also means dance-like movement, or *chisō* (馳走) or *gochisō* (御馳走), which literally means running around (to prepare food with utmost consideration). See Murai, *Cha no Bunkashi*, p. 165.
121. Surak, *Making Tea*, p. 47, emphasis added.
122. Joy Hendry, *Wrapping Culture*, p. 63, emphasis added.
123. Yasutaka Sai, *The Eight Core Values of the Japanese Businessman: Toward an Understanding of Japanese Management* (New York: International Business Press, 1995), p. 57, emphasis added.
124. For a more detailed exploration of the aesthetics involved in Japanese packaging, see my "Japanese Aesthetics of Packaging," *The Journal of Aesthetics and Art Criticism* 57/2 (1999), pp. 257–65. For a more general discussion including packaging, food, and garden, see "The Moral Dimension of Japanese Aesthetics," *The Journal of Aesthetics and Art Criticism* 65/1 (Winter 2007), pp. 85–97.
125. I owe this point to Arnold Berleant.
126. Another set of examples that demonstrate the power of aesthetics that leads to extremely problematic consequences regards human (and to some extent non-human animal) appearances. For humans, the examples range from contemporary obsession with a thin body for females and muscular physique for males, youthful appearance, tanning, tattooing, and body piercing, to high heels, cosmetics, and tight-fitting jeans. Their problematic consequences include various health issues, such as anorexia, use of steroids, infection, and injury, as well as financial implications. As for non-human animals, various forms of body modification, such as tail docking and ear cropping for Doberman, inflict pain on animals simply to satisfy human desires for their specific appearance. I will not address these examples here

because there is a growing literature particularly on human body aesthetics, such as *Beauty Matters*, ed. Peg Zeglin Brand (Bloomington: Indiana University Press, 2000); Deborah L. Rhode, *The Beauty Bias: The Injustice of Appearance in Life and Law* (Oxford: Oxford University Press, 2010); *Beauty Unlimited*, ed. Peg Zeglin Brand (Bloomington: Indiana University Press, 2012); *Body Aesthetics*, ed. Sherri Irvin (Oxford: Oxford University Press, 2016). For animal body modification, see Yi-Fu Tuan, *Dominance & Affection: The Making of Pets* (New Haven: Yale University Press, 1984).

127. Leddy, *Extraordinary*, p. 211.

7

The Power of Everyday Aesthetics in World-Making

I concluded the last chapter by advocating the need for developing aesthetic literacy regarding everyday life. We need to recognize *that* and *how* the quality of life and the state of the world are affected, sometimes determined, by the aesthetic considerations in our daily life. In this chapter, I want to go even further by exploring whether it is sufficient to raise awareness of the power of the aesthetic.

7.1 What to Do with the Power of the Aesthetic

Is recognizing this power of the aesthetic and developing aesthetic literacy enough? Once recognized, what should we do with this power of the aesthetic? We have two options regarding this potent power of the aesthetic. One is to end everyday aesthetics inquiry at this point, that is, by simply exposing its potency. The other is to go further by engaging in a normative discourse to guide this power in a certain direction.

The first option is to separate the aesthetic from the other life values, such as the moral, political, and environmental, and train ourselves to act only on the basis of the latter, without being affected by any aesthetic considerations. So, for example, we should decide on the issues regarding preservation of unscenic landscapes and unattractive creatures by their environmental values, *despite* their lack of aesthetic value. We should accept wind turbines and laundry hanging, *disregarding* their eyesore-like appearance. We should also *give up* our ideal green lawns and instead train ourselves to *tolerate* brownish spots and weeds. We should also try to *resist* the allure of the newer, stylish, and fashionable clothes, shoes, and iPhones and hang on to the obsolete-looking current ones as long as the functional performance is satisfactory.

This way of promoting social, political, and environmental good may be supported by the advocates of Kantian ethics who would want to appeal only to one's rationality as a moral compass. The separation of the aesthetic and other life values will also be supported by those who object to a kind of social engineering or "nudging" of our aesthetic life to conform to what Marcia Eaton calls "aesthetic ought."[1] Furthermore, after considering the precedents in which the powerful effect of aesthetics promoted dubious political ends as well as leading us away from an environmentally sound future, one may be inclined to choose this option and sever the tie between the aesthetic dimensions and other value-laden aspects of things.

However, the fact that the power of the aesthetic can be dangerous underscores its potential to be utilized to direct people's world-making project toward a better quality of life and state of the world. Indeed, for every problematic use of the power of the aesthetic, there are examples of contributions made by the same power for better world-making, such as the American Civil Rights movement that cannot be separated from the moving qualities of folk songs.[2] I also cited in Chapter 6 (note 24) the power of the aesthetics of cherry blossoms as a healing agent for the victims of the Japanese tsunami disaster in 2011.

While Plato's censorship of arts in his Republic, let alone his blueprint for his utopia, may be unacceptable to many, what I take to be the most important insight behind his discussion of the arts is that they can be a powerful enemy but also an equally powerful ally for building a good society. He was fully cognizant of the power of the aesthetic: "musical training is a more potent instrument than any other, because rhythm and harmony find their way into the inward places of the soul, on which they mightily fasten, imparting grace, and making the soul of him who is rightly educated graceful."[3] We have encountered similar recognition of the power of music and other aesthetic pursuits in Confucianism in Chapter 6. Similarly, Sir Philip Sidney emphasizes poetry's power to instruct people accompanied by "delight": "poesy ... is an art of imitation, for so Aristotle termeth [archaic spelling in the original] it in his word *mimesis*, that is to say, representing, counterfeiting, or figuring forth—to speak metaphorically, a speaking picture—with this end, to teach and *delight*"; in short, "poesy is full of virtue-breeding delightfulness."[4] For him, moral teaching can go down easier when it is accompanied by the delight engendered by aesthetic pleasure. It leads a man toward virtuous path "as if they took a medicine of cherries" similar to the way in which "the child is often brought to take most wholesome things by hiding them in such other as have a pleasant taste."[5]

As I pointed out when discussing the aesthetics of care and respect in Chapter 6, Friedrich Schiller is most clear in his vision of the aesthetic education of man that humans are affected by and operate on the sensible as well as on the rational level, and what really moves us to act is that which appeals to the sensible part.[6] Arnold Berleant points out that aesthetics' significance "lies not only in the ability...to serve as a critical tool for probing social practice but as a beacon for illuminating the direction of social betterment."[7] Those who have been promoting a sustainable future also recognize the potential of aesthetics to serve this cause and argue for its utilization. To cite only one example, David Orr holds that "we are moved to act more often, more consistently, and more profoundly by *the experience of beauty* in all of its forms than by intellectual arguments, abstract appeals to duty or even by fear." Therefore, he continues, "we must be inspired to act by examples that we can see, touch, and experience," toward which we can develop an "emotional attachment" and a "deep affection."[8]

Given the potent power of the aesthetic, not utilizing it and steering it toward better world-making seems like a missed opportunity. Those professional world-makers cognizant of this power of the aesthetic have been advocating uniting the aesthetic appeal of design with other values, such as environmental and social. For example, one landscape architect argues for the need to align aesthetics with ecology by making sustainable landscape design attractive and appealing, so that people cherish, maintain, care for, and protect it, rendering it "culturally sustainable."[9] Another landscape architect observes that "this separation of art, ethics, utility and nature can leave aesthetics with an atrophied, and indeed, frivolous role in landscape education" and calls for the need to "make explicit a developing aesthetic criteria related to both ethics and utility."[10]

But what about those of us non-professionals who are nonetheless engaged in the world-making project through our everyday aesthetic decisions? I would characterize the current situation in which we are affected by the power of the aesthetic as *laissez faire*. We are letting the power of the aesthetic be used for any purposes or agenda irrespective of its cumulative and collective consequences. There is a compelling reason for supporting this *laissez faire* attitude: when it comes to aesthetic matters, we favor complete freedom and reject any attempt to regulate aesthetic taste, even if such legislation of aesthetic taste were possible.

However, the problem is that the power of the aesthetic has already been co-opted by those who seek to guide our aesthetic life toward a certain direction. We have already looked at examples of coercion, such as the prohibition of laundry hanging and the pressure to keep up with the Joneses' green grass. We have also found that aesthetic strategies "nudge" us toward certain choices in every corner of commercial enterprise today, ranging from branding of goods and food styling to creating a specific multisensory ambience in a store. If we continue to endorse a *laissez faire* attitude, we are in effect supporting these existing "aesthetic ought" and "nudge" by default. As Richard Thaler and Cass Sunstein point out, "there is...no way of avoiding nudging in some direction, and whether intended or not, these nudges will affect what people choose."[11] So, can everyday aesthetics promote an alternative or competing "aesthetic ought" and "nudge" to steer our aesthetic tastes, choices, and judgments toward a sustainable future, good life, and better society? I propose that everyday aesthetics engage in a normative discourse to guide the non-professionals among us toward more informed aesthetic judgments which move our decisions and actions toward better world-making.[12]

7.2 Objections to Everyday Aesthetics as a Normative Discourse

There are several objections to guiding the aesthetics discourse in a normative direction. Most prominently, there is a persistent resistance to connecting the aesthetic and other life values, particularly the moral, within contemporary Anglo-American aesthetics discourse. The primary reason is the worry that developing a normative discourse will compromise the core of the aesthetic, namely the sensuous and the free play of the imagination. This resistance is understandable when considering the development of modern Western aesthetics. Since the eighteenth century, Western aesthetic discourse evolved by declaring its independence from other considerations, in particular the moral. It culminated in the aestheticism of the late nineteenth century, promoted notably by Oscar Wilde and J. A McNeill Whistler as a response to the prevailing moralistic view of art, followed by the aesthetic formalism of the early twentieth century proposed by Clive Bell and Roger Fry as a defense for the then emerging abstract art.

7.2.1 Perceptual autonomy of aesthetics

The concern for protecting the autonomy of aesthetics is still alive and well today, as summarized by Marcia Eaton (who is critical of this view): "when one looks, reads, or listens to works of art or aesthetic objects, the only genuinely aesthetic experiences are those solely or exclusively directed at intrinsic features," and "the intrusion of any other kind of consideration necessarily destroys or dilutes an aesthetic experience."[13] This view regarding the perceptual autonomy of aesthetic experience generally takes the following two formulations: (1) the sensuous appeal of an object *is not* affected by the cognitive, such as moral and environmental, associations with the object; (2) the sensuous appeal of an object *should not* be affected by such associations.

For the first of these claims, take the following questions posed by David E. Cooper: "Can the look of a lawn really change according to ecological savvy?

Or wind farms begin to look beautiful when their benefits are explained at a consultation meeting?"[14] There are two responses to these questions. First, consider the two already established discourses in aesthetics: art criticism and nature aesthetics. The mainstream aesthetics discourse regarding art presupposes that the interpretation and judgment regarding art is not merely a matter of subjective opinion but should be amenable to reasoned and critical discussion. Although there may not be *one* correct interpretation and evaluation of a work of art, within all-too-familiar disagreements, we do disregard those appreciations which are derived from highly idiosyncratic personal associations or not based upon sufficient or correct information. In a critical discourse on art, therefore, we expect not only the relevance, but indeed the necessity, of connecting the sensuous with other considerations, such as the object's art-historical context, the technique used in production, the artist's *oeuvre*, and the like.

These extra-sensory considerations are then expected to modify the sensuous appearance of a work of art. The clearest example may be the change in our perception of a painting after we discover that it is a forgery. What we appreciated as a brilliant composition of Vermeer no longer appears to be brilliant, although we may see it now as being cleverly deceptive. Or, as pointed out by Arthur Danto in his theory of the artworld, the same writing that constitutes Cervantes' *Don Quixote* changes its meaning and expressive quality if it was written in the twentieth century by Jorge Luis Borges' fictional writer Pierre Menard. Similarly, as Kendall Walton argues, the category in which an art object is experienced determines its expressive property, so that Picasso's *Guernica* will appear placid and peaceful if it is experienced under a fictional artistic category consisting of the same monochrome pattern of this painting with differing degrees of three-dimensional protrusion and recession.[15]

Nature aesthetics is following suit by developing the possibility of engaging in a critical discourse and educating one's aesthetic sensibility through scientific study, nature walks, nature writings, and works of art that represent or comment on nature. Despite considerable debates about the relevance and relative importance of scientific, historical, mythological, poetic, and imaginative associations in nature aesthetics, there is a sense in which some of these associations in certain contexts do render our aesthetic experience of nature richer, possibly more appropriate, and less trivial. Even those who advocate the imaginative aesthetic appreciation of nature seem to distinguish between "serious" and "trivial" associations, as well as between "imagining well" and the undisciplined "imagination let loose [which] can lead to the manipulation of the aesthetic object for one's own pleasure-seeking ends."[16]

The seemingly monotonous and boring appearance of a salt marsh becomes richer and more complex when we associate its diverse environmental functions as well as its rather complex structure that negotiates varied saline content of the surrounding water.[17] Furthermore, after discovering that the brilliant sunset is caused by air pollution, our perception of its crimson color is modified, because we experience what Cheryl Foster calls "aesthetic disillusionment," perhaps similar to when we discover a painting is a forgery.[18] The aesthetics of the green lawns certainly has to be based upon the green color and its texture, and the aesthetics of a sunset its color. However, as I argued in Chapter 2, it is not clear whether the aesthetic appreciation of a color and texture can be based strictly on the object's sensuous quality in isolation from what it is and its context, and it seems to me that the context also includes cognitive considerations such as its cause, consequences, and the like. In fact, Eaton wonders whether there can be any aesthetic qualities that do not involve cognitive and other considerations: "I would wager most aesthetic terms are 'impure'—they reflect, even require, beliefs and values: sincere, suspenseful, sentimental, shallow, subtle, sexy, sensual, salacious, sordid, sobering, sustainable, skillful...and that, of course, only scratches the surface of the s-words!"[19]

But when it comes to everyday artifacts and activities, we have not yet developed an equivalent discourse in which to analyze the appropriateness of our response or a strategy for educating and improving it. If everyday aesthetic responses are considered trivial because they lack a critical discourse, it is not clear whether the absence of such a discourse is endemic to everyday aesthetics or rather a lacuna that needs to be filled. My proposal is to pursue the latter possibility by leading everyday aesthetics to explore what sort of considerations are relevant and necessary to modify our aesthetic response so as to guide it toward better world-making.

There is another response to the objection that the cognitive considerations do not alter the aesthetic quality of an object. Admitting that the cognitive can modify or transform the sensuous does not necessarily commit us to allowing the cognitive considerations to *determine* its aesthetic value by *nullifying* the sensuous. As I have argued previously, recognizing the aesthetic relevance of conceptual considerations does not and should not commit us to determinism whereby a moral, political, or environmental value *determines* the aesthetic value of green lawns, wind turbines, and laundry hanging. Making connections to other life values instead enriches the experience, sometimes in a positive way and other times negatively.

7.2.2 *Protection of everyday aesthetics from moral censure*

The preceding discussion demonstrates that the cognitive considerations do in fact alter, though not determine, the aesthetic qualities of an object. The next challenge is to consider whether they *should*; that is, shouldn't the aesthetic realm be protected from what may amount to a kind of moral censure? Do we want to share Arnold Toynbee's predicament regarding the aesthetics of pyramids?

When we admire aesthetically the marvelous masonry and architecture of the Great Pyramid or the exquisite furniture and jewelry of tut-ankh-Amen's tomb, there is a conflict in our hearts between our pride and pleasure in such triumphs of human art and our moral condemnation of the human price at which these triumphs have been bought: the hard labour unjustly imposed on the many to produce the fine flowers of civilization for the exclusive enjoyment of a few who reap where they have not sown. During these last five or six thousand years, the masters of the civilizations have robbed their slaves of their share in the fruits of society's corporate labours as cold-bloodedly as we rob our bees of their honey. The moral ugliness of the unjust act mars the aesthetic beauty of the artistic results.[20]

If we agree with Toynbee regarding the pyramids and other Egyptian treasures, many objects, including the Taj Mahal, that we currently admire for their aesthetic values, would lose some of their appeal. Do we want to take this route?

Many would not want to take this route. Jane Forsey presents a typical view regarding the aesthetics of designed objects: the fact that some objects are made "in a third-world factory under dismal conditions...will certainly affect our moral judgements of the objects depending on our view on international trade and labour laws but not our aesthetic judgment of their beauty."[21] Another version of the same point is suggested by Thomas Leddy, who questions whether there is anything objectionable to aesthetically appreciating junkyards and roadside clutter. He points out that artists are particularly "sensitive observers of our world and capture aesthetic features in their works that we might not normally notice" and argues that it is important "to clear a space for a form of aesthetic appreciation that is freer, more imaginative, and more in tune with important discoveries of modernist art than is allowed by current morally-centered views in aesthetics."[22]

Leddy, however, recognizes the pragmatic importance of morally based aesthetics and proposes the "toggle between interested and disinterested perception" of an object particularly when its other life values are problematic.[23] The junkyard *as a* junkyard should be experienced with all of its life values, particularly when pragmatic concerns are at stake, for example, in deciding whether or not to clean up the environment. However, there may be no compelling reason to *always* experience a junkyard in such a way. It will certainly diminish our aesthetic life if we never experience things like junkyards and roadside clutter for their interesting colors and textures. Thus, there is a need to protect aesthetic experience free of concerns from other life values.

The equivalent situation exists in art aesthetics. Although Kendall Walton is right in proposing putting a work of art in its category to appreciate a work of art properly, there may be occasions in which deviating from the work's proper category is beneficial, such as viewing a representational painting as a non-representational painting in order to focus on its formal structure. So, the legitimacy of my environmentally informed aesthetic response to green lawns and laundry-hanging, one could argue, is *context-dependent*, and we have much to gain from recognizing the value of aesthetic experience unencumbered by the life values associated with the object. The important point to be emphasized, then, is that we cannot make an *indiscriminate* case for or against one kind of aesthetic appreciation of everyday objects with other values or disvalues. A further consideration is needed to determine the appropriateness of a certain kind of judgment in a particular context. So, the normative dimension of everyday aesthetics discourse consists not so much of a set of 'correct' or 'appropriate' judgments as the determination of a particular context which further determines what relevant factors should be considered.

However, we need to carefully distinguish these different examples. A case could be made that when it regards objects like the pyramids, ancient Egyptian treasures, and the Taj Mahal, even if their creation involved a huge sacrifice of human lives, we are not in a position to correct such injustice. In comparison, we cannot ignore that our aesthetic desire is primarily responsible for the continuing production of consumer goods created in sweatshops overseas with devastating environmental destruction and human rights violation as well as ever-growing junkyards. Here, the Kantian notion of how the judgment of taste has to be disinterested in the sense we are not interested in the object's existence does not seem to apply, nor is the mainstream aesthetic theory's characterization of the experiencing agent as a distanced spectator. Whether or not we are aware, most of us are implicated in creating problems, enticed by aesthetic considerations. Everyday aesthetics aims at addressing the reality that we are actively engaged in our everyday life by *acting* on aesthetic preferences and judgments. I thus agree with the following statement by Marcia Eaton:

Our experiences, our encounters with and in the world, and the decisions we make as a result do not typically come in separate packets, with the moral, aesthetic, economic, religious, political, scientific, and so on serving as viewing stands distanced from one another so that we look at the world first from one and then from another standpoint. I do not claim that aesthetic experiences or considerations are never separable from other sorts. What I insist is that it is *not a requirement* of the aesthetic that all other interests or concerns are blocked off or out.[24]

I would venture to go further by insisting that it is not only "not required" of the aesthetic that all other interests or concerns are blocked off but rather it is "required" that they *not* be blocked off when the aesthetic leads to problematic consequences. Even if we cannot correct the past problems like in the case of the pyramids and Taj Mahal, we *are* in the position to determine the future state of the world. Unless we change our current aesthetic paradigm, the future generation will have to contend with more ugliness caused by deforestation, burgeoning landfills, and aesthetic deprivation of sweatshops, and I believe that everyday aesthetics has a responsibility to address this issue. Speaking specifically of the aesthetics of windfarms, Tyson-Lord Gray proposes a forward-looking aesthetics for "its potential to enrich future aesthetic judgments," and I think this can be generalized to apply to other issues that I have dealt with.[25]

7.2.3 Aesthetic paradigm shift

One may continue to be skeptical, if not of the desirability, then the feasibility of effecting a change of people's aesthetics. For example, is it possible to transform people's current aesthetic taste and preference by educating them about various facts, such as the environmental ramifications, injustice against certain group of people, political agenda, unbridled capitalistic motive, and the like?

If history is any indication, it seems quite possible. We can refer to the dramatic shift in European people's landscape aesthetics from "mountain gloom" to "mountain glory" that occurred during the eighteenth century.[26] This is followed by the nineteenth-century transformation of wilderness from something aesthetically negative to positive in the United States. As mentioned in the last chapter, this transformation is a part of the relatively young nation's attempt to formulate and promote its own national identity. The Japanese aesthetics of *wabi* and *sabi*, a celebration of imperfection, defect, and insufficiency, prominently advocated in the tea ceremony, emerged in sixteenth century as an alternative to the prevailing penchant for perfection and opulence. It was motivated not only by aesthetic reasons but also by existential and political reasons, and it became established as one of the quintessential Japanese aesthetic tastes for years to come.[27]

Today, too, we are witnessing that some prevailing everyday aesthetic tastes are going through transformation, often instigated by reasons other than aesthetics. Case in point is the recent movement gaining in popularity that celebrates 'ugly' fruits and vegetables. It is not only that misshapen, deformed, blemished, 'inglorious' fruits and vegetables became 'accepted' by consumers, largely thanks to initiatives by supermarkets in Europe, UK, and Australia,[28] but also there are even artistic treatments of such fruits and vegetables, such as German photographer Uli Westphal's *Mutatoes*. Furthermore, with the understanding that organic produce tends to have more blemishes and misshapen appearance, consumers are increasingly embracing its appearance as a sign of health and well-being. One writer suggests that

there's also the growing prevalence of organics, which, because they tend to be less uniformly "pretty" than industrial mass-produced crops, have conditioned consumers to seeing less than ideal looking product. In fact, it may have conditioned them to view imperfectly formed fruits and veggies as being "better" because of their organic connotations.[29]

But how exactly do we cultivate an everyday aesthetic sensibility to contribute to a better world-making? I suggest that we begin by questioning the prevalent notion of beauty underlying our common aesthetic responses. David Orr proposes a new standard of beauty "as that which causes no ugliness somewhere else or at some later time."[30] It contrasts with the current situation where ugliness is rendered largely invisible:

The problem is that we do not often see the true ugliness of the consumer economy and so are not compelled to do much about it. The distance between shopping malls and the mines, wells, corporate farms, factories, toxic dumps, and landfills, sometimes half a world away, dampens our perceptions that something is fundamentally wrong.[31]

We can add to his list the current disconnect between the beautiful garment and the sweatshop where it is manufactured.

Jonathan Maskit also calls for "the aesthetics of elsewhere" as "an environmentalist everyday aesthetics" that needs to be cultivated along with environmentalist everyday ethics. For example, in addition to the environmental harm caused by logging and mining, the aesthetics of elsewhere will expose the *aesthetic* devastation caused by them: "mines, particularly open pit mines or mountain-top removal mines are seen by many as ugly. So too with logging sites as well as the various industrial facilities from which the raw materials for even the most beautiful buildings and artworks are sourced."[32] He argues for the role art can play in this regard, such as photographs of Edward Burtynsky and others that document various forms of ugliness caused by resource extraction and afterlife of manufactured goods such as discarded electronics and automobiles.[33]

Just as it is impossible to predict future environmental consequences of wind energy, as discussed in Chapter 4, one may claim that Orr's definition of beauty is impossible to put into practice because, lacking omniscience, we can never predict the future aesthetic consequences of our activities and products. Future ugliness may be unforeseen, just as environmentally harmful consequences can be unexpected. After all, a silent spring was not predicted by the use of DDT, nor was fish kill by the application of fertilizer. While this skepticism is justified and we may be taken by surprises in the future, we already know the negative aesthetic effects of mining, logging, chemical fertilizers, and disposal of electronic devices and automobiles. Disfigured landscapes, the visual blight and foul stench of fish kill, ever-expanding junkyards, and the aesthetic deprivation of sweat-shops already exist. The fact that we are not fully cognizant of future aesthetic consequences is no argument for ignoring current aesthetic harm. We can rephrase Martin Luther King Jr's famous statement: "Injustice anywhere is a threat to justice everywhere"[34] to read: "Ugliness anywhere is a threat to beauty everywhere."

Orr's definition of beauty can also be put in a more positive manner. That is, even if something may not strike us immediately as beautiful in the conventional sense, its contribution to producing aesthetically positive values elsewhere or at a later time can shed a different light on the object's aesthetics. Recall my reference in Chapter 4 to William James' anecdote regarding a cleared field in North Carolina and the increasingly popular community gardens in American urban areas. Neither of them satisfies the aesthetic ideals related to picturesque landscape or green lawns. Both often appear to be crudely created and messily arranged, but they embody communal pride and collaborative spirit, or "a very paean of duty, struggle, and success," as James characterizes the North Carolina coves.[35]

Wildflower gardens featuring indigenous plants are also beginning to be accepted and appreciated, despite their seemingly messy, disorderly, and chaotic appearance. Piet Oudolf, the designer of Chicago Millennium Park's Lurie Garden consisting of indigenous wildflowers, as well as New York City's Highline, is clear about challenging the prevailing aesthetic paradigm: "I think it's the journey in your life to find out what real beauty is, of course, but also discover beauty in things that are at first sight not beautiful."[36] Because native wildflowers don't need extra water, fertilizer, pesticide, and herbicide, they also attract birds, butterflies, and other wildlife, contributing to a vibrant atmosphere. If an environmentally prob-lematic green lawn falls short of Orr's definition of beauty, community gardens and wildflower gardens earn a new sense of aesthetic value based upon their contribu-tion to enlivening the area community for both humans and nature.

Consider also the recent project of "Edible Estates" spearheaded by Fritz Haeg. Specifically dubbed as an "attack on the front lawn," this project replaces green lawns in residential front yards with gardens with fruits and vegetables.[37]

This project challenges the uniformity and monoculture of the green lawn as "an icon of beauty," as well as the assumption that "plants that produce food are ugly and should not be seen."[38] Haeg instead calls for a paradigm shift in American domestic aesthetics, advocating fecundity, productivity, and "chaotic abundance of biodiversity." Furthermore, in addition to the literal fruits of labor harvested from such gardens, there are a number of other benefits, ranging from environmental stewardship to promoting neighborliness by initiating conversations among neighbors about how the crops are doing and by sharing bumper crops. Their seemingly messy, chaotic, and disorderly appearance can begin to appear aesthetically positive when we consider their fecundity, productivity, and contribution to biodiversity and neighborliness. At the same time, the green lawn's beauty becomes compromised by its sterility, inhospitability toward living creatures, and the downright environmental harm it causes as well as the health hazards it poses. As Diana Balmori comments on Edible Estates:

Beauty has many dimensions, and...is a rather...complex concept that has cultural and moral dimensions. Will you look at this established icon deemed beautiful for generations with the same eyes once you know the effects it has on our environment? Ecological thinking has transformed how we see the lawn, and our concept of beauty has been transformed with it.[39]

In short, it is not possible to surgically remove life values from aesthetic values.

The aesthetic paradigm shift, however, may require evolution instead of revolution. For those whose aesthetic taste is entrenched in conventional standards, a drastic and sudden change may be too much and too fast for acceptance. Joan Nassauer thus calls for introducing biodiversity and environmentally friendlier urban landscapes with enough conventional cues and signs to make them "culturally sustainable."

In an urban or countryside context, people tend to perceive landscapes that exhibit biodiversity as messy, weedy, and unkempt. A central problem in introducing greater biodiversity and heterogeneity to the urban landscape is that these characteristics tend to be mistaken for a lack of care.... Cues to human care, expressions of neatness and tended nature, are inclusive symbols by which ecologically rich landscapes can be presented to people and can enter vernacular culture.[40]

Landscapes that attract the admiring attention of human beings may be more likely to survive than landscapes that do not attract care or admiration. Survival that depends on human attention might be called *cultural sustainability*. Landscapes that are ecologically sound, and that also evoke enjoyment and approval, are more likely to be sustained by appropriate human care over the long term. People will be less likely to redevelop, pave, mine, or "improve" landscapes that they recognize as attractive. In short, the health of the landscape requires that humans enjoy and take care of it.[41]

Nassauer suggests utilizing recognizable cues indicative of human care, such as a neat border and a fence, to frame an otherwise unkempt and messy looking indigenous garden. Eaton also points out that "a wetland initially read as a dirty swamp may be read as a park if there are boardwalks or species markers."[42] Cultural sustainability of a landscape, whether it be a residential front yard or a farm land, requires development of a new aesthetic vocabulary that is informed by other considerations, such as ecological health, cultural values, and community engagement. Eaton states that one of the challenges for designers and aestheticians is "developing an aesthetic 'language' that will communicate ethical ecological health... Experimental farming techniques will not be seen as beautiful until ecologically valuable properties of landscape types are more readily recognized."[43]

Recall Robert Thayer's discussion of the aesthetics of sustainability I cited in Chapter 4. He stresses the importance of developing a new set of aesthetic vocabulary that makes "the emotional state provoked by the landscape's *surfaces*" to be "congruent with and not contradictory to the manner in which the *core* properties of the same landscape provide for our functional needs and well-being."[44] Thayer insists that the embodiment of sustainable design be made fully visible and accessible, contrary to the prevailing tendency to hide signs of technology, as we have seen in the debate over wind turbines. That is, this new aesthetic sensibility should be facilitated and nurtured by our experiencing and living with those mechanisms which are its major players, such as wind turbines, solar panels, constructed wetlands, and natural storm drainage.[45] Thayer calls these "conspicuous nonconsumption" and regards them as "essential markers along the road to a more sustainable world."[46] They will provide, according to him, "an accrual of positive environmental symbolism"[47] and add to the cumulative and collective memories of our cultural landscape.

Do these views in favor of aesthetic paradigm shift sound too preachy? Do they resemble a forced effort to push nutritional food, exercise, and other constituents of a healthy lifestyle *despite* any lack of appeal other than the health benefits? Not necessarily if we succeed in effecting the paradigm shift on the *aesthetic* level.

Eaton argues that developing such new aesthetic sensibility will not take the fun out of our aesthetic life. Instead, she claims:

We aim for a public that does not... mistake a well-kept prairie park for a weed patch. Hedgerows that maintain diversity can come to be perceived as creating beautiful contoured patterns. Colorful native flowers can be perceived and reflected upon as an indication of soil unpoisoned by harsh chemicals. An adequate canopy will signify the presence of songbirds. Too rapid runoff of rainwater will result in one's seeing concrete curbs as ugly rather than neat.[48]

Early advocates of ecological design Sim Van der Ryn and Stuart Cowan make a similar point regarding storm drainage systems.

With a conventional storm-drain system...water quickly disappears into subterranean arteries, picking up various toxins along the way. The water is hidden, and so are the impacts of the system itself—contamination of downstream rivers or wetlands, altered hydrology, and decreased groundwater recharge.[49]

In comparison, a drainage system that lets "water flow on the surface into drainage ponds" has not only an ecological advantage but also an aesthetic benefit:

The *delightful* thing about such a design is that people love to watch it in action, rushing out in the rain to watch the water flow. All of this suggests a new kind of *aesthetic* for the built environment, one that explicitly teaches people about the potentially symbiotic relationship between culture, nature, and design.

I have also mentioned in Chapter 4 the transformation of NIMBYism into YIMBYism in some communities in the State of Rhode Island regarding wind turbines. Overall, one could claim that the loss suffered when "what is ecologically bad begins to be seen as aesthetically bad"[50] is made up by the opposite: what is ecologically good begins to be seen as aesthetically good.

7.3 Practicing Body Aesthetics

Section 7.2.3 explored the feasibility of an aesthetic paradigm shift in developing an aesthetic sensibility toward everyday life informed by associated life values. Our participation in such a paradigm shift is primarily judgment-based (such as developing a positive aesthetic judgment of an edible estate and laundry hanging) that may inspire some actions (such as creating an edible garden and hanging laundry).

However, I argued in Chapter 2 that an equally important aspect of everyday aesthetics regards our experience as an acting agent. In this regard, I want to advocate another way in which to develop a normative dimension of everyday aesthetics: *practicing* body aesthetics. Here, as before, the Japanese aesthetic tradition is helpful.

As mentioned before, the Japanese aesthetic tradition is primarily concerned with instructions for art practitioners' training, which ultimately turns out to be an instruction on how to live one's life. Mostly Zen priests or students of Zen Buddhism, Japanese art masters and their disciples all emphasize selfless devotion, rigorous self-discipline, and constant practice in the chosen artistic medium not only as a means to achieve artistic excellence but more importantly as a way of experiencing enlightenment and self-fulfillment. Furthermore, such self-discipline, whether toward Zen enlightenment, artistic mastery, or the good life, requires bodily engagement and practice. Zazen (座禅), sitting and meditating, the specific training method of the Sōtō (曹洞) sect of Zen Buddhism established by Dōgen, engages both body and mind, where bodily engagement requires sitting still, keeping an erect posture, breathing mindfully, and locating one's center of gravity in the middle of the abdomen.

Zen bodily training goes beyond Zazen to encompass all daily activities, ranging from cooking and eating to cleaning and washing one's face. From his own experience at a Zen monastery, Richard Shusterman relates how his Roshi's instructions to the trainees were directed toward "the way we handled our bowls and chopsticks, how we chewed and swallowed our food, how we passed food to our eating companions" by showing them "the aesthetically proper way to pick up and put down one's chopsticks and to hold one's rice bowl and cup."[51] The goal is to achieve "performative grace and thoughtful elegance" facilitated when each movement is "executed and experienced as the focus of careful, mindful, loving attention."[52] Zen bodily training contributes to cultivating an open-minded sensibility to recognize aesthetic values in diverse objects and qualities, as well as mindful living by paying careful attention to things and surroundings.

I mentioned in Chapter 1 that, though her focus is not specifically on body aesthetics, Sherri Irvin argues for the aesthetic dimension of ordinary experiences, including scratching an itch, drinking coffee and petting her cat. The benefit of cultivating aesthetic sensibility toward these mundane acts of daily life, she claims, is enriching one's life: "insofar as we are led to ignore it [everyday experience] or regard it as unworthy of attention, we deprive ourselves of a source of gratification," and "if we attend to the aesthetic aspects of everyday experience, our lives can come to seem more satisfying to us, even more profound."[53]

I agree that cultivating an aesthetic sensibility regarding everyday objects and activities contributes to living more mindfully and appreciatively, as well as encouraging a more open-minded approach to objects and human affairs. However, there is a potential danger in accounting for the value of practicing aesthetic mindfulness as self-improvement, self-enrichment, and acting as an artist of one's own life, if the social ramifications of these are not also taken into account. Particularly with respect to practicing aesthetics through specific body movements, we need to emphasize the social and interpersonal dimensions, as the examples in Chapter 6 have shown.[54] The ultimate reason why it is important to practice specific body movements is because it contributes to cultivating other-regarding moral virtues, for which self-improvement may be a necessary step.

As we have seen in Dōgen's instructions regarding serving and eating food, concern for specific body movements is directed toward how best to express one's respect and care for others. Through repeated practice, we are cultivating ourselves to be a civic-minded member of a society who contributes to creating a humane environment respectful of other members' dignity.

It is instructive that in the Japanese language, the written character for social discipline or cultivation of manners, *shitsuke* (躾), is a Japanese invention which combines two Chinese characters: body (身) and beauty (美).[55] The significant part of learning proper behavior concerns body movements of daily activities such as opening and closing a door, holding a cup, serving a drink, giving and receiving a name card, opening a gift, and bowing, to name only a few. *Shitsuke* training requires that we practice engaging in these acts gently, carefully, respectfully, and mindfully. If we act carelessly, roughly, and with no regard to how the appearance and sound affect others, our actions would appear not only inelegant but also disrespectful, even if it is unintended and despite the fact that the task gets accomplished.[56] The aesthetic appeal of an elegant body movement thus is not for the sake of aesthetic effect alone but more importantly a sensuous display of one's other-regarding considerations.

Arnold Berleant's notion of "social aesthetics" is instructive here. His long-held aesthetics of engagement is an attempt to overcome modern Western aesthetics' deeply entrenched framework of subject–object separation as well as a disembodied, disinterested spectator as the ideal agent for having an aesthetic experience. One of the consequences of the aesthetics of engagement is that there is no limit to what can inspire aesthetic engagement. He challenges the traditional aesthetics discourse by arguing that "disinterestedness confines appreciation to a state of mind, that is, to a psychological attitude, and *unduly excludes the somatic and social dimensions of experience,* thus directing aesthetic appreciation improperly."[57] The 'disinterested' attitude that is regarded as a requirement for an aesthetic experience and judgment also isolates aesthetic matters from other human concerns. Interpersonal interactions and social situations involve various sensuous, hence aesthetic, dimensions, which determine their character, such as acceptance, respect for uniqueness, and reciprocity, or lack thereof. These characteristics underlie our aesthetic engagement, but they also characterize ethical relationships between humans. Social aesthetics thus highlights "the essential relatedness of the aesthetic and the social" and "ethical values lie at the heart of social aesthetics."[58]

Thus conceived, social aesthetics necessarily leads to a more 'activist'-oriented aesthetics, as discussed in Chapter 2. That is, we cannot remain an uninvolved, disinterested spectator of a social situation by making an aesthetic judgment as a distant observer. Most of the time, we are an active agent and take part in creating a social situation by interacting with others. The examples of body aesthetics in Chapter 6 indicate that we need to practice body movements in daily life as a way of cultivating moral virtues, thereby contributing to a civil discourse and humane society. That is, we cannot simply study virtues or will ourselves to develop them. As Robert Carter points out, "correct ethical action most often grows out of concrete, physical training, or repetition, and is best described as a cluster of attitudes about who one is in the world and how to properly and effectively interact with others. Ethics is not a theoretical, intellectual 'meta' search, but a way of walking (or being) in the world."[59] Similarly, Megan Laverty states, "civility is a learned behavior—individuals develop civility by habitually practicing civil interactions."[60]

Various theories and cultural traditions testify to the fact that practicing these movements will make civil behavior a kind of second nature so that it flows spontaneously as if one is acting purely on one's inclination without recourse to rational deliberation. Citing an empirical research result, Nancy Sherman concludes that "emotional change can sometimes work from the outside in" and "we nurse a change from the outside in" because "outward emotional demeanor can sometimes move inward and effect deeper changes of attitude."[61]

Testimonies of Japanese art practitioners and those who had a proper *shitsuke* discipline sufficiently demonstrate that, through repeated bodily engagement and practice, the artistic skills and respectful conduct *tend to* become internalized so that one becomes a certain kind of person who, at the masterful stage, will 'naturally' exhibit virtuous qualities. The training of geisha best illustrates this process of internalizing outward bodily training. Literally meaning a person accomplished in the arts, a geisha practices classical music, dance, and the art of entertaining guests. The arduous physical regimen of all of these activities, according to a first-person account, is "as much a discipline of the self as the technical mastery of an art form" and "if art is life for a geisha, then her life must also become art." Accordingly, "a geisha's professional ideal is to become so permeated with her art that everything she does is informed by it, down to the way she walks, sits, and speaks."[62] One may not achieve a perfectly virtuous self, but that does not nullify the *ideal* of cultivating moral virtues through bodily engagement both within and outside of artistic training.[63]

Such an ideal of a virtuous self underlies Schiller's aesthetic education of man. As a response to Kantian ethics, Schiller argues for the crucial importance of the sensuous and the emotive in our moral life, as he believes that following the heart is necessary in effecting an action dictated by reason. His vision of a moral person is not someone who simply carries out duties dictated by reason, often against his inclination; rather, it is someone who has a "great soul when the moral sense has finished assuring itself of all the affections, to the extent of abandoning without fear the direction of the senses to the will, and never incurring the risk of finding himself in discord with its decisions."[64] Such a person acts with grace. For Schiller, grace is located between willful movements instigated by rational deliberation and those activated by natural endowment. Although he is not as explicit as Confucius explained below, he seems to hold that a person needs to practice to act gracefully so as to appear to deny any trace of willful practice, as indicated by this passage: "The true grace...ought always to be pure nature, that is to say, involuntary (or at least appear to be so), to be graceful. The subject even ought not to *appear to know that it possesses grace.*"[65]

Confucianism in comparison is clear about the role of performing and practicing aesthetic movements through arts and rituals. For example, Mencius teaches:

...sages literally "image" the virtues in their bodies and make even more evident the fusion of the good, the elegant, and the beautiful. Learning *li* 禮 is essentially a "discipline of the body," and the literal meaning of teaching by examples (*shenjiao* 身教), which is to be preferred over teaching by words (*yanjiao* 言教), means "body teaching."[66]

When such training is successful, "the beauty of such a creation [of an elegant, harmonious, and balanced soul] is reflected in the person's demeanor as well as in her face, limbs, and back."[67] While practicing and training imply intentional activity and sustained effort, it is believed that such continuous devotion will help one internalize the expression of virtues so that ultimately it becomes almost like one's second nature, wherein a virtuous action naturally and spontaneously follows. This ideal state of a virtuous self is what Confucius describes as having achieved at the age of seventy: "I could follow my heart's desires without overstepping the bounds of propriety."[68]

I have been devoting this chapter to making a case for developing the normative direction for everyday aesthetics by going beyond cultivating aesthetic literacy of our everyday life. My thesis is that, through an aesthetic paradigm shift and practicing body aesthetics, we are better equipped to contribute positively to the project of world-making. I will now address the final challenge to this normative direction for everyday aesthetics.

7.4 Instrumental Value of Everyday Aesthetics

Some may object to reducing aesthetic dimensions of our lives to a means for serving some other ends, like better world-making. So, is aesthetics valuable merely as an instrument for bettering the quality of our life and society? It is

214 THE POWER OF EVERYDAY AESTHETICS IN WORLD-MAKING

instructive that John Dewey describes the moral function of art as follows: it is "to remove prejudice, do away with the scales that keep the eye from seeing, tear away the veils due to wont and custom, (and) perfect the power to perceive," because, according to him, "works of art are means by which we enter . . . into other forms of relationship and participation than our own."[69] Appreciating art on *its own*, rather than *our*, terms helps us cultivate this moral capacity for recognizing and understanding the other's reality through sympathetic imagination, thereby widening our horizons and ultimately laying the foundation for a civil society.

Similarly, as we have seen, the Japanese aesthetic tradition, whether regarding practice of art or engagement in everyday activities, can be characterized as providing an instrument for leading a good life, whether in terms of spiritual discipline or cultivation of moral virtues. There is no indication that this understanding of aesthetics as having an instrumental value compromises the aesthetic value of art, our experience of it, or our engagement with everyday practice.

I would go even further by advocating that everyday aesthetics *must* pursue its instrumental value. This is particularly important for exposing and addressing 'negative aesthetics' that unfortunately is prevalent today. If one is wedded to the honorific understanding of the term 'aesthetics,' as Arnold Berleant points out, 'negative aesthetics' may sound like "an oxymoron."[70] However, as I argued in Chapter 1, particularly when it comes to everyday aesthetics, it is critical that we adopt the classificatory sense of the term so as to allow the possibility of negative aesthetics. It is because my thesis of this book is that everyday aesthetics has a surprisingly important role to play in humanity's world-making project, and one of the most important dimensions of such a project is for us to be able to detect and explore parts of our lives and environments that are aesthetically negative. Hideous, offensive, malodorous, dreary, and tedious qualities found in everyday life *are* aesthetic qualities insofar as they result from our reactions through sensibility. While it is possible to adopt a distanced and disinterested attitude toward them and derive a positive aesthetic experience, as in seeing the junkyard for its interesting combination of colors and texture as I discussed previously, it is crucial that these negative qualities be experienced as negative in the context of the world-making project. How else are we going to detect that something is amiss or wrong with the artifacts with which we interact, our environment, or social engagement? Isn't it important to recognize these negative qualities, diagnose the cause of the problem, think of a way to improve the situation, and ultimately act on it?

Arnold Berleant and Katya Mandoki stand out among everyday aesthetics advocates for exploring negative aesthetics. By identifying aesthetics as "the theory of sensibility," Berleant rejects the "common association of aesthetics with art and its connotation of art that is good or great" and calls attention to occasions and environments where sensory experience "offends, distresses, or has harmful or damaging consequences."[71] Berleant provides two kinds of negative aesthetics. One is caused by absence of any positive aesthetic values due to utter blandness. The examples include: "tract housing, big box stores, and ritual conversation"; "the bland anonymity of suburban housing tracts and sterile blocks of low income housing,... sitcoms that pander to the emptiness and crassness of ordinary life, and pulp novels that breed on people's dissatisfaction by offering escape into fictional romance or adventure."[72] He calls these instances "aesthetic deprivation" because it "extinguishes our capacity for sensory experience" and "conditions of such deprivation may be harmful and produce aesthetic damage either through the loss of the capacity for perceptual satisfaction or by withholding aesthetic occasions."[73]

The other kind of negative aesthetics "is the actual presence of negative aesthetic value."[74] Various forms of intrusion and pollution damage not only the environment and health but also our sensibility. Examples include "cacophony of the roar of traffic and the blaring of loudspeakers in public places... the soporific blanket of canned music and intrusive private conversations over cell phones... the gaudy, intense colors of advertising circulars and the bath of all the commercial impingements on our sensibility...," as well as street litter, utility lines, telephone poles, and billboards.[75]

One may quibble over the specifics of examples, but the important point to be gained from his discussion is the existence of negative aesthetics in today's world and in our lives. As I argued when discussing the body aesthetics in social context, we can also insist that some problematic social interactions, such as rudeness, inconsiderateness, and lack of care and concern, are unfortunately common occurrences punctuating contemporary everyday life, and body aesthetics has a significant role to play in their detection as well as providing a strategy for improvement.

Katya Mandoki also calls attention to "aesthetic poisoning."[76] She diagnoses modern Western aesthetics to suffer from what she calls the "Pangloss Syndrome," which she characterizes as "the tendency to deal only with things that are nice and worthy, good and beautiful," through "a surgical operation of systematic exclusion of all phenomena that are not positive and useful in their supply of pleasure and nice thoughts."[77] According to her, this syndrome "explains why aesthetics has dealt only with art and beauty, so when other qualities that are not as pleasing become apparent, they are either only mentioned superficially or swept under the rug."[78] But, she observes, in our daily life, we are confronted with negative aesthetic qualities every day, such as "the disgusting, the obscene, the coarse, the insignificant, the banal, the ugly, the sordid."

Although I would not use the terms "unaesthetic" and "anaesthetic," Marcia Eaton also makes the same observation: "questions concerning aesthetic value become particularly daunting when one considers the extent to which the world daily grows not only more unaesthetic—(ugly, graceless, even repulsive) but also more anaesthetic—(dulling, numbing, alienating)."[79]

Unfortunately, we do not live in an aesthetic utopia; I don't think anyone would believe that the world which we inhabit and the life we lead are aesthetically perfect with no room for improvement. If everyday aesthetics sometimes encourages adoption of not-so-ordinary attitudes toward those aesthetic negatives, it should also encourage exposing negative aesthetics in our life and in the world as negative. If one does not pursue this latter option, one fails to acknowledge that the power that everyday aesthetics wields is considerable in determining the quality of life, not just for oneself, but for the society and humanity at large. The sharpened aesthetic sensibility should thus be directed not simply to enhance one's pleasures and enrichment but, perhaps more importantly, to detect negative qualities which are impoverishing or harming the quality of life and environment. I agree with Mandoki's criticism that "we as aestheticians have evaded our *social responsibility* of contributing to the knowledge of human beings from our particular perspective, and thus lost for this field of inquiry the *relevance* it deserves" and that "aesthetic theory has to deal with social reality here and now to safeguard the quality of life and the respect for the integrity of human sensibility."[80] In short, everyday aesthetics will be derelict if it does not recognize the existence of negative aesthetics for what it is and explore ways in which our aesthetic life can be improved.

One may continue to be uneasy about this normative direction and instrumental value of everyday aesthetics. The objection will point out that we simply don't have a consensus as to what constitutes good life and good society. These fundamental disagreements result in differing life values that inform the 'thick' sense of aesthetic values of things such as a luscious-looking green lawn and an elegant gated community, as discussed previously. Some of us are ardent defenders of free enterprise, while others believe socialism is a better societal system; furthermore, we disagree over whether it is better to be a dissatisfied Socrates than a satisfied pig. On the one hand, aesthetics cannot be expected to solve these perennial debates. However, on the other hand, it seems to me that there are some basic facts and values that I believe can be accepted as common to humanity's flourishing, such as health, a sustainable future, a humane and civil society based upon mutual respect, and a comfortable, stable, and welcoming environment, among others, although their specific ingredients will depend upon cultural, historical, and other contexts.

It will be difficult to maintain complete relativism when it comes to forming an aesthetic judgment on things like a stench from a nearby factory, a public space, such as the aforementioned Providence train station, with no welcoming and comforting amenities or visitor-friendly signage, and a deafening and pounding noise from a car stereo.[81] At the same time, I can't think of any objections to what Yrjö Sepänmaa calls "aesthetic welfare,"[82] a sensuous manifestation that our lived experience is attended and responded to with care. Care, thoughtfulness, and respect expressed in the objects and environments that surround us and in the way in which others interact with us cannot but encourage us to 'pay it forward,' so to speak. If aesthetics can be a powerful ally in enhancing basic amenities for human flourishing, I cannot think of any good reason for not utilizing its powerful influence. On the other hand, if aesthetics can be a formidable enemy, as some of the examples have shown, then I believe that it is our collective responsibility to not only expose its role but also to counter it. Examples include supporting and promoting things like edible estate, laundry hanging, designed objects and spaces that reflect care and thoughtfulness, and products made in a manner that is environmentally benign and respectful of human rights and dignity. What needs to be emphasized in order for these efforts to remain *aesthetic* instead of purely ethical and environmental is that the focus be on each object's and activity's sensuous surface. That is, the environmental benefit by itself cannot justify the aesthetics of *any* edible estate, wind farm, or laundry hanging; neither can respect for human rights by itself override the aesthetics of a piece of garment that is simply ugly or poorly put together.

This normative, hence educational, dimension of aesthetics is summarized by Eaton as a challenge to aesthetic educators: "how can one instill aesthetic and ethical values that will contribute to healthy citizens and communities?"[83] Her own response with which I agree is that "aesthetic educators share responsibility— a responsibility that I believe can best be met with and through an aes-ethical education." I also share the following observation made by D. W. Prall:

... if aesthetic possibilities are to be realized at all fully, we must find most of our aesthetic satisfaction not in truant excursions from business, but in the forms and surroundings of our main activities and tools, graciousness or even physical grace in daily human relations and transactions, and colors and forms and sounds that are not intolerably unpleasant and chaotic in factory-buildings, streets, traffic, and office-furniture, as well as in public monuments and parks and school-houses and gardens, where aesthetic concern is normally, if vaguely and too often unsuccessfully, taken into account.[84]

I believe every aesthetician will agree that a life without any aesthetic dimension (even if such were possible) greatly impoverishes one's experience. But I will go further by maintaining that an aesthetic life without any connection to the rest of life, moral, social, political or otherwise, (again, even if such were possible) also greatly compromises the quality of life.

Conceived this way, I believe that characterizing aesthetics' significance as an instrumental value does not diminish its place in our life. Instead, it provides an ultimate justification why the aesthetic in our life is indispensable, rather than some luxury, frills, or fluff. We need to respond to a rather widespread and unfortunate perception that "aesthetic considerations are 'extras'—luxuries to be indulged in after real concerns have been taken care of,"[85] which is often manifested by the fact that arts are the first thing to be cut in education and public funding, particularly in the United States. The isolation of the aesthetic from the social and the cultural, Raymond Williams, warns, "can be damaging, for there is something irresistibly displaced and marginal about the now common and limiting phrase 'aesthetic considerations,' especially when contrasted with *practical . . . considerations*."[86] Our aesthetic life is an important instrument for shaping the state of the society and world and improving the quality of life. Thus, it behooves everyday aesthetics to continue developing a critical discourse to improve our aesthetic life beyond art and nature appreciation so that we become better equipped to participate in the collective project of world-making. In conclusion, we need to reclaim aesthetics' prominent place in the project of world-making and its inseparable connection with the rest of life.

Notes

1. The notion of "nudge" to assist better decision-making is discussed in *Nudge: Improving Decisions About Health, Wealth, and Happiness* by Richard H. Thaler and Cass R. Sunstein (New York: Penguin Books, 2008). Marcia Eaton's "aesthetic ought" appears in *Merit, Aesthetic and Ethical* (Oxford: Oxford University Press, 2001), p. 176.
2. I owe this example to Tom Leddy.
3. Plato, *The Republic*, Book III, in *Philosophies of Art and Beauty*, eds. Albert Hofstadter and Richard Kuhns (New York: The Modern Library, 1964), p. 28.
4. Sir Philip Sidney, *An Apology for Poetry*, originally published in 1595, in *Philosophical Issues in Art*, ed. Patricia H. Werhane (Englewood Cliffs: Prentice-Hall, 1984), pp. 86–7, emphasis added, and p. 89.
5. Sidney, *An Apology*, p. 88.
6. Friedrich Schiller, *On the Aesthetic Education of Man*, tr. Reginald Snell (New York: Frederick Ungar Publishing Co., 1977).

7. Arnold Berleant, *Sensibility and Sense: The Aesthetic Transformation of the Human World* (Exeter: Imprint Academic, 2010), p. 193.

8. David Orr, *The Nature of Design: Ecology, Culture, and Human Intention* (Oxford: Oxford University Press, 2002), pp. 178–9, emphasis added, 185, 25, and 26. A parallel reminder was issued by Aldo Leopold, who claims that "we can be ethical only in relation to something we can see, feel, understand, love" and that it is "inconceivable...that an ethical relation to land can exist without love, respect, and admiration for land, and a high regard for its value." *A Sand County Almanac* (New York: Ballantine Books, 1966), pp. 251 and 261.

9. Joan Iverson Nassauer, "Cultural Sustainability: Aligning Aesthetics with Ecology," in *Placing Nature: Culture and Landscape Ecology*, ed. Joan Iverson Nassauer (Washington, D.C.: Island Press, 1997), p. 68.

10. Catherine Dee, "Form, Utility, and the Aesthetics of Thrift in Design Education," *Landscape Journal* 29/1 (2010), p. 21.

11. Thaler and Sunstein, *Nudge*, p. 10.

12. Paul Duncum proposes that art education should also engage in a similar normative discourse: "Without denying children the opportunity to find pleasure in constructing identities for themselves through the visual appeal of consumer goods, it is central to the art educational task *to offer alternatives*." Paul Duncum, "Aesthetics, Popular Visual Culture, and Designer Capitalism," *Journal of Art and Design Education* 26/3 (2007), p. 293.

13. Eaton, *Merit*, pp. 63–4.

14. David E. Cooper, "Look of Lawns," *Times Literary Supplement* 5525 (February 20, 2009), p. 23.

15. For Danto's theory of the artworld, see "The Artworld" in *Philosophy Looks at the Arts*, ed. Joseph Margolis (Philadelphia: Temple University Press, 1978), pp. 132–44. For Walton's categories of art, see "Categories of Art," in *Philosophy Looks at the Arts*, ed. Joseph Margolis (Philadelphia: Temple University Press, 1978), pp. 88–116.

16. The distinction between "serious" and "trivial" associations in nature aesthetics is discussed by Ronald Hepburn, "Trivial and Serious in the Aesthetic Appreciation of Nature," in *The Reach of the Aesthetic* (Hants: Ashgate, 2001), pp. 1–15. The notion of imagining well/not well is discussed by Emily Brady, "Imagination and the Aesthetic Appreciation of Nature," in *The Aesthetics of Natural Environment*, eds. Allen Carlson and Arnold Berleant (Peterborough: Broadview Press, 2004), p. 164.

17. My claim here is not that bringing in such knowledge is the *only* way to have a complex, enriching aesthetic experience of a salt marsh. As Tom Leddy points out, the experience can be enriched if one attends closely to the play of light, creatures in the marsh, and the like, particularly by physically interacting with the environment instead of taking in a view as a distanced spectator. What I need to establish here is that the cognitive *can* affect the perceptual.

18. Cheryl Foster, "Aesthetic Disillusionment: Environment, Ethics, Art," *Environmental Values* 1 (1992), pp. 205–15.

19. Marcia M. Eaton, "Kantian and Contextual Beauty," in *Beauty Matters*, ed. Peg Zeglin Brand (Bloomington: Indiana University Press, 2000), p. 34. In her *Merit*, Eaton cites Malcolm Budd's statement: "Artistic value does not exist in a watertight

compartment impermeable by other values" (p. 68). Though his reference is to artistic values, I think it applies to aesthetic value in general.

20. Arnold Toynbee, from *Civilization on Trial* cited in *Puzzles about Art: An Aesthetics Casebook*, eds. Margaret P. Battin et al. (New York: St. Martin's Press, 1989), pp. 172–3.

21. Jane Forsey, *The Aesthetics of Design* (Oxford: Oxford University Press, 2013), p. 186.

22. Thomas Leddy, "The Aesthetics of Junkyards and Roadside Clutter," *Contemporary Aesthetics* (2008), sec. 5, http://www.contempaesthetics.org/newvolume/pages/article. php?articleID=511.

23. Thomas Leddy, *The Extraordinary in the Ordinary: The Aesthetics of Everyday Life* (Peterborough: Broadview Press, 2012), p. 114. His most recent work, such as "Everyday Aesthetics and Happiness," emphasizes the importance of addressing the consequences of everyday aesthetics such as consumer aesthetics. In *Aesthetics of Everyday Life*, eds. Liu Yuedi and Curtis L. Carter (Newcastle upon Tyne: Cambridge Scholars Publishing, 2014), pp. 26–47.

24. Eaton, *Merit*, p. 62.

25. Tyson-Lord Gray, "Beauty or Bane: Advancing an Aesthetic Appreciation of Wind Turbine Farms," in *Environmental Aesthetics: Crossing Divides and Breaking Ground*, eds. Martin Drenthen and Jozef Keulartz (New York: Fordham University Press, 2014), pp. 171, 170.

26. The best account of this shift in the aesthetics of mountains is Marjorie Hope Nicolson's *Mountain Gloom and Mountain Glory: The Development of the Aesthetics of the Infinite* (New York: W.W. Norton & Company, 1959).

27. I explored this aspect of Japanese aesthetics in "The Japanese Aesthetics of Imperfection and Insufficiency," *The Journal of Aesthetics and Art Criticism* 55/4 (1997), pp. 377–85.

28. Dan Mitchell points out regarding the "ugly food" movement that "despite the popular name of the movement, marketers generally aren't using the word 'ugly.' More artful terms are favored. A French supermarket chain is selling 'inglorious' foods. The British chain ASDA uses 'wonky' (which to American ears might sound as bad as 'ugly.') Canada's Loblaws uses 'naturally imperfect.'" Dan Mitchell, "Why People Are Falling in Love with 'Ugly Food'," *Times.com* (March 27, 2015) http://time.com/3761942/why-people-are-falling-in-love-with-ugly-food/.

29. Mike Buzalka, "Is Ugly the New Beautiful?" *Food Management* (March 30, 2015) http://food-management.com/blog/ugly-new-beautiful?eid=forward. In fact, Leddy was making exactly the same point two decades ago before there was a movement to embrace and celebrate 'inglorious' fruits and vegetables:

… unblemished fruits sell more readily *because* they are more aesthetically pleasing. (But note also that what the general populace may find to be a blemish in a piece of fruit may be considered an attraction to others. Thus, 'blemished' apples might sell better in communities that are sensitive to possible ecological damage caused by processes used to insure the clean appearance of an apple. The apples may even come to *look* better to these people. Thus, moral as well as practical issues enter into our aesthetic discriminations at this level.)

Thomas Leddy, "Everyday Surface Aesthetic Qualities: 'Neat,' 'Messy,' 'Clean,' 'Dirty,'" *The Journal of Aesthetics and Art Criticism* 53/3 (1995), p. 264.
30. David Orr, *The Nature of Design*, p. 134.
31. David Orr, *The Nature of Design*, p. 179.
32. Jonathan Maskit, "The Aesthetics of Elsewhere: An Environmentalist Everyday Aesthetics," *Aesthetic Pathways* 1/2 (2011), p. 99.
33. In addition to Burtynski's work, see photos compiled from Deep Ecology Foundation in "PLANET NEWS: WHAT HUMANS ARE DOING TO EARTH: 19 photos that will shake up your thinking about consumption and waste" by Skylar Harrison (August 21, 2015) http://www.purpleclover.com/lifestyle/4507-planet-news-what-humans-are-doing-earth/item/screen-shot-2015-05-13-18/.
34. Martin Luther King, Jr. "Letter from Birmingham City Jail" (1963), p. 3, http://www.thekingcenter.org/archive/document/letter-birmingham-city-jail-0#.
35. William James, "On a Certain Blindness in Human Being," in *Talks to Teachers* (New York: Henry Holt and Company, 1915), p. 234.
36. Documentary film on Piet Oudolf trailer "Fall, Winter, Spring, Summer, Fall," dir. Thomas Piper (2014) https://www.youtube.com/watch?v=Eb8LoJyuIC8.
37. Fritz Haeg, *Edible Estates: Attack on the Front Lawn*, 2nd ed (New York: Metropolis Books, 2010). I thank my student, Adrianna Gallo for this reference.
38. Fritz Haeg, "Full-Frontal Gardening," in *Edible Estates*, pp. 16, 17. The next passage is from p. 22.
39. Diana Balmori, "Beauty and the Lawn: A Break with Tradition," in *Edible Estates*, p. 13.
40. Joan Iverson Nassauer, "Messy Ecosystems, Orderly Frames," *Landscape Journal* 14/2 (1995), p. 163.
41. Joan Iverson Nassauer, "Cultural Sustainability: Aligning Aesthetics with Ecology," in *Placing Nature: Culture and Landscape Ecology*, ed. Joan Iverson Nassauer (Washington, D.C.: Island Press, 1997), p. 68. The effort to marry environmental health and aesthetics seems to be gaining more popularity, as indicated by "The Low-Impact (but Still Lush) Landscape" article in *Consumer Report* (May 2015).
42. Eaton, *Merit*, p. 195.
43. Eaton, *Merit*, p. 193.
44. Robert Thayer, Jr., "Gray World," excerpt from *Gray World, Green Heart: Technology, Nature, and the Sustainable Landscape*, in *Theory in Landscape Architecture*, ed. Simon Swaffield (Philadelphia: University of Pennsylvania Press, 2002), pp. 189, 190.
45. In addition to these, Thayer includes material recycling facilities, minimum tillage and organic farming practices, drip irrigation systems, bicycle transportation networks, and multipurpose wastewater treatment wetlands which double as wildlife reserves or recreation areas. Robert L. Thayer, Jr., *Gray World, Green Heart: Technology, Nature, and the Sustainable Landscape* (New York: John Wiley & Sons, 1994), p. 126. I thank my student, Erica Chung, for calling my attention to the city of Los Gatos, CA, which recently enacted an ordinance, in pursuit of "architectural excellence," cracking down on the placement of solar panels on top of the buildings that "threaten(s) to make their upscale Silicon Valley village an ugly place." Paul Rogers,

"Solar Panels' Problem in Los Gatos: Visibility," *San Jose Mercury News* (Aug. 3, 2003).

46. Taken from "Gray World," in *Theory in Landscape Architecture*, p. 192.

47. Cited by Robert W. Righter, "Exoskeletal Outer-Space Creations," in *Wind Power in View: Energy Landscape in a Crowded World*, eds. Martin J. Pasqualetti, Paul Gipe, and Robert W. Righter (San Diego: Academic Press, 2002), p. 36.

48. Eaton, *Merit*, p. 196.

49. Sim Van der Ryn and Stuart Cowan, *Ecological Design* (Washington, D.C.: Island Press, 1996), p. 164. The next passage is from p. 165, emphases added.

50. Eaton, *Merit*, p. 179.

51. Richard Shusterman, "Everyday Aesthetics of Embodiment," in *Rethinking Aesthetics: The Role of Body in Design*, ed. Ritu Bhatt (New York: Routledge, 2013), pp. 30 and 31.

52. Shusterman, "Everyday Aesthetics," p. 30.

53. Sherri Irvin, "The Pervasiveness of the Aesthetic in Ordinary Experience," *The British Journal of Aesthetics* 48/1 (2008), p. 41.

54. I have discussed in Chapter 1 that Irvin does go further by pointing out the specific moral benefit of deriving satisfaction and pleasure from things and activities which incur no moral, social, or environmental cost, such as avoiding participating in consumerism and practicing vegetarian eating.

55. I owe this point regarding the Japanese character to Kazuo Inumaru. Eiko Ikegami also discusses this character and further points out that the same term is also used for "basting" in sewing, which is a preliminary rough sewing to put the fabric's shaping and folding in place to prepare it for the bona fide sewing. This process may be compared to "training" a material such as a plant material to create a desired shape and the analogy extends to the training of the body so that it expresses moral virtues (Eiko Ikegami, *Bonds of Civility: Aesthetic Networks and the Political Origins of Japanese Culture* (Cambridge: Cambridge University Press, 2005), p. 344).

56. During the Edo period in Japan (1603–1868), various rules of etiquette involving bodily movements were established, sometimes formally written as manuals and sometimes as townspeople's cumulative wisdom referred to as *Edo Shigusa* (Edo Way of Acting). For various written documents, see Ikegami's chapter on "Hierarchical Civility and Beauty: Etiquette and Manners in Tokugawa Manuals," pp. 324–59. For *Edo Shigusa*, specific body movements are discussed in *Nihonjin Reigi Sahō no Shikitari* (*Japanese Custom of Etiquette and Manners*) by Iikura Harutake (Tokyo: Seishun Shuppansha, 2008).

57. Berleant, *Sensibility*, p. 85, emphasis added.

58. Berleant, *Sensibility*, pp. 7 and 95.

59. Robert E. Carter, *The Japanese Arts and Self-Discipline* (Albany: SUNY Press, 2008), p. 5.

60. Megan Laverty, "Civility, Tact, and the Joy of Communication," *Philosophy of Education* (2009), p. 235.

61. Nancy Sherman, "Of Manners and Morals," *British Journal of Educational Studies* 53/3 (Sept. 2005), pp. 277, 277, 278.

62. Liza Crihfield Dalby, "The Art of the Geisha," *Natural History* 92/2 (Feb. 1983), p. 51. Geisha training of body and mind is analogous to the artistic training of medieval

performing arts. Ikegami points out that "the distinctive characteristic of medieval performing arts was their emphasis on the relationship between a careful aesthetic training of the corporeal body and personal and internal cultivation. It was through the repeated training of body movements in the performing arts that unity of body and mind might be actualized" (Ikegami, *Bonds of Civility*, p. 345).

63. The point here is similar to Aldo Leopold's discussion on land ethic. "We shall never achieve harmony with land, any more than we shall achieve absolute justice or liberty for people. In these higher aspirations the important thing is not to achieve, but to strive." *A Sand County Almanac* (New York: Ballantine Books, 1977), p. 210. Eric Mullis points out that Confucius himself "is quite clear that the moral ideals that he espouses are difficult to attain." "The Ethics of Confucian Artistry," *The Journal of Aesthetics and Art Criticism* 65/1 (Winter 2007), p. 106.

64. Friedrich Schiller, "On Grace and Beauty," in *Essays Aesthetical and Philosophical* (London: George Bell & Sons, 1882), p. 203.

65. Schiller, "On Grace and Beauty," p. 186.

66. Nicholas F. Gier, "The Dancing *Ru*: A Confucian Aesthetics of Virtue," *Philosophy East & West* 51/2 (2001), p. 283.

67. Gier, "The Dancing *Ru*," p. 292. Speaking of the art of calligraphy as an example, Eric Mullis also emphasizes the moral and aesthetic importance of "gestural communication" and points out that "the human body is at the intersection of the moral and the aesthetic, as the ability to intelligently form habits enables one to become both a good person and a good artist." The reference to "gestural communication" is on p. 103 and p. 104, and the quoted passage is on p. 101 of Mullis, "The Ethics of Confucian Artistry."

68. Confucius, *Analects* in *Analects with Selections from Traditional Commentaries*, trans. Edward Slingerland (Indianapolis: Hackett Publishing Company, 2003), p. 9. The entire passage reads: "At fifteen, I set my mind upon learning; at thirty, I took my place in society; at forty, I became free of doubts; at fifty, I understood Heaven's Mandate; at sixty, my ear was attuned, and at seventy, I could follow my heart's desire without overstepping the bounds of propriety."

69. John Dewey, *Art as Experience* (New York: Capricorn Books, 1958), pp. 325, 333.

70. Berleant, *Sensibility*, p. 166.

71. Berleant, *Sensibility*, p. 155.

72. Berleant, *Sensibility*, p. 164. The second passage is from Berleant, *Aesthetics Beyond the Arts: New and Recent Essays* (Farnham: Ashgate Publishing Limited, 2012), p. 206.

73. Berleant, *Sensibility*, p. 164.

74. Berleant, *Aesthetics*, p. 206.

75. Berleant, *Sensibility*, p. 46. Other examples include "the sound from music systems and television sets that infiltrates into virtually every public place, from supermarkets to doctors' waiting rooms, airport lobbies, restaurants, bars, and even public streets." *Aesthetics*, p. 206.

76. Katya Mandoki, *Everyday Aesthetics: Prosaics, the Play of Culture and Social Identities* (Aldershot: Ashgate Publishing Limited, 2007), p. 38.

77. Mandoki, *Everyday Aesthetics*, all from p. 37.

78. Mandoki, *Everyday Aesthetics*, pp. 37–8, 38.

79. Eaton, *Merit*, p. 210.

80. Mandoki, *Everyday Aesthetics*, p. 97, emphases added.

81. I noted, when discussing the Providence train station in Chapter 6, that the desire for clear and welcoming signage in such a space may not be universally shared, as there are those who would prefer to make an adventure into an unknown place without any guidance. Similarly, as Leddy pointed out on my draft, some with a blaring car stereo obviously enjoy such deafening volume. I responded to the skeptic's concern regarding the train station in section 6.2.1 of Chapter 6. As for the blaring car stereo, Leddy himself pointed out that they can blast their ear drums by putting on earphones, thereby avoiding disturbing others around.

82. Yrjö Sepänmaa, "Aesthetics in Practice: Prolegomenon," in *Practical Aesthetics in Practice and in Theory*, ed. Martti Honkanen (Helsinki: University of Helsinki, 1995), p. 15.

83. Eaton, *Merit*, p. 210. The next passage is from p. 216.

84. D. W. Prall, *Aesthetic Judgment* (New York: Thomas Y. Crowell Company, 1967), pp. 40–1.

85. Prall, *Aesthetic Judgment*, p. 70.

86. Raymond Williams, *Keywords: A Vocabulary of Culture and Society* (New York: Oxford University Press, 1983), rev. ed., entry on "aesthetic," p. 32.

Conclusion

One mission of everyday aesthetics is to unearth hidden potentials behind the façade of ordinariness that makes up our daily lives. The art of living includes cultivating a capacity and sensibility to shed light on the all-too-familiar and to be able to derive a fresh aesthetic experience. Enriching individual lives in this way is one important role of everyday aesthetics.

However, I am becoming increasingly concerned with what I call 'the power of the aesthetic.' Against the rather unfortunate, but prevalent, assessment of aesthetic matters as a dispensable, superficial icing on the cake, I argue that aesthetics is deeply entrenched in our daily lives, decisions, and actions, all of which have serious consequences. Particularly today, aesthetics has become the prime mover behind capitalistic enterprises and a major factor in the political domain. We have also seen that the power of the aesthetic can determine the future sustainability of this world. Furthermore, aesthetics can make or break our interactions with others, whether human or non-human, physical environments, and artifacts. Finally, aesthetics can promote civil discourses, respectful and fulfilling interactions, and a humane and inclusive atmosphere. Conversely, it can exacerbate alienation, indignity, disrespect, and indifference. Unfortunately, these effects of negative aesthetics exist in many pockets of today's societies as well as in human lives.

In light of this power of the aesthetic, I believe that it is no longer tenable for aesthetics to ignore its social responsibility. Instead, I propose that the social mission of everyday aesthetics be taken seriously. That is, we need to explore ways to cultivate aesthetic sensibility and what I call aesthetic literacy beyond the already established discourses on art and more recently nature. Something like 'aesthetic' education, distinct from the existing educational programs on visual arts, music, literary arts, theater, and dance, may be worth exploring and developing. Such education may include critically analyzing the aesthetic effects of familiar objects and environments in our lives, as well as creating positive aesthetic effects through designing objects and environments and practicing respectful and caring interactions.

Emphasizing the importance of developing everyday aesthetics by no means diminishes the importance and value of cultivating aesthetic sensibility through arts. They are the best means available for sharpening our aesthetic sensibility, and we certainly imagine a life without any recourse to arts (if we can imagine such a life) to be impoverished. At the same time, I consider to be inadequate a life that is full of art appreciation but without any understanding or consideration of the significance and consequences of our everyday aesthetic judgments, decisions, and actions. Furthermore, ignoring the power of the aesthetic amounts to abandoning responsibility for the collective and cumulative project of world-making in which, I maintain, we are all implicated, whether we recognize it or not. This world-making project cannot but include macro-level considerations such as environmental consequences, human rights violation, and problematic political causes, and micro-level concerns such as human interactions and caring for non-human objects. I have devoted this book to demonstrating that our everyday aesthetic experiences and judgments have an often unrecognized, but profound, role to play in this world-making project. As such, it behooves everyday aesthetics to expose the role it plays in this ongoing task for humanity and to harness its power toward better world-making.

Bibliography

Alexander, Christopher et al. *A Pattern Language: Towns, Buildings, Construction.* New York: Oxford University Press, 1977.

Allsop, Laura. "Sky Fidelity: The World Turned Upside Down." *Art Review* 56.3 (2006): 37–8.

Ando, Tadao. *Chichu Art Museum: Tadao Ando Builds for Walter de Maria, James Turrell, and Claude Monet.* Ostfildern: Hatje Cantz, 2005.

Arafat Al Qudwa, Salem Y. "Reinventing Aesthetic Values of Minimalist Architecture in the Gaza Strip, Palestine." Presented at The First Jordanian and International Conference on Architecture and Design, 2014.

Balmori, Diana. "Beauty and the Lawn: A Break with Tradition." In *Edible Estates: Attack on the Front Lawn,* 2nd ed. Edited by Fritz Haeg. New York: Metropolis Books, 2010: 13.

Bartley, Nancy. "Clothesline Crusaders Calling Laundry Flap Overblown." *Seattle Times* (August 13, 2013).

Battin, Margaret P. et al. *Puzzles about Art: An Aesthetics Casebook.* New York: St. Martin's Press, 1989.

BBC (co-production with Time Inc.). *American Visions: The History of American Art and Architecture.* Written and presented by Robert Hughes, 1996.

Beardsley, John. *Earthworks and Beyond.* Abbeville Press: New York, 1989.

Berleant, Arnold. *The Aesthetics of Environment.* Philadelphia: Temple University Press, 1992.

Berleant, Arnold. *Living in the Landscape.* Lawrence: The University Press of Kansas, 1997.

Berleant, Arnold. *Aesthetics and Environment: Variations on a Theme.* Aldershot: Ashgate, 2005.

Berleant, Arnold. *Sensibility and Sense: The Aesthetic Transformation of the Human World.* Exeter: Imprint Academic, 2010.

Berleant, Arnold. *Aesthetics beyond the Arts: New and Recent Essays.* Farnham: Ashgate, 2012.

Berleant, Arnold. "Environmental Aesthetics: Overview." In *Encyclopedia of Aesthetics,* 2nd ed. Edited by Michael Kelly. Oxford: Oxford University Press, 2014: Vol. 2, 493–500.

Bhatt, Ritu, ed. *Rethinking Aesthetics: The Role of Body in Design.* New York: Routledge, 2013.

Blatt, Harvey. *America's Food: What You Don't Know About What You Eat.* Cambridge: MIT Press, 2008.

Böhme, Gernot. "Atmosphere as the Fundamental Concept of a New Aesthetics." Translated by David Roberts. *Thesis Eleven* 36 (1993): 113–26.

Böhme, Gernot. "Atmosphere as an Aesthetic Concept." *Daidallos* 68 (1998): 112–15.

Böhme, Gernot. "Contribution to the Critique of the Aesthetic Economy." *Thesis Eleven* 73 (2003): 71–92.

Böhme, Gernot. "On Beauty." *The Nordic Journal of Aesthetics* 39 (2010): 22–33.

Borasi, Giovanna. *Journeys: How Travelling Fruit, Ideas and Buildings Rearrange Our Environment.* Montreal: Canadian Centre for Architecture, 2010.

Bormann, F. Herbert et al. *Redesigning the American Lawn: A Search for Environmental Harmony.* New Haven: Yale University Press, 1993.

Brand, Peg Zeglin, ed. *Beauty Matters.* Bloomington: Indiana University Press, 2000.

Brand, Peg Zeglin, ed. *Beauty Unlimited.* Bloomington: Indiana University Press, 2012.

Brady, Emily. "Imagination and the Aesthetic Appreciation of Nature." In *The Aesthetics of Natural Environments.* Edited by Allen Carlson and Arnold Berleant. Peterborough: Broadview Press, 2004: 156–69.

Brady, Emily. "Environmental Aesthetics: Contemporary." In *Encyclopedia of Aesthetics*, 2nd ed. Edited by Michael Kelly. Oxford: Oxford University Press, 2014: Vol. 2, 500–3.

Bright, Richard. *James Turrell: Eclipse.* London: Michael Hue-Williams Fine Art, 1999.

Brittan, Gordon G., Jr. "The Wind in One's Sails: a Philosophy." In *Wind Power in View: Energy Landscape in a Crowded World.* Edited by Martin J. Pasqualetti, Paul Gipe, and Robert W. Righter. San Diego: Academic Press, 2002.

Buffalo Bird Woman. "from *Buffalo Bird Woman's Garden.*" In *Cooking, Eating, Thinking: Transformative Philosophies of Food.* Edited by Deane W. Curtin and Lisa M. Heldke. Bloomington: Indiana University Press, 1992: 270–9.

Bullough, Edward. "'Psychical Distance' as a Factor in Art and an Aesthetic Principle." *The British Journal of Psychology* 5 (1912–13): 87–118.

Burke, Edmund. *A Philosophical Enquiry into the Origin of Our Ideas of the Sublime and Beautiful.* Oxford: Oxford University Press, 1990.

Burkett, Elinor. "A Mighty Wind." *The New York Times Sunday Magazine* (June 15, 2003).

Buss, Sarah. "Appearing Respectful: The Moral Significance of Manners." *Ethics* 109.4 (1999): 795–826.

Buzalka, Mike. "Is Ugly the New Beautiful?" *Food Management* (March 30, 2015) http://food-management.com/blog/ugly-new-beautiful?eid=forward.

Calhoun, Cheshire. "The Virtue of Civility." *Philosophy & Public Affairs* 29.3 (2000): 251–75.

Callicott, J. Baird. "The Land Aesthetic." *Orion Nature Quarterly* 3 (1984): 16–23.

Camus, Albert. *The Myth of Sisyphus and Other Essays.* Translated by Justin O'Brien. New York: Vintage Books, 1955.

Carlson, Allen. "On Aesthetically Appreciating Human Environments." *Philosophy & Geography* 4.1 (2001): 9–24.

Carlson, Allen. *Nature and Landscape: An Introduction to Environmental Aesthetics.* New York: Columbia University Press, 2009.

Carlson, Allen. "The Dilemma of Everyday Aesthetics." In *Aesthetics of Everyday Life East and West.* Edited by Liu Yuedi and Curtis L. Carter. Newcastle upon Tyne: Cambridge Scholars Publishing, 2014: 48–64.

Carlson, Allen. "Environmental Aesthetics." *Stanford Encyclopedia of Philosophy* (revised 2014) http://plato.stanford.edu/entries/environmental-aesthetics/.

Carlson, Allen. "Nature: Contemporary Thought." In *Encyclopedia of Aesthetics*, 2nd ed. Edited by Michael Kelly. Oxford: Oxford University Press, 2014: Vol. 4, 474–8.

Carlson, Allen and Arnold Berleant, eds. *The Aesthetics of Natural Environments*. Peterborough: Broadview Press, 2004.

Carter, Robert E. *The Japanese Arts and Self-Discipline*. Albany: SUNY Press, 2008.

Charles, Dorothée. *Cai Guo-Qiang*. London: Thames & Hudson, 2000.

Clair, Jean. *Cosmos: From Romanticism to Avant-garde*. Munich: Prestel Verlag, 1999.

Clark, Edie. "Summer's Scent." *Yankee* 65.6 (July/Aug. 2001): 144.

Cleary, Thomas. *Shōbōgenzō: Zen Essays by Dōgen*. Honolulu: University of Hawaii Press, 1986.

Cole, Thomas. "Essay on American Scenery," first appeared in *The American Monthly Magazine*, I (January 1836). In *The American Landscape: A Critical Anthology of Prose and Poetry*. Edited by John Conron. New York: Oxford University Press, 1974: 568–78.

Confucius. *Analects with Selections from Traditional Commentaries*. Translated by Edward Slingerland. Indianapolis: Hackett Publishing Company, 2003.

Consumer Report. "Your Ultimate Laundry Guide." *Consumer Report* 79.8 (Aug. 2014): 36–9.

Consumer Report. "The Low-Impact (but Still Lush) Landscape." *Consumer Report* 80.5 (May 2015): 33–42.

Cooper, David E. "Look of Lawns." *Times Literary Supplement* 5525 (February 20, 2009): 22–3.

Cotel, Orli. "The Answer, My Friend." *Sierra* 92.5 (Sept./Oct. 2007): 8.

Dalai Lama. *The Universe in a Single Atom: The Convergence of Science and Spirituality*. New York: Morgan Road Books, 2005.

Dalby, Liza Crihfield. "The Art of the Geisha." *Natural History* 92.2 (1983): 47–54.

Danto, Arthur. "The Artworld." In *Philosophy Looks at the Arts*. Edited by Joseph Margolis. Philadelphia: Temple University Press, 1978: 132–44.

Danto, Arthur. *Transfiguration of the Commonplace*. Cambridge: Harvard University Press, 1983.

Danto, Arthur. *The Abuse of Beauty: Aesthetics and the Concept of Art*. Chicago: Open Court, 2004.

Darsø, Lotte. *Artful Creation: Learning-Tales of Arts-in-Business*. Frederiksberg, Denmark: samfundslitteratur, 2004.

Davis, Philip E. *A Pragmatic Theory of Public Art and Architecture*. North Charleston: CreativeSpace Independent Publishing Platform, 2015.

Dean, Andrea Oppenheimer and Timothy Hursley. *Proceed and Be Bold: Rural Studio After Samuel Mockbee*. New York: Princeton Architectural Press, 2005.

Dee, Catherine. "Form, Utility, and the Aesthetics of Thrift in Design Education." *Landscape Journal* 29.1 (2010): 21–35.

Deep Ecology Foundation. "PLANET NEWS: WHAT HUMANS ARE DOING TO EARTH: 19 photos that will shake up your thinking about consumption and waste" (August 21, 2015) http://www.purpleclover.com/lifestyle/4507-planet-news-what-humans-are-doing-earth/item/screen-shot-2015-05-13-18/.

Dewey, John. *Art as Experience*. New York: Capricorn Press, 1958.

Dickie, George. "The Myth of the Aesthetic Attitude." In *Introductory Readings in Aesthetics*. Edited by John Hospers. New York: The Free Press, 1969: 28–44.

Didi-Huberman, Georges. "The Fable of the Place." In *James Turrell: The Other Horizon.* Edited by P. Noever. Vienna: MAK, 2002: 45–56.

Dillard, Annie. "Seeing," originally in *Pilgrim at Tinker Creek* (1974). In *Environmental Ethics: Divergence and Convergence.* Edited by Richard G. Botzler and Susan J. Armstrong. New York: McGraw-Hill, 1998: 114–21.

Dirksen, Kirsten. "Clothesline Wars: The Solar Dryer." *Faircompanies Sustainable News.* (March 11, 2008).

Dōgen. *Shōbōgenzō: The Eye and Treasury of the True Law.* Translated by Kōsen Nishiyama and John Stevens. Tokyo: Nakayama Shobō, 1975.

Dōgen. *Shōbōgenzō: Zen Essays by Dōgen.* Translated by Thomas Cleary. Honolulu: University of Hawaii Press, 1986.

Dōgen. *Fushuku-Hampō (Meal-Time Regulations).* In *Cooking, Eating, Thinking: Transformative Philosophies of Food.* Edited by Deane W. Curtin and Lisa M. Heldke. Bloomington: Indiana University Press, 1992: 153–63.

Dōgen. *Tenzo Kyōkun (Instruction for the Tenzo).* In *Cooking, Eating, Thinking: Transformative Philosophies of Food.* Edited by Deane W. Curtin and Lisa M. Heldke. Bloomington: Indiana University Press, 1992: 280–5.

Dōgen. "Guidelines for Studying the Way." In *Moon in a Dewdrop: Writings of Zen Master Dōgen.* Translated by Kazuaki Tanahashi. New York: North Point Press, 1995: 31–43.

Douglas, Mary. *Purity and Danger: An Analysis of Concept of Pollution and Taboo.* London: Routledge, 2002.

Dowling, Christopher. "The Aesthetics of Daily Life." *British Journal of Aesthetics* 50.3 (2010): 225–42.

Drobnick, Jim. "Volatile Effects: Olfactory Dimensions of Art and Architecture." In *Empire of the Senses: The Sensual Culture Reader.* Edited by David Howes. Oxford: Berg, 2005, 265–80.

Duerksen, Christopher J. and R. Matthew Goebel. *Aesthetics, Community Character, and the Law.* Chicago: American Planning Association, 1999.

Duncum, Paul. "A Case for an Art Education of Everyday Aesthetic Experiences." *Studies in Art Education* 40.4 (1999): 295–311.

Duncum, Paul. "Aesthetics, Popular Visual Culture, and Designer Capitalism." *Journal of Art and Design Education* 26.3 (2007): 285–95.

Duncum, Paul. "Reasons for the Continuing Use of an Aesthetic Discourse in Art Education." *Art Education* 60.2 (March 2007): 46–51.

Eagleton, Terry. *The Ideology of the Aesthetic.* Oxford: Basil Blackwell, 1990.

Eaton, Marcia Muelder. *Aesthetics and the Good Life.* Rutherford: Farleigh Dickinson University Press, 1989.

Eaton, Marcia Muelder. "Kantian and Contextual Beauty." In *Beauty Matters.* Edited by Peg Zeglin Brand. Bloomington: Indiana University Press, 2000: 27–36.

Eaton, Marcia Muelder. *Merit, Aesthetic and Ethical.* Oxford: Oxford University Press, 2001.

Etter-Turnbull, Cindy. *Fine Lines: A Celebration of Clothesline Culture.* East Lawrencetown, Nova Scotia: Pottersfield Press, 2006.

Evernden, Neil. *The Social Creation of Nature.* Baltimore: The Johns Hopkins University Press, 1992.

Fei, Dawei. "Amateur Recklessness: On the Work of Cai Guo-Qiang." In *Cai Guo-Qiang*. Edited by Dorothée Charles. London: Thames & Hudson, 2000: 7–14.

Felski, Rita. "Introduction." *New Literary History* 33. 4 (2002): 607–22.

Felski, Rita. "Everyday Aesthetics." *The Minnesota Review* 71–72 (2009): 171–9.

Forsey, Jane. *The Aesthetics of Design*. Oxford: Oxford University Press, 2013.

Foster, Cheryl. "Aesthetic Disillusionment: Environment, Ethics, Art." *Environmental Values* 1 (1992): 205–15.

Fox, Louis, Dir. *The Story of Stuff*. Written by Annie Leonard et al. Free Range Studios, 2007 http://storyofstuff.org/movies/story-of-stuff/.

Fukasawa, Naoto and Jasper Morrison. *Super Normal*. Translated by Mardi Miyake. Baden: Lars Müller Publishers, 2008.

Giard, Luce. "Doing Cooking." In *The Practice of Everyday Life*. Volume 2: Living & Cooking. Edited by Luce Giard. Translated by Timothy J. Tomasik. Minneapolis: University of Minnesota Press, 1998: 149–247.

Gier, Nicholas F. "The Dancing *Ru*: A Confucian Aesthetics of Virtue." *Philosophy East & West* 51.2 (2001): 280–305.

Gilfoyle, Timothy J. *Millennium Park: Creating a Chicago Landmark*. Chicago: The University of Chicago Press, 2006.

Gipe, Paul. "Design As If People Matter: Aesthetic Guidelines for a Wind Power Future." In *Wind Power in View: Energy Landscape in a Crowded World*. Edited by Martin J. Pasqualetti, Paul Gipe, and Robert W. Righter. San Diego: Academic Press, 2002.

Godlovitch, Stan. "Ice Breakers: Environmentalism and Natural Aesthetics." *Journal of Applied Philosophy* 11.1 (1994): 15–30.

Gould, Stephen Jay. "The Golden Rule–A Proper Scale for Our Environmental Crisis." In *Environmental Ethics: Divergence and Convergence*. Edited by Susan J. Armstrong and Richard G. Botzler. New York: McGraw Hill, 1993: 310–15.

Gould, Stephen Jay. "An Evolutionary Perspective on Strengths, Fallacies, and Confusions in the Concept of Native Plants." In *Nature and Ideology: Natural Garden Design in the Twentieth Century*. Edited by Joachim Wolschke-Bulmahn. Washington, D.C.: Dumbarton Oaks Research Library and Collection, 1997: 11–19.

Gray, Tyson-Lord. "Beauty or Bane: Advancing an Aesthetic Appreciation of Wind Turbine Farms." In *Environmental Aesthetics: Crossing Divides and Breaking Ground*. Edited by Martin Drenthen and Jozef Keulartz. New York: Fordham University Press, 2014: 157–73.

Grilli, Peter. *Pleasures of the Japanese Bath*. New York: Weatherhill, 1992.

Groening, Gert and Joachim Wolschke-Bulmahn. "Some Notes on the Mania for Native Plants in Germany." *Landscape Journal* 11.2 (Fall 1992): 116–26.

Guinness, Sebastian. "James Turrell." In *Chichu Art Museum: Tadao Ando Builds for Walter de Maria, James Turrell, and Claude Monet*. Ostfildern: Hatje Cantz, 2005: 122–8.

Gumbrecht, Hans Ulrich. "Aesthetic Experience in Everyday Worlds: Reclaiming an Unredeemed Utopian Motif." *New Literary History* 37 (2006): 299–318.

Haapala, Arto. "On the Aesthetics of the Everyday: Familiarity, Strangeness, and the Meaning of Place." In *The Aesthetics of Everyday Life*. Edited by Andrew Light and Jonathan M. Smith. New York: Columbia University Press, 2005: 39–55.

Haeg, Fritz. *Edible Estates: Attack on the Front Lawn*, 2nd ed. New York: Metropolis Books, 2010.

Hanhardt, John G. "A Great Experiment: Otto Piene and the Center for Advanced Visual Studies." In *Otto Piene: Retrospektive 1952–1996*. Edited by Stephan von Wiese and Susanne Rennert. Köln: Wienand, 1996: 39–45.

Hara, Kenya. *White*. Translated by Jooyeon Rhee. Baden: Lars Müller Publishers, 2010.

Hara, Kenya. *Nihon no Dezain—Biishiki ga Tsukuru Mirai (Japanese Design—Future Created by Aesthetic Sensibility)*. Tokyo: Iwanami Shoten, 2012.

Harris, Daniel. *Cute, Quaint, Hungry and Romantic: The Aesthetics of Consumerism*. Cambridge: Da Capo Press, 2000.

Hendry, Joy. *Wrapping Culture: Politeness, Presentation and Power in Japan and Other Societies*. Oxford: Clarendon Press, 1993.

Hepburn, Ronald. "Aesthetic Appreciation of Nature." In *Aesthetics in the Modern World*. Edited by Harold Osborne. London: Thames and Hudson, 1968: 18–35.

Hepburn, Ronald. "Trivial and Serious in the Aesthetic Appreciation of Nature." In *The Reach of the Aesthetic: Collected Essays on Art and Nature*. Aldershot: Ashgate, 2001: 1–15.

Hextall, Janie and Barbara McNaught, eds. *Washing Lines: A Collection of Poems*. Lechlade: Lautus Press, 2011.

Highmore, Ben, ed. *The Everyday Life Reader*. Abingdon, Oxon. 2002.

Highmore, Ben. "Homework: Routine, Social Aesthetics and the Ambiguity of Everyday Life." *Cultural Studies* 18.2/3 (2004): 306–27.

Highmore, Ben. *Everyday Life and Cultural Theory: An Introduction*. Oxon: Routledge, 2010.

Highmore, Ben, ed. *Everyday Life*. Abingdon, Oxon. 2011.

Highmore, Ben. *Ordinary Lives: Studies in the Everyday*. Oxon: Routledge, 2011.

Hisamatsu, Shin'ichi. *Sadō no Tetsugaku (The Philosophy of the Way of Tea)*. Tokyo: Kōdansha, 1991.

Hogarth, William. *The Analysis of Beauty* (1753). In *A Documentary History of Art*. Edited by Elizabeth G. Holt. Garden City: Doubleday, 1958: Vol. II, 261–72.

Holdforth, Lucinda. *Why Manners Matter: What Confucius, Jefferson, and Jackie O Knew and You Should Too*. New York: Plume, 2009.

Hospers, John. *Meaning and Truth in the Arts*. Hamden: Archon Books, 1964.

Howes, David. "HYPERESTHESIA, or, the Sensual Logic of Late Capitalism." In *Empire of the Senses: The Sensual Culture Reader*. Edited by David Howes. Oxford: Berg, 2005: 281–303.

Howes, David. "Selling Sensation." *New Scientist* 219/2934 (2013): 28–9.

Howes, David and Constance Classen. *Ways of Sensing: Understanding the Senses in Society*. London: Routledge, 2014.

Howland, Jon. "Clothesline Bans Void in 19 States." *Sightline Daily* (February 21, 2012) http://daily.sightline.org/2012/02/21/clothesline-bans-void-in-19-states/.

Hughes, Kathleen A. "To Fight Global Warming, Some Hang a Clothesline." *The New York Times* (April 12, 2007).

Hume, David. "Of Qualities Immediately Agreeable to Others." In *An Inquiry Concerning the Principles of Morals*. Edited by Charles W. Hendel. New York: The Liberal Arts Press, 1957: 83–9.

Huxley, Aldous. *The Doors of Perception*. New York: Harper & Row, 1954.

Iikura, Harutake. *Nihonjin Reigi Sahō no Shikitari (Japanese Custom of Etiquette and Manners)*. Tokyo: Seishun Shuppansha, 2008.

Ikegami, Eiko. *Bonds of Civility: Aesthetic Networks and the Political Origins of Japanese Culture*. Cambridge: Cambridge University Press, 2005.

Irvin, Sherri. "The Pervasiveness of the Aesthetic in Ordinary Experience." *British Journal of Aesthetics* 48.1 (2008): 29–44.

Irvin, Sherri. "Scratching an Itch." *The Journal of Aesthetics and Art Criticism* 66. 1 (2008): 25–35.

Irvin, Sherri. "Aesthetics and the Private Realm." *The Journal of Aesthetics and Art Criticism* 67.2 (2009): 226–30.

IVAM Institut Valencia d'Art Modern. *Cai Guo-Qiang: On Black Fireworks*. Valencia: IVAM Institut Valencia d'Art Modern, 2005.

Jacob, Mary Jane. "Being with Cloud Gate." In *Anish Kapoor: Past Present Future*. Edited by Nicholas Baume. Cambridge: MIT Press, 2008: 120–33.

James, Simon. "For the Sake of a Stone? Inanimate Things and the Demands of Morality." *Inquiry* 54.4 (2011): 384–97.

James, William. "On a Certain Blindness in Human Beings." In *Talks to Teachers*. New York: Henry Holt and Company, 1915: 231–4.

James, William. *The Principles of Psychology*. Vol. 1. New York: Dover Publications, 1950.

Jenkins, Virginia Scott. *The Lawn: A History of an American Obsession*. Washington, D.C.: Smithsonian Institution Press, 1994.

Kakishita, Yoshinori. *Rojō no Geijutsu [Fukkoku ban] (Art on the Street [Reprint Edition])*. Tokyo: Hobby Japan, 2015.

Kanai, Masaaki et al. *Muji*. New York: Rizzoli, 2013.

Kant, Immanuel. *Critique of Judgment*. Translated by J. H. Bernard. New York: Hafner Press, 1974.

Karatani, Kōjin. "Japan as Museum: Okakura Tenshin and Ernest Fenollosa." In *Japanese Art After 1945: Scream Against the Sky*. Edited by Alexandra Munroe. New York: Harry N. Abrams, 1994: 33–40.

Karatani, Kōjin. "Uses of Aesthetics: After Orientalism." In *Edward Said and the Work of the Critic: Speaking Truth to Power*. Edited by Paul A. Bove. Durham: Duke University Press, 2000: 139–51.

Keane, Marc Peter. *Japanese Garden Design*. Rutland: Charles E. Tuttle, 1996.

Kennedy, Randy. "A Most Public Artist Polishes a New York Image." *The New York Times* (August 20, 2006).

King, Jr., Martin Luther. "Letter from Birmingham City Jail" (1963) http://www.thekingcenter.org/archive/document/letter-birmingham-city-jail-0#.

Komanoff, Charles. "NIMBYs Everywhere: Even Wind Power Can't Be Invisible." *The Providence Journal* (June 6, 2003).

Lailach, Michael. *Land Art*. Köln: Taschen, 2007.

Laverty, Megan. "Civility, Tact, and the Joy of Communication." *Philosophy of Education* (2009): 228–37.

Leddy, Thomas. "Everyday Surface Aesthetic Qualities: 'Neat,' 'Messy,' 'Clean,' 'Dirty.'" *The Journal of Aesthetics and Art Criticism* 53.3 (1995): 259–68.

Leddy, Thomas. "Sparkle and Shine." *British Journal of Aesthetics* 37.3 (1997): 259–73.

Leddy, Thomas. "The Nature of Everyday Aesthetics." In *The Aesthetics of Everyday Life*. Edited by Andrew Light and Jonathan M. Smith. New York: Columbia University Press, 2005: 3–22.

Leddy, Thomas. "The Aesthetics of Junkyards and Roadside Clutter." *Contemporary Aesthetics* 6 (2008) http://www.contempaesthetics.org/newvolume/pages/article.php?articleID=511.

Leddy, Thomas. "Defending Everyday Aesthetics and the Concept of 'Pretty.'" *Contemporary Aesthetics* 10 (2012) http://www.contempaesthetics.org/newvolume/pages/article.php?articleID=654.

Leddy, Thomas. *The Extraordinary in the Ordinary: The Aesthetics of Everyday Life*. Peterborough: Broadview Press, 2012.

Leddy, Thomas. "Everyday Aesthetics and Happiness." In *Aesthetics of Everyday Life*. Edited by Liu Yuedi and Curtis L. Carter. Newcastle upon Tyne: Cambridge Scholars Publishing, 2014: 26–47.

Leddy, Thomas. "The Experience of Awe: An Expansive Approach to Everyday Aesthetics." *Contemporary Aesthetics* 13 (2015) http://www.contempaesthetics.org/newvolume/pages/article.php?articleID=727.

Lee, Jessica. "Home Life: Cultivating a Domestic Aesthetic." *Contemporary Aesthetics* 8 (2010) http://www.contempaesthetics.org/newvolume/pages/article.php?articleID=587.

Leopold, Aldo. *A Sand County Almanac*. New York: Ballantine Books, 1966.

Light, Andrew. "Urban Ecological Citizenship." *Journal of Social Philosophy* 34.1 (2003): 44–63.

Lippard, Lucy. *The Lure of the Local: Senses of Place in a Multicultural Society*. New York: The New Press, 1997.

Lorde, Audre. "from *Zami: A New Spelling of My Name*." In *Cooking, Eating, Thinking: Transformative Philosophies of Food*. Edited by Deane W. Curtin and Lisa M. Heldke. Bloomington: Indiana University Press, 1992: 286–93.

Maki, Fumihiko. "Japanese City Spaces and the Concept of *Oku*." *The Japan Architect* 264 (1979): 50–62.

Mandoki, Katya. *Everyday Aesthetics: Prosaics, the Play of Culture and Social Identities*. Aldershot: Ashgate, 2007.

Mandoki, Katya. "The Third Tear in Everyday Aesthetics." *Contemporary Aesthetics* 8 (2010) http://www.contempaesthetics.org/newvolume/pages/article.php?articleID=606.

Marin, Rick. "A Scholar Tackles the Wash." *The New York Times* (September 29, 2005).

Marx, Leo. *The Machine in the Garden: Technology and the Pastoral Ideal in America*. Oxford: Oxford University Press, 2000.

Maskit, Jonathan. "Subjectivity, Desire, and the Problem of Consumption." In *Deleuze/Guattari & Ecology*. Edited by Bernd Herzogenrath. New York: Palgrave Macmillian, 2008: 129–44.

Maskit, Jonathan. "The Aesthetics of Elsewhere: An Environmentalist Everyday Aesthetics." *Aesthetic Pathways* 1.2 (2011): 92–107.

Matilsky, Barbara, *Fragile Ecologies: Contemporary Artists' Interpretations and Solutions*. New York: Rizzoli, 1992.

Maysles, David, Dir. *Running Fence: Christo's Project for Sonoma and Marin Counties, State of California.* New York: Maysles Films, 1978.

McGlone, Conor. "Asda's Ugly Veg Drive Divides Supermarkets." *ENDS Report* 480 (Feb. 2015): 39–40.

Melchionne, Kevin. "Aesthetic Experience in Everyday Life: A Reply to Dowling." *British Journal of Aesthetics* 51.4 (2011): 437–42.

Melchionne, Kevin. "Definition of Everyday Aesthetics." *Contemporary Aesthetics* 11 (2013) http://www.contempaesthetics.org/newvolume/pages/article.php?articleID=663.

Mendelson, Cheryl. *Laundry: The Home Comforts: Book of Caring for Clothes and Linens.* New York: Scribner, 2005.

Miller, M. H. "James Turrell Allowing Limited Visitors to Roden Crater for $6,500 a Person." *ARTNEWS* (Feb. 19, 2015) http://www.artnews.com/2015/02/19/james-turrell-allowing-limited-visitors-to-roden-crater-for-6500-a-person/.

Mitchell, Dan. "Why People Are Falling In Love with 'Ugly Food'." *Times.com* (March 27, 2015) http://time.com/3761942/why-people-are-falling-in-love-with-ugly-food/.

Miyahara, Kōjirō and Fujisaka Shingo. *Shakai Bigaku e no Shōtai (Invitation to Social Aesthetics).* Kyoto: Minerva Shobō, 2012.

Miyahara, Kōjirō and Fujisaka Shingo. "Exploring Social Aesthetics: Aesthetic Appreciation as a Method for Qualitative Sociology and Social Research." *International Journal of Japanese Sociology* 23 (2014): 63–79.

Mock, Freida Lee, Dir. *Maya Lin: A Strong Clear Vision.* Santa Monica: American Film Foundation, 2003.

Mollar, Dan. "The Boring." *The Journal of Aesthetics and Art Criticism* 72.2 (2014): 181–91.

Morris, William. "The Lesser Arts" first published in 1877. In *William Morris on Art & Design.* Edited by Christine Poulson. Sheffield: Academic Press, 1996: 156–78.

Moss, Hilary and Desmond O'Neill. "The Art of Medicine: Aesthetic Deprivation in Clinical Settings." *Lancet* 383 (March 22, 2014): 1032–3 http://www.thelancet.com/journals/lancet/article/PIIS0140-6736(14)60507-9/fulltext?rss=yes.

Mullis, Eric. "The Ethics of Confucian Artistry." *The Journal of Aesthetics and Art Criticism* 65.1 (Winter 2007): 99–107.

Murai, Yasuhiko. *Cha no Bunkashi (Cultural History of Tea).* Tokyo: Iwanami Shinsho, 1979.

Murdoch, Iris. *Sartre: Romantic Rationalist.* New Haven: Yale University Press, 1969.

Nakamura, Hajime. *Shin Bukkyō Jiten (New Dictionary of Buddhism).* Tokyo: Seishin Shobō, 1962.

Nakane, Kazuko. "Naoshima: Art off the Waters of Industrialized Japan." *Sculpture* 24.5 (2005): 10–11.

Nanbō, Sōkei. *Nanbōroku* in *Nanbōroku wo Yomu (Reading Nanbōroku).* Edited by Kumakura Isao. Kyoto: Tankōsha, 1989.

Nash, Roderick. *Wilderness and the American Mind.* New Haven: Yale University Press, 1982.

Nassauer, Joan Iverson. "Messy Ecosystems, Orderly Frames." *Landscape Journal* 14.2 (1995): 161–70.

Nassauer, Joan Iverson. "Cultural Sustainability: Aligning Aesthetics with Ecology." In *Placing Nature: Culture and Landscape Ecology*. Edited by Joan Iverson Nassauer. Washington, D.C.: Island Press, 1997: 67–83.

Naukkarinen, Ossi. "What Is 'Everyday' in Everyday Aesthetics?" *Contemporary Aesthetics* 11 (2013) http://www.contempaesthetics.org/newvolume/pages/article. php?articleID=675.

Naukkarinen, Ossi. "Everyday Aesthetic Practices, Ethics and Tact." *Aisthesis* 7.1 (Jan. 2014): 23–44.

Naukkarinen, Ossi and Yuriko Saito. *Artification*. Special volume of *Contemporary Aesthetics* (2012) http://www.contempaesthetics.org/newvolume/pages/journal.php? volume=49.

Nicolson, Marjorie Hope. *Mountain Gloom and Mountain Glory: The Development of the Aesthetics of the Infinite*. New York: W.W. Norton & Company, 1959.

Nietzsche, Friedrich. *Beyond Good and Evil*. Translated by Walter Kaufmann. In *Basic Writings of Nietzsche*. Translated and edited by Walter Kaufmann. New York: Modern Library, 1968: 179–436.

Nietzsche, Friedrich. *The Birth of Tragedy*. Translated by Walter Kaufmann. In *Basic Writings of Nietzsche*. Edited by Walter Kaufmann. New York: Modern Library, 1968: 1–144.

Nietzsche, Friedrich. *On the Genealogy of Morals*. Translated by Walter Kaufmann. In *Basic Writings of Nietzsche*. Edited by Walter Kaufmann. New York: Modern Library, 1968: 437–600.

Nietzsche, Friedrich. *The Gay Science*. Translated by Walter Kaufmann. New York: Vintage Books, 1974.

Nikkei Design. *Mujirushi Ryōhin no Dezain (Mujirushi Ryōhin's Design)*. Tokyo: Nikkei BP sha, 2015.

Nishimura, Kiyokazu. *Nichijōsei no Kankyō Bigaku (Aesthetics of Ordinary Environment)*. Tokyo: Keisō Shobō, 2012.

Noddings, Nel. "An Ethics of Care." In *Introduction to Ethics: Personal and Social Responsibility in a Diverse World*. Edited by Gary Percesepe. Englewood Cliffs: Prentice Hall, 1995: 175–89.

Norman, Donald A. *The Design of Everyday Things*. New York: Doubleday, 1990.

Norman, Donald A. *Emotional Design: Why We Love (or Hate) Everyday Things*. New York: Basic Books, 2004.

Novitz, David. *The Boundaries of Art: A Philosophical Inquiry into the Place of Art in Everyday Life*. Philadelphia: Temple University Press, 1992.

Oakes, Baile. *Sculpting with the Environment*. New York: Van Norstrand Reinhold, 1995.

Ohnuki-Tierney, Emiko. *Kamikaze, Cherry Blossoms, and Nationalisms: The Militarization of Aesthetics in Japanese History*. Chicago: The University of Chicago Press, 2002.

Orr, David. *The Nature of Design: Ecology, Culture, and Human Intention*. Oxford: Oxford University Press, 2002.

Pallasmaa, Juhani. "Toward an Architecture of Humility." *Harvard Design Magazine* 7 (Winter/Spring, 1999): 22–5.

Pallasmaa, Juhani. *The Eyes of the Skin: Architecture and the Senses*. Chichester: John Wiley & Sons, 2007.

Panza di Biumo, Count Giuseppe. "Artists of the Sky." In *Occluded Front: James Turrell.* Edited by Julia Brown. Los Angeles: Museum of Contemporary Art, 1985: 61–88.

Papanek, Victor. *The Green Imperative: Natural Design for the Real World.* New York: Thames and Hudson, 1995.

Parsons, Glenn, and Allen Carlson. *Functional Beauty.* Oxford: Oxford University Press, 2008.

Pasqualetti, Martin J. "Living with Wind Power in a Hostile Landscape." In *Wind Power in View: Energy Landscape in a Crowded World.* Edited by Martin J. Pasqualetti, Paul Gipe, and Robert W. Righter. San Diego: Academic Press, 2002: 153–72.

Pavlides, Lefteris. "The Aesthetics of Wind Power." *The Providence Journal* (March 5, 2005).

Pearson, David. "Making Sense of Architecture." *Architectural Review* 1136 (1991): 68–70.

Petersen, Will. "Stone Garden." In *The World of Zen: An East-West Anthology.* Edited by Nancy W. Ross. New York: Vintage Books, 1960: 104–11.

Piene, Otto. *Light Ballet.* New York: Howard Wise Gallery, 1965.

Piene, Otto. *More Sky I.* Cambridge: Migrant Apparition, 1970.

Pine II, Joseph and James H. Gilmore. "Welcome to the Experience Economy." *Harvard Business Review* (July/August 1998): 97–105.

Piper, Thomas, Dir. *Fall, Winter, Spring, Summer, Fall* (2014) https://www.youtube.com/watch?v=Eb8LoJyuIC8.

Plato. *The Republic*, Book III. In *Philosophies of Art and Beauty.* Edited by Albert Hofstadter and Richard Kuhns. New York: The Modern Library, 1964: 3–77.

Postrel, Virginia. *The Substance of Style: How the Rise of Aesthetic Value is Remaking Commerce, Culture, and Consciousness.* New York: HarperCollins Publishers, 2003.

Prall, D. W. *Aesthetic Judgment,* first published in 1929. New York: Thomas Y. Crowell Company, 1967.

Prose, Francine. "A Dirty Tablecloth, Deconstructed." *ARTnews* 98.9 (1999): 126–7.

Quinton, Amy. "Clothesline: Solar Device or Eyesore?" *New Hampshire Public Radio* (Nov. 1, 2007) http://nhpr.org/post/clothesline-solar-device-or-eyesore.

Rancière, Jacques. *Aesthetics and its Discontents.* Translated by Steven Corcoran. Cambridge: Polity Press, 2009.

Rautio, Pauliina. "On Hanging Laundry: The Place of Beauty in Managing Everyday Life." *Contemporary Aesthetics* 7 (2009) http://www.contempaesthetics.org/newvolume/pages/article.php?articleID=535.

Rawlings, Irene and Andrea Vansteenhouse. *The Clothesline.* Layton: Gibbs Smith, Publisher, 2002.

Rawson, Philip. *Sacred Tibet.* London: Thames & Hudson, 1991.

Rhode, Deborah L. *The Beauty Bias: The Injustice of Appearance in Life and Law.* Oxford: Oxford University Press, 2010.

Righter, Robert W. *Wind Energy in America: A History.* Norman: University of Oklahoma Press, 1996.

Righter, Robert W. "Exoskeletal Outer-Space Creations." In *Wind Power in View: Energy Landscape in a Crowded World.* Edited by Martin J. Pasqualetti, Paul Gipe, and Robert W. Righter. San Diego: Academic Press, 2002: 19–41.

Rogers, Paul. "Solar Panels' Problem in Los Gatos: Visibility." *San Jose Mercury News.* (Aug. 3, 2003).

Runte, Alfred. *National Parks: The American Experience.* Lincoln: University of Nebraska Press, 1989.

Runte, Alfred. *Yosemite: The Embattled Wilderness.* Lincoln: University of Nebraska Press, 1990.

Russell, Jeanna. "Clothesline Rule Creates Flap." *The Boston Globe* (March 13, 2008).

Ryūkyo Teien Kenkyūsho. *Arukukoto ga Tanoshikunaru Tobiishi Shikiishi Sahō (How to Make Stepping Stones and Pavement for Enjoyable Walking).* Tokyo: Kenchiku Shiryō Kenkyūsha, 2002.

Sai, Yasutaka. *The Eight Core Values of the Japanese Businessman: Toward an Understanding of Japanese Management.* New York: International Business Press, 1995.

Saito, Katsuo and Sadaji Wada, *Magic of Trees & Stones: Secrets of Japanese Gardening.* New York: Japan Publication Trading Company, 1970.

Saito, Yuriko. "Appreciating Nature on Its Own Terms." *Environmental Ethics* 20 (Summer, 1986): 135–49.

Saito, Yuriko. "The Japanese Aesthetics of Imperfection and Insufficiency." *The Journal of Aesthetics and Art Criticism* 55.4 (1997): 377–85.

Saito, Yuriko. "The Aesthetics of Unscenic Nature." *The Journal of Aesthetics and Art Criticism* 56.2 (1998): 101–11.

Saito, Yuriko. "Japanese Aesthetics of Packaging." *The Journal of Aesthetics and Art Criticism* 57.2 (1999): 257–65.

Saito, Yuriko. "Machines in the Ocean: The Aesthetics of Wind Farms." *Contemporary Aesthetics* 2 (2004) http://www.contempaesthetics.org/newvolume/pages/article.php?articleID=247.

Saito, Yuriko. "Response to Jon Boone's Critique." *Contemporary Aesthetics* 3 (2005) http://www.contempaesthetics.org/newvolume/pages/article.php?articleID=321.

Saito, Yuriko. *Everyday Aesthetics.* Oxford: Oxford University Press, 2007.

Saito, Yuriko. "The Moral Dimension of Japanese Aesthetics." *The Journal of Aesthetics and Art Criticism* 65.1 (Winter 2007): 85–97.

Saito, Yuriko. "The Role of Aesthetics in Civic Environmentalism." In *The Aesthetics of Human Environments.* Edited by Arnold Berleant and Allen Carlson. Peterborough: Broadview Press, 2007: 203–18.

Saito, Yuriko. "Cultural Construction of National Landscapes and its Consequences: Cases of Japan and the United States." In *Humans in the Landscape.* Edited by Emily Brady and Sven Arntzen. Oslo: Oslo Academic Press, 2008: 219–47.

Saito, Yuriko. "The Power of the Aesthetic." *Aesthetic Pathways* 1.2 (2011): 11–25.

Saito, Yuriko. "Everyday Aesthetics and World-Making." *Contrastes: Revista Internacional de Filosofía* Suplemento 17 (2012): 255–74.

Saito, Yuriko. "Consumer Aesthetics and Environmental Ethics: Problems and Possibilities." *The Journal of Aesthetics and Art Criticism* 76.4 (Fall 2018): 429–39.

Salemme, Elisabeth. "The Right to Dry." *Time* (Dec. 2, 2007): 100.

Sanburn, Josh. "The Joy of Less." *Time* (March 23, 2015): 44–50.

Sartre, Jean-Paul. *Nausea.* Translated by Lloyd Alexander. New York: New Directions Publishing, 1964.

Schama, Simon. *Landscape and Memory.* London: HarperCollins, 1995.

Schiller, Friedrich. "On Grace and Beauty." In *Essays Aesthetical and Philosophical*. London: George Bell & Sons, 1882: 168–223.

Schiller, Friedrich. *On the Aesthetic Education of Man*. Translated by Reginald Snell. New York: Frederick Ungar Publishing Co., 1977.

Scruton, Roger. *The Aesthetics of Architecture*. Princeton: Princeton University Press, 1979.

Sei Shōnagon. *The Pillow Book of Sei Shōnagon*. Translated by Ivan Morris. Harmondsworth: Penguin Books, 1982.

Sen, Sōshitsu. *Shoho no Sadō (Introductory Way of Tea)*. Kyoto: Tankōsha, 1965.

Sepänmaa, Yrjö. "Aesthetics in Practice: Prolegomenon." In *Practical Aesthetics in Practice and in Theory*. Edited by Marti Honkanen. Helsinki: University of Helsinki, 1995: 13–17.

Sharp, Deborah. "Neighborhood Rules on the Line; Want to Hang Clothes Outside? Better Check City, Local Bylaws." *USA Today* (Dec. 10, 2004).

Sharpe, Tim. "The Role of Aesthetics, Visual and Physical Integration in Building Mounted Wind Turbines—An Alternative Approach." In *Paths to Sustainable Energy*. Edited by Jatin Nathwami. Rijeka, Croatia: InTech, 2010: 279–300.

Sherman, Nancy. "Of Manners and Morals." *British Journal of Educational Studies* 53.3 (2005): 272–89.

Shiotsuki, Yaeko. *Washoku no Itadakikata: Oishiku, Tanoshiku, Utsukushiku (How to Eat Japanese Cuisine: Deliciously, Enjoyably, Beautifully)*. Tokyo: Shinchōsha, 1983.

Short, Lawrence. "Wind Power and English Landscape Identity." In *Wind Power in View: Energy Landscape in a Crowded World*. Edited by Martin J. Pasqualetti, Paul Gipe, and Robert W. Righter. San Diego: Academic Press, 2002: 43–58.

Shusterman, Richard. "Aesthetic Experience: From Analysis to Eros," *The Journal of Aesthetics and Art Criticism* 64.2 (2006): 217–29.

Shusterman, Richard. "Everyday Aesthetics of Embodiment." In *Rethinking Aesthetics: The Role of Body in Design*. Edited by Ritu Bhatt. New York: Routledge, 2013: 13–35.

Sidney, Sir Philip. *An Apology for Poetry*, originally published in 1595. In *Philosophical Issues in Art*. Edited by Patricia H. Werhane. Englewood Cliffs: Prentice-Hall, 1984: 86–90.

Silverman, David. "Routine Pleasures: The Aesthetics of the Mundane." In *The Aesthetics of Organization*. Edited by Stephen Linstead and Heather Höpfl. London: SAGE Publications, 2000: 130–53.

Skydell, Robert. "While Tilting at Windmills, Consider the Aesthetics." *Martha's Vineyard Gazette* (Nov. 11, 2003).

Smart-Grosvenor, Verta Mae. "from *Vibration Cooking: or The Travel Notes of a Geechee Girl*." In *Cooking, Eating, Thinking: Transformative Philosophies of Food*. Edited by Deane W. Curtin and Lisa M. Heldke. Bloomington: Indiana University Press, 1992: 294–7.

Sollins, Marybeth, ed. *Art: 21: Art in the Twenty-First Century*. New York: Harry N. Abrams, 2001.

Steinberg, Ted. *American Green: The Obsessive Quest for the Perfect Lawn*. New York: W.W. Norton, 2006.

Stohr, Karen. *On Manners*. New York: Routledge, 2012.

Stolnitz, Jerome. "The Aesthetic Attitude." In *Introductory Readings in Aesthetics*. Edited by John Hospers. New York: The Free Press, 1969: 17–27.

Stolnitz, Jerome. "On the Origins of 'Aesthetic Disinterestedness'." In *Aesthetics: A Critical Anthology*. Edited by George Dickie and R. J. Sclafani. New York: St. Martin's Press, 1977: 607–25.

Surak, Kristin. *Making Tea, Making Japan: Cultural Nationalism in Practice*. Stanford: Stanford University Press, 2013.

Suzuki, David. "They're Welcome in My Backyard." *New Scientist* 186/2495 (April 16, 2005): 20.

Takashina, Shūji. *Nihonjin ni totte Utsukushisa to wa Nanika (What is Beauty to the Japanese?)*. Tokyo: Chikuma Shobō, 2015.

Tansman, Alan. *The Aesthetics of Japanese Fascism*. Berkeley: University of California Press, 2009.

Tavin, Kevin. "Eyes Wide Shut: The Use and Uselessness of the Discourse of Aesthetics in Art Education." *Art Education* 60.2 (March 2007): 40–5.

Taylor, Nigel. "Ethical Arguments about the Aesthetics of Architecture." In *Ethics and the Built Environment*. Edited by Warwick Fox. London: Routledge, 2000: 193–206.

Tenner, Edward. *Why Things Bite Back: Technology and the Revenge of Unintended Consequences*. New York: Alfred A. Knopf, 1996.

Teysott, Georges. "The American Lawn: Surface of Everyday life." In *The American Lawn*. Edited by Georges Teysott. New York: Princeton Architectural Press, 1999: 1–39.

Thaler, Richard H. and Cass R. Sunstein. *Nudge: Improving Decisions about Health, Wealth, and Happiness*. New York: Penguin Books, 2008.

Thayer, Robert L., Jr. *Gray World, Green Heart: Technology, Nature, and the Sustainable Landscape*. New York: John Wiley & Sons, 1994.

Thayer, Robert L., Jr. "Gray World." In *Theory in Landscape Architecture*. Edited by Simon Swaffield. Philadelphia: University of Pennsylvania Press, 2002: 189–96.

Tuan, Yi-Fu. *Topophilia: A Study of Environmental Perception, Attitudes, and Values*. Englewood Cliffs: Prentice-Hall, 1974.

Tuan, Yi-Fu. *Dominance & Affection: The Making of Pets*. New Haven: Yale University Press, 1984.

Tuan, Yi-Fu. *Passing Strange and Wonderful: Aesthetics, Nature, and Culture*. Washington, D.C.: Island Press, 1993.

Turrell, James. "Roden Crater Project." In *James Turrell Light & Space*. New York: Whitney Museum of American Art, 1980: 15–41.

Ueda, Makoto. *Literary and Art Theories in Japan*. Cleveland: Press of Case Western Reserve University, 1967.

United States Department of the Interior. *Draft Environmental Impact Statement for the Proposed Cape Wind Energy Project*, 2004 http://www.nae.usace.army.mil/projects/ma/ccwf/deis.htm.

Van der Ryn, Sim and Stuart Cowan. *Ecological Design*. Washington, D.C.: Island Press, 1996.

Vihma, Susann. "Artification for Well-Being: Institutional Living as a Special Case." *Contemporary Aesthetics*, special volume 4 on Artification (2012) http://www.contempaesthetics.org/newvolume/pages/article.php?articleID=645.

Vileisis, Ann. *Discovering the Unknown Landscape: A History of America's Wetlands.* Washington, D.C.: Island Press, 1997.

von Wiese, Stephen and Susanne Rennert. *Otto Piene: Retrospektive 1952–1996.* Köln: Wienand, 1996.

Walker, Lucy, Dir. *Tsunami and the Cherry Blossom.* Supply and Demand Integrated, 2011.

Walton, Kendall L. "Categories of Art." In *Philosophy Looks at the Arts.* Edited by Joseph Margolis. Philadelphia: Temple University Press, 1978: 88–116.

Washing Lines: A Collection of Poems. Selected by Janie Hextall and Barbara McNaught. Lechlade: Lautus Press, 2011.

Welsch, Roger. "Musings from the Mud Porch." *Successful Farming* 99.7 (May–June 2001): 62.

Whiteley, Nigel. *Design for Society.* London: Reaktion Books, 1993.

Wilkinson, Nancy Lee. "No Holier Temple: Responses to Hodel's Hetch Hetchy Proposal." *Landscape* 31.1 (1991): 1–9.

Williams, Raymond. *Keywords: A Vocabulary of Culture and Society.* New York: Oxford University Press, 1983.

Wilson, Craig. "Three Sheets to the Wind: The Only Way to Dry." *USA Today* (April 8, 1999).

Woodside, Christine. "Drawing a Line on Outdoor Clothes Drying." *The New York Times* (Dec. 2, 2007).

Worth-Baker, Marcia. "HOME WORK: The Quiet Pleasures of a Line in the Sun." *The New York Times* (July 23, 2006).

Wortz, Melinda. "Introduction." In *James Turrell Light & Space.* New York: Whitney Museum of American Art, 1980: 7–13.

Wu, Hung. "Once Again, Painting as Model: Reflections on Cai Guo-Qiang's Gunpowder Painting." In *Cai Guo-Qiang: On Black Fireworks.* Edited by IVAM Institut Valencia d'Art Modern. Valencia: IVAM Institut Valencia d'Art Modern, 2005: 54–72.

Yanagita, Kunio. *Mame no Ha to Taiyō (Leaves of Bean and the Sun).* Tokyo: Sōgensha, 1942.

Yuedi, Liu. "'Living Aesthetics' from the Perspective of the Intercultural Turn." In *Aesthetics of Everyday Life East and West.* Edited by Liu Yuedi and Curtis L. Carter. Newcastle upon Tyne: Cambridge Scholars Publishing, 2014: 14–25.

Ziff, Paul. "Anything Viewed." In *Oxford Readers: Aesthetics.* Edited by Susan L. Feagin and Patrick Maynard. Oxford: Oxford University Press, 1997: 23–30.

Index

The manufacturer's authorised representative in the EU for product
safety is Oxford University Press España S.A. of El Parque Empresarial
San Fernando de Henares, Avenida de Castilla, 2 - 28830 Madrid
(www.oup.es/en or product.safety@oup.com). OUP España S.A. also acts
as importer into Spain of products made by the manufacturer.
Printed and bound by CPI Group (UK) Ltd, Croydon, CR0 4YY

18/03/2025

01834353-0008